Jason Webster first mov... receiving a degree in Arabic and Islamic history at the University of Oxford. He is the author of a dozen books on Spanish themes, including *Duende: A Journey in Search of Flamenco*; *Andalus: Unlocking the Secrets of Moorish Spain*; *¡Guerra!: Living in the Shadows of the Spanish Civil War*; and *The Spy with 29 Names: The Story of the Second World War's Most Audacious Double Agent*. He is married to the Flamenco dancer Salud and has two children. He and his family divide their time between Spain and Dorset.

Violencia

A New History of Spain
Past, Present and the Future of the West

Jason Webster

CONSTABLE

CONSTABLE

First published in Great Britain in 2019 by Constable
This paperback edition published in 2020

1 3 5 7 9 10 8 6 4 2

A CIP catalogue record for this book
is available from the British Library.

ISBN: 978-1-47212-983-3

Typeset in Electra by SX Composing DTP, Rayleigh, Essex
Printed and bound in Great Britain by Clays Ltd, Elcograf S.p.A.

Constable
An imprint of
Little, Brown Book Group
Carmelite House
50 Victoria Embankment
London EC4Y 0DZ

An Hachette UK Company
www.hachette.co.uk

www.littlebrown.co.uk

For Arturo and Gabi

'The Spanish prefer war to resting, and if they have no enemy abroad, look for one at home.'

Pompeius Trogus (first century BC)

'The Spanish have made great discoveries in the New World, yet still do not know their own continent: there are sections of her rivers which they have not explored, and in her mountains live nations which are unknown to them.'

Charles de Montesquieu

'Perhaps no other country except Turkey is so little known and so ill judged by the rest of Europe as Spain.'

Karl Marx

'Spain never changes.'

George Borrow, *The Bible in Spain*

CONTENTS

AUTHOR'S NOTE

This book describes in part how a geographical reality has at times been turned into a political one. 'Spain' can refer to both. As this double meaning creates complications, for the sake of simplicity I often refer to the geographical Spain as 'the Peninsula' for short.

In a similar vein, Castilian Spanish spellings for cities and individuals are generally used, except where an English rendition is more common. Hence 'Ferdinand' is preferred in the case of the Catholic Monarch and husband of Queen Isabella, but the nineteenth-century king of the same name is referred to as 'Fernando'. As the book is mostly focused on Spain, the Holy Roman Emperor Charles V goes under the Spanish version of his name, Carlos.

INTRODUCTION

Spain is a Cassandra, forever predicting the future of those around her; what happens there foreshadows events elsewhere.

But as with Homer's doomed prophetess, Spain is rarely heard, for her prescient gifts are unrecognised. A more commonly held view is that, in most matters, Spain is generally behind her European neighbours (if in a Romantic kind of way).

Even a brief glance at Spanish history, however, bears out the fact that, on highly important issues, she is almost always in the lead: the Crusades, the European Renaissance, the Discovery of the Americas, Western imperialism, Liberalism, post-colonialism, the Second World War, the Cold War and the recent Occupy movement are all either driven by, presaged by, or built on, Spanish endeavour and experience. Without Spain, emblematic aspects of 'Western' civilisation as diverse as rational thought, modern surgery and the American cowboy would all be missing. Not only that: in a theoretically 'Spain-less' world, there is no desert-island story, no courtly or romantic love, no chivalry, no 'modern' literature or painting, no *Animal Farm* or *1984* and the warnings they still sound for contemporary society. On all kinds of levels – culturally, politically and socially – developments in Spain present powerful indications of the way things will go in the rest of Europe and the West.

Given this tendency, you might be forgiven for assuming that all eyes would be fixed on Madrid and Barcelona both for mapping out the past and for indications of what is to come. Yet this is very far from the case. In 1969, Kenneth Clark wrote this in the introduction to his *Civilisation*:

> *Some of the most offensive omissions were dictated by*
> *my title. If I had been talking about the history of art,*
> *it would not have been possible to leave out Spain;*
> *but when one asks what Spain has done to enlarge the*
> *human mind and pull mankind a few steps up the hill,*
> *the answer is less clear.*

Extraordinarily, for Clark the Spanish had done nothing to advance 'the European mind', and so had no place in his magnum opus. Echoing a generally held view, the country had played little part in the history of ideas, so why look to it for the future?

As with Cassandra, so with Spain: the rest of the world ignores her and carries on, convinced that their own particular Troy will never fall. Spain may be viewed as a pleasant tourist destination, as one of a handful of economically fragile Mediterranean countries propped up by the rest of the European Union, as a nation of passion, colour and *fiesta* – in all manner of ways – but it is seldom seen as pathfinder or harbinger, despite acting as a gauge of the winds of time over many hundreds of years.

The cause for this myopia lies as much with the Spanish themselves as with outsiders. As with most peoples, Spaniards are generally proud of their country's achievements. But ask what those achievements are and many would struggle to recognise a large number of the examples given above. In fact, an average Spanish person is more likely to inform you that the (admittedly laudable) pastime of table football was invented by one of his compatriots, than that the scalpel, speculum and over two hundred other common surgical instruments were first devised by a Cordoban of the twelfth century. Or that a clunking long-distance train known as the *Talgo* was the fruit of Spanish industrial design, than that the concept of 'human rights' was first debated over four hundred years ago in Valladolid.

And this is because Spain is locked in perpetual civil conflict: every century in the country's history has witnessed at least one major civil war, often several. In consequence, Spain periodically blinds herself to huge swathes of her own past in an attempt to forge new national identities. By drawing a veil over aspects of her history, pretending that they never happened or placing them in some sanitising parenthesis, she tries to create a positive out of a negative aimed at uniting a notoriously disunited people: If we are not *that*, then we must be *this*.

The most recent example of this collective act of forgetting came in the wake of the dictator Franco's death in 1975. In what was actually called the 'pact of forgetting' or the 'pact of silence', the bloodshed and crimes of the previous decades were made to vanish in what was viewed as a pragmatic move to help pacify the many forces which might have brought down the nascent democratic state. 'Don't mention the war!' became the unspoken watchword.

Another lasting and perhaps more serious example is found in how the Moorish period of Spanish history is viewed to this day.

The orthodoxy is that the Moors are 'Other', are 'them', and that the 'Spanish' side of that particular chapter involves nothing more than the defeat and expulsion of the 'invader' (over the course of some eight hundred years, no less). That a thriving and highly advanced civilisation could exist in a country for almost a millennium and then be effectively wiped from the national story – by pretending that 'we' had nothing to do with it – is clearly absurd. And yet the reason why an average Spaniard can't tell you that, to take our example, modern surgery was invented by one of his own, is because that man was a Muslim, spoke Arabic and went by the name of Al-Zahrawi. In the Spanish imagination he is, at a stroke, removed from the collective narrative as a 'non-Spaniard'.

The trouble with not knowing your own history, however – or only having a partial grasp of it – is that you lay yourself open to the risk of repeating patterns of behaviour, many of which can be destructive. Expunging what doesn't fit, or what is uncomfortable, only brings more problems in its wake. The 'pact of forgetting' which acted as midwife to the modern Spanish state may have seemed a good idea in its day, but the multiple and dangerous divisions within Spain now can largely be understood as a split between supporters and detractors of the nation constructed in the late 1970s. Many of the problems lie in the lack of honesty about how it was built and what preceded it. Pretending that the ghosts from the past don't exist only makes them stronger in the long run.

This is the story that Spanish history consistently tells, of trying to remove unwanted truths from its past only to fall back into repeated patterns of behaviour. The tendency is so integral to the country's experience that it is even embodied in its patron saint, St James – Santiago. As Islamic Iberian kingdoms were gradually conquered during the Middle Ages, a collective identity on the

Christian side coalesced around 'not being Moorish'. Hence Santiago's nickname 'Matamoros', the Moor-Slayer, and his depiction astride a horse slicing off be-turbanned heads. For centuries Santiago provided a symbol around which the Christian Spanish peoples could find some kind of shared identity: 'We are not *them*.' But beyond being a warrior for Christ, Santiago doesn't in turn supply much in the way of what being Spanish actually is. Because 'Spanishness' is a particularly slippery quality to define. And so the poor saint is frozen in his martial pose, forever fending off perceived threats to national unity. In consequence, the handful of 'Moors' at his feet turn into a form-changing Hydra, stubbornly growing new heads whenever any are cut off.

The role Santiago represents has been played many times over the course of Spanish history, often predating the saint's icono- graphical metamorphosis from Apostle into bloodthirsty Knight. The Visigoths, the Almohad caliphs, Philip II, and Franco, all tried in some way to forge a Spain in their own image, and all, ultimately, failed. For the job of killing off the enemy is a perpetual and thankless task; Spain is a conglomeration of nations, witnessed by the fact that today, with a population of some forty million, it has five official languages (one of which, Basque, is not even Indo- European). In such circumstances national unity can at best be a work in progress, and threats against it can never be annihilated; in recent times it has risen again in the shape of Catalan separatism. Santiago would be better served by turning his sword towards himself and studying his own face reflected in its steel surface. Then he might understand that, in fact, there is no Other, only him, multifaceted, complex and endlessly fascinating.

Some of the greats of Spanish culture have at times performed this very act, placing a looking glass before their audience:

Cervantes with his multi-layered depiction of the impoverished yet aristocratic *hidalgo* Don Quixote; Goya in the psychological and satirical acuity of his royal portraits, of which his sitters were (presumably) unaware; and most obviously Velázquez in his masterpiece, *Las Meninas*, by deliberately placing a mirror at its heart, reflecting the royal couple watching him work while he paints their daughter. In all of these, the invitation is to look at ourselves – and for the Spanish to look at themselves.

Yet despite these individual moments of clarity, the tendency (as elsewhere: the Spanish have no monopoly on this) is towards partial collective amnesia. If history is viewed at all, it is generally less in order to shed light on the present than to support one or other current world view or perspective. And this in turn condemns the country blindly to follow routes it has taken many times before; the details change, but the structure remains the same.

Part of the problem is that learning from past mistakes requires a certain humility. Yet if one Deadly Sin were to define the Spanish national character, it would be Pride. Anyone who has spent time in the country and with its people will know what I mean. Many examples could be given by way of illustration, but here is one taken almost at random:

At a party in France once I met a Swiss woman who ran a luxury car-valeting service in Berne.

'I used to employ Spaniards,' she told me, 'but not any more.'

I asked her to explain.

'They were too quick to take offence. If they felt a customer wasn't treating them with enough respect they would simply refuse to clean his car.'

Images flashed through my mind of imperious Ferrari-driving bankers ordering valet boys around, and a secret sympathy for the put-down-upon Spaniards came with it. But the woman went on:

'You can't run a business like that. I only employ Portuguese now.'

Things in Spain are rarely what they seem. Black and white do not lie in binary opposition, but tend to coexist side by side in paradoxical union. How else can one explain that in a perpetually divided nation (which has no words to its national anthem because no one can agree what they should be) there are those who, with no sense of irony, use terms such as *la España eterna* – 'eternal Spain' – as though it had been created by God Himself? The country's geographical positioning goes a long way to explaining this curious state of affairs: seen from above, it becomes clear that Spain is a crossroads – between Europe and Africa, the Mediterranean and the Atlantic, between East and West, North and South.[1] As such it is simultaneously all of these seemingly contradictory things, a springboard from one to the other, while also being essentially itself.

This mixing of so many elements over the centuries from so many different quarters has had the effect of turning Spain into a crucible, where multiple and apparently inharmonious ingredients have long been combined in alchemical experimentation. Sometimes gold is produced; at other times, base lead. And this contradiction explains the inner tensions which define the country: her influence – the product of her refining – spreads far beyond her borders, while she herself continues to bubble in agitation, caught between pulls to the dark and pulls to the light, both equally strong.

In a similarly paradoxical fashion, this book is both a history and not a history. History, to my mind, while fascinating in itself, best serves us when it functions as a tool in which understanding

---

1 Beyond Spain, it is frequently overlooked that in her African exclaves of Ceuta and Melilla, there are actual land borders between the developed and developing worlds.

yesterday helps bring a better awareness of today and tomorrow. Spain's story is told here from her very beginnings to the present day, and includes a liberal sprinkling of anecdote and personal observation. It is history viewed from a macro-perspective, one in which patterns emerge that might be invisible when focusing at a micro-level. As such there will inevitably be gaps, but it is my intention that the overall story of Spain's past will shed light on the country's current state and the choices facing it. And in consequence, the choices which will be facing other Western countries in the near future.

Spain has given me so much – my passion, interests, and my livelihood. Without Spain I would be much the poorer person, for it is the birthplace of both my wife and my two children. I have been enamoured of it since I was a teenager, when a chance glimpse of images of the Alhambra captivated me and subsequently shaped the course of my life, leading me to a degree in Arabic and Islamic History at Oxford, and from there to making Spain my home. This book is a distillation of much thinking, reading and writing about the country over the past thirty-five years, but most importantly of living there, absorbing the language and culture, and, as far as I am able, going 'native'. It is in part a homage to the best of Spain, an indefinable yet instantly recognisable essence, a precious kernel which has held me spellbound my entire adult life. The Spain which enchants and enraptures; a powerhouse of art, beauty, wisdom and mystery; a crossroads for civilisations and a country which has given so much to the rest of the world – this is the Spain I love and champion.

Yet Spain is currently going through moments of great stress, and these are intrinsically bound up with patterns and structures which have governed events in the country for well over a thousand years: moments of brightness, of openness and experimentation in her past regularly give way to insularity, self-obsession and darkness. In that way she is a prisoner of her own history. Unless she can come to a swift and better position of self-awareness, she appears destined to follow one of two paths into the future. Neither will be pleasant; both involve bloodshed.

And why that matters is because what happens in Spain today and tomorrow will predict in large part what takes place elsewhere the day after.

THE THREE FACES OF
ST JAMES

St James – Santiago – patron saint of Spain, icon and symbol of a country. The man who, officially, lies buried at Compostela in the north-western corner of the Iberian Peninsula, final destination of the most important pilgrimage in Christendom[1]: Christianity's 'Mecca'.

As with many saints, James's story is complicated. Yet where other national patrons may be easily identified – St George with his dragon, St Andrew with his X-shaped cross, or St Patrick with his snakes – Santiago comes in very different guises, ones which in ordinary circumstances would be mutually exclusive.

In fact, pilgrims crossing the Pyrenees might be forgiven for wondering who St James really is, not because the source material about him dates from remote times, but because he has what today could be termed 'branding issues'. There isn't a single, clearly recognised image of the man. Instead there are three.

---

1 *Dixit* Dante.

Let's take the first. This shows James as an Apostle of Christ. He is not just any Apostle: James is one of the three closest disciples of Jesus, along with John (James's younger brother and author of the Gospel that bears his name) and Peter. These men are the only ones who witness the Transfiguration. A fisherman by trade and son of Zebedee, this is James the Greater, so called to distinguish him from another Apostle of the same name, James the Less. (The original Ya'akov became Iacobus in Latin, which eventually turned into the English James. In Spain it evolved into both 'Jaime' and 'Iago'. 'Sant Iago' was elided into 'Santiago', which then went on to become Diego, or Tiago in Portuguese.)

St James the Greater was a hothead. Luke's Gospel mentions how, when Jesus and his disciples were turned away from a Samaritan town, James and John suggested burning the place to the ground in a scorched-earth reprisal. Similar, eyebrow-raising behaviour appears in an anecdote related in Mark's Gospel, when James and John ask to sit at Jesus's right and left side 'in glory'. On both occasions they are rebuked, and receive the nickname 'Boanerges', the 'sons of thunder' in reference to their fiery nature.

Be that as it may, James's status as a senior disciple was confirmed by his being the only Apostle whose martyrdom is mentioned in the New Testament: he was put to the sword in AD 44 by the order of King Herod Agrippa, friend of the Emperor Claudius.

What happened next introduces the Spanish connection. Stories linking St James to the Iberian Peninsula began to appear around the early seventh century. According to these sources, after his death James's friends placed his body in a boat made of stone which had neither sails, oars nor sailors. The boat then made its own miraculous way along the Mediterranean, through the Strait of Gibraltar, and up the western Iberian coast till it landed in Galicia at a place called Iria Flavia[2]. After a number of adventures, the body was finally buried, only to be discovered – again, miraculously – several hundred years later in the ninth century, an event which initiated the famous pilgrimage in his name.

The reason why, according to the stories, James's body found its way to Spain is because in the years before his death he had already visited the Peninsula. Again, the legends developed centuries afterwards, but following the 'speaking in tongues' at Pentecost, the Apostles dispersed to preach Jesus's message. James got the task of converting the Diaspora Jews. By the seventh century, in an anonymous text known as the *Breviarium Apostolorum*, this mission had been specified to 'Spain and the West'. It was shortly after his return to Judea from Spain that James was executed.

We shall return to the legends of St James in more detail when we reach the Middle Ages and the establishment of the pilgrimage to Compostela. For the time being, consider this pattern, for it will crop up again several times: a man very close to a prophet or a deity travels from the East to perform great deeds in Spain; thanks to his efforts, a new culture develops, and a new connection between Spain and the rest of the world is established.

Now, given his importance as a disciple, you would assume that images of St James would draw inspiration from the New Testament. It's true that as you progress along the pilgrimage route – or travel throughout Spain – paintings or sculptures of him with a beard and biblical-looking robes can be found. But not very often, or at least not as often as you might think.

For St James has two other manifestations.

---

2 Today's Padrón, home of Spain's occasionally spicy chilli peppers 'Pimientos de Padrón'. Whether there is a connection here with St James's alleged hotheadedness is not known.

The second is that of Santiago as a pilgrim, dressed as a typical medieval foot-traveller with long robes, a staff, a leather satchel over his shoulder, and a wide-brimmed hat with a scallop shell – symbol of the pilgrimage – attached to the front. There is, of course, no mention of him dressing or acting in this manner in the Bible, but in this guise he acts as a kind of mirror, reflecting the pilgrim back to himself. He is a seeker, a man alone in the world, on a quest, in search of answers, a distant and sacred destination in mind. He is open and friendly, at the mercy of whatever Life or Fate may send his way. He is gentle and harmless, barely leaving an imprint on the world he is passing through, his mind focused on the next world, on the world beyond worlds. He is a mystic, a person for whom this life represents a mere moment, a passage, a journey through illusion.

This Santiago is a traveller and a man of peace. He seeks answers and wishes to cure ills.

What greater contrast, then, could there be with the third and final manifestation of Spain's patron saint?

This is St James as he is commonly seen in every corner of the country. The apostolic robes have been exchanged for armour, the pilgrim's staff for a sword. And the saint no longer walks, he rides a white horse. Most importantly, preaching a message of turning the other cheek has been replaced by the more vigorous activity of slaughtering the enemy. And in case you're wondering who the saint is violently despatching to the other side, observe the turbans on their severed heads.

This is Santiago 'Matamoros', the 'Moor-Slayer', symbol of military might, the soldier, the victor, the oppressor, the killer. A bloodstained hero who crashes in and smites whoever needs to be smitten in the name of Spain, its purity, its unity, its very being. He is the sword and shield of the country, its creator and defender, the man in whose name it exists and continues to exist. No mercy, no discussion, no subtlety. Mere might and righteousness, and a simple answer: the use of extreme violence to oppress and exterminate the enemy, the Other.

One saint, three very different images: the Saint, the Seeker and the Slayer.

It is common when referring to Spain and Spanish history to talk about *las dos Españas* in reference to a poem by twentieth-century poet Antonio Machado coining the phrase.[3] Two versions of the country, according to the idea, are perpetually at loggerheads, trying to annihilate each other. Yet this is only a partial truth. As the manifestations of Santiago, Spain's patron and symbol, indicate, there are in fact three Spains, two in direct opposition, while the third watches from the sidelines, generally patiently but sometimes wearily, trying to explain to the other two the folly of their struggle.

This is Spain.

And these are her three faces.

---

3 *Epañolito que vienes / al mundo, te guarde Dios. / Una de las dos Españas / ha de helarte el corazón.* 'Oh little Spaniard, fresh in the world, may God protect you. For one of the two Spains will chill your heart.'

PART ONE

PRE-SPAIN

GEOGRAPHY

Geography can give clues to much of a country's national character and behaviour, even determine it. This holds no less for Spain, whose location and landscape explain some of her essential paradoxes: her simultaneously open and yet closed, almost bunker-like tendencies; her singular coherence and perpetual regional struggles; her strong sense of self coexisting with constant debate over her own identity.

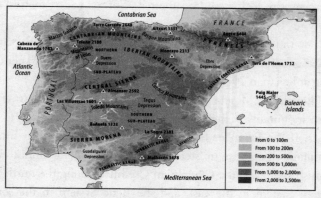

Geographically, Spain is a series of castles within a greater castle

Like Britain, Spain is at once part of and yet semi-detached from Europe. But while the sea marks Britain's divide from the Continent, Spain is at one remove thanks to the high mountains of the Pyrenees. These were formed from the Cretaceous Period to the Eocene Epoch as the Iberian Plate, a tectonic land mass in its own right, rotated anticlockwise and smashed into southern France. In a similar fashion to India, whose movement northwards has caused the rising of the Himalayas, Spain is akin to a subcontinent, if on a much smaller scale.

This geological separateness reflects both a certain uniqueness about Spain and its enormous internal complexity.

Mountains are a key feature of the Spanish landscape. A surprising fact, perhaps, when the vast, flat, and quintessentially Spanish plains of the interior are conjured in the imagination. Yet much of these areas, despite their relative lack of high peaks, lie at well over 600 metres, or 2,000 feet – the generally accepted minimum height for a mountain. In fact the average height of the whole country is 660 metres, making it the second-most mountainous country in Europe after Switzerland, with an average altitude of 1,350 metres. Compare this to France (375 metres), Germany (263 metres) and low-lying Britain (162 metres) and you get a sense of quite how high up much of Spain really is. As much as a quarter of the country has an altitude of over 1,000 metres, with only about 10 per cent lying at less than 200 metres above sea level.

The central Meseta, or Tableland, apart, what's curious about these mountains is that many of them lie along or close to the coasts. If the Pyrenees form a barrier with France, then similar mountain chains rise up steeply from the sea along almost every Spanish shoreline: the Cantabrian Cordillera along the north, the Iberian System in the east, and the Betic System in the south.

Where any strip between sea and mountains exists at all, it is usually quite narrow. Geographically, Spain appears like a fortress or castle, with high walls defending its outer perimeter.

Yet contrast this with its location, and the first paradox becomes apparent. Spain is nothing if not a crossing point: it touches Europe to the north and is only eight miles away from Africa at its southern tip; half of its coastline is Mediterranean, the other Atlantic – passage from one body of water to the other can only take place by skirting the Spanish shoreline. Not surprising, then, that it was the springboard for the Old World's discovery of the New. And also why it has been settled throughout history by peoples from all quarters, from Germanic tribes to Berbers and from Jews to Celts.

But this openness and expansiveness comes hand in hand with a tendency towards isolationism. For the walls that constitute the coastline mountain ranges are not alone: further ranges stretch inland, dividing this subcontinent into natural zones, with widely varying climates. Andalusia, for example, has its own dividing line from the rest of the country in the shape of the Sierra Morena, rising from the northern banks of the River Guadalquivir. So emblematic is the only pass through this range – the Despeñaperros gorge – that it is used in much the same way as the English talk of the Watford Gap to denote a geographical marker between north and south.

Castilla–León, the heartland of old, Catholic Spain and birthplace of El Cid, is walled in both to the south by the Sierra de Guadarrama, which divides it from Madrid, and the Cantabrian chain to the north cutting it off from the sea. Castilla–La Mancha contains such a richness of natural barriers that until the past thirty years there were no direct transport communications between Madrid and its nearest port city (as the crow flies), Valencia. Only recent developments in civil engineering have allowed Man finally to conquer it, several decades after landing on the Moon . . .

The various rivers cutting through these mountain ranges offer only small chinks in the defensive walls: both the Ebro and the Tagus become unnavigable a short way inland as they bend and twist their way past towering rock faces. The Guadalquivir is the only exception, and allowed the Moors to establish their capital deep in the Andalusian heartland at Cordoba. But silting problems made this passage short-lived: any modern visitor to the city struggles to imagine today's shallow waters once constituting one of the most important shipping lanes in the world.

Historically speaking, travel and communication across the Peninsula have been, if not impossible, then complicated. Which brings us to the second paradox: geologically and geographically, Spain has a clear, unified sense of self (*pace* Portugal). Seen from outer space, it is one of the world's more easily identifiable countries, its boundaries clearly visible in the shape of coastlines, or the Pyrenees mountains. And yet this unity fails to provide cohesion within the country itself because those same mountain barriers also form internal divisions which historically have delineated the various segments which make up the country. Standing on the edge of a green Galician fjord-like *Ría* with grey, melancholy Atlantic winds blowing in, you feel far closer in spirit to Ireland or Brittany than to the toehold of the Sahara Desert which has leapt the Mediterranean and established itself on the opposite corner of the Peninsula at Almería. Likewise at Tarifa, Spain's most southerly tip, where Africa is so close you feel you could reach out and touch it, your imagination struggles to grasp that you are in the same country as the temperate ash and oak forests of northern Navarre.

Such geographical differences heighten and strengthen the many regional identities within Spain. Seen from one level, a micro-level, they are distinct nations. Yet from a macro-level they are obviously one. Both views are correct; at one time or another, either one or the other has prevailed, and the perpetual question that hangs over Spain and its identity has been the cause of much violence and bloodshed.

PEOPLES

Few countries in the Old World enjoy Spain's rich mixture of cultures. For many thousands of years, peoples have travelled to the Iberian Peninsula from all directions. And while the country has been the final destination for many of these migrations, it has also – in a tradition that continues to this day – acted as the launch pad for large exoduses, some voluntary, others forced.

Something of this pattern emerges from very early human times, when the Peninsula became the last bastion of the much-maligned (although increasingly respected) Neanderthals. It was at the southern tip of Spain, the Rock of Gibraltar, that the last of their kind are thought to have holed up, a small, final group of a hominid that had once roamed the European Continent. Pushed out by their smaller but presumably more capable Cro-Magnon cousins (with an occasional inter-species sexual encounter en route), they lived in caves, unable to escape across the Strait to possible safety on the other side. Had they done so, perhaps the history of humanity would have been quite different.

Millennia later, these last remaining Neanderthals provided the first evidence to modern scientists of their existence. The joke goes that 'Neanderthal Man' should really be called 'Gibraltarian Woman'. In 1846, Lieutenant Edmund Flint of the Royal Navy was involved in excavations for the construction of a new fortification at the northern end of the Rock. Stone for the structure came from nearby Forbes' Quarry, and it was there that one day Flint came across what appeared to be an ancient human skull. As well as a naval officer, he was also secretary of the Gibraltar Scientific Society, and two years later, in 1848, he presented the skull to the learned members, describing it as an ancient human who had died 'before the Flood'.

Not much more was thought of the skull, and it was left for several years in a cupboard in the Garrison Library.

In late 1859, Darwin published *On the Origin of Species* and a new interest in ancient bones and relics was kindled. In 1862, a couple of palaeontologists visiting Gibraltar, George Busk and Hugh Falconer, examined the skull, and two years later they presented a report on it to the British Association for the Advancement of Science in London, concluding, as Darwin himself did after examining it, that it belonged to an extinct human species and should be named *Homo Calpicus*, after the ancient Greek name for Gibraltar, 'Calpe'.

Only later did Busk realise that it was the same species as the one discovered a few years earlier, in 1856, in the Neander valley near Dusseldorf. The Gibraltarian female skull was in fact *Homo Neanderthalis*.

If the Strait served as a barrier for the Neanderthals, however, it acted as a bridge for later cultures. The Neolithic period begins in Spain with the arrival of farmers from North Africa some seven thousand years ago. Genetic studies suggest they had originated in the Fertile Crescent and made their way down into Arabia before crossing the Horn of Africa into today's Sudan, pushing up through Egypt and from there westwards to the Maghreb. On reaching Spain, they seem to have limited their presence to the southern and eastern coasts, leaving the hunter-gatherers further inland to their own devices. These new arrivals brought crop-growing techniques with them, living off cereals and legumes, as well as pork and rabbit and, that most typical of Mediterranean foods, olives.

Skip forward a few thousand years, and we move into the Copper Age and the emergence of the first-known Spanish cities. Los Millares, just to the north of modern Almería, was established around 3100 BC. It was discovered in 1891 during the building of a new railway line.[1]

Los Millares was a proper city state, home to upwards of a thousand people who dominated much of the local area. The culture, however, was martial and violent, as witnessed by its four lines of defensive walls. Archaeologists have found many arrowheads in the area, most of them bent or broken where they were fired by enemy forces against the residents. Life expectancy was not much more than thirty years, with high levels of child mortality. It was also a very hierarchical society, in which religion played a key role in establishing and maintaining strict social structures.

While the Los Millares culture eventually died out, it was quickly replaced by a new civilisation just a few miles away at a place known as El Algar, whose dominance came from a new technology, bronze-making.

Established around 2200 BC, the El Algar culture turned into

---

[1] The British were responsible for much of the expansion of the Spanish railway network in the nineteenth century, a fact reflected in the nearby coastal town of Águilas, where many of the local railway workers lived. To this day, Anglicanism is the majority religion in the town.

a proper unified state whose boundaries stretched up towards the central Spanish Meseta highlands, and from today's Murcia in the east to Granada and Jaén in the west. The bronze was used essentially to make weapons; knives, spearheads and arrowheads, swords and large curved axes abound at El Algar sites. When it came to killing, bronze gave you the edge, and this south-eastern corner of Spain turned into the Peninsula's undisputed centre of metallurgy.

Archaeologists have argued over whether these Bronze Age cultures developed on their own (the so-called 'Occidentalist' theory) or whether they were imports from the East (the 'Orientalists'). For the time being the Occidentalists have the upper hand, but some form of contact with the eastern Mediterranean continued in this period, as shown by some of the dead at El Algar being buried in jars, a tradition presumably borrowed from the Ancient Greeks, who carried out the same practice.

While these cultures were dominating the south, however, a new wave of immigrants was pouring in from the north towards the end of the Bronze Age in what would turn out – genetically speaking – to be the most important influx into the Iberian Peninsula.

Over the next few hundred years, waves of people from Europe would cross the Pyrenees, first the Urnfield culture (known as 'proto-Celts') who spread along the Mediterranean coast into modern Catalonia, and then in the Iron Age, waves of the Hallstatt peoples ('proper' Celts), who settled mostly in central and western areas. Today around two thirds of Spanish and Portuguese men carry R1b haplogroup Y-DNA, suggesting their ancestors arrived during this time. Celtic languages were still being spoken in some parts of Spain at the time of the Roman conquest.

Meanwhile, southern Spain was playing host to its own new wave of immigrants. The Phoenicians, master traders of the ancient world, had reached Iberian shores and in 1104 BC founded the city of Cádiz, the oldest surviving city in Western Europe. Shortly afterwards they also founded Malaga, Almuñécar and Lisbon. Along with things like writing, potter's wheels and iron, they also introduced wine-making.

The genetic imprint which the Phoenicians left behind is interesting because it is quite localised. Perhaps not surprisingly, it is relatively high in the modern city of Cádiz, where some 10 per cent of the population can boast Phoenician blood. Meanwhile Ibiza, which also became a Phoenician colony, has as much as 13 per cent.

By the eighth century the Greeks were also alive to trading opportunities in the Peninsula – which they called 'Iberia' – and were spreading southwards from their colony in Marseille, setting up posts at Ampurias and along the eastern coastline as far south as Alicante. Unlike the Phoenicians, however, they appear to have kept their sexual activities in-house, as there is little Greek DNA in the general Spanish gene pool.

As their power waned, the Phoenicians and Greeks were respectively replaced by the Carthaginians and Romans. The most celebrated clash between these Mediterranean superpowers – the Second Punic War – started in Spain. Eventually, as we know, the Romans emerged victorious, Hannibal's elephants notwithstanding. In the wake of the Carthaginian defeat, the Peninsula was slowly conquered by Rome's legions.

Roman culture left an indelible mark on Spain, not least in the various Spanish languages spoken today (apart from Basque). But when it comes to genetics, the picture is murkier, as Roman DNA looks like a mixture of Celtic and Greek. Yet this may go some way to explaining the preponderance of the R1b haplogroup among contemporary Spaniards.

During the Roman period, another group from the East decided to make its way to Spanish shores. There is growing evidence to suggest that Jews migrated to the Peninsula long before the Diaspora of the first century AD, and that sizeable communities had existed for some centuries when the later influx arrived. In fact, the Sephardic Jews, as they became known (from the Hebrew word for Spain, 'Sefarad') maintained their own traditions that this was indeed so. The Jewish community played an important part in Spanish life for some two thousand years. The order in 1492 for them to convert to Catholicism or face expulsion came as a shock. Many stayed, demonstrated by the fact that today as many as 25 per cent of Spanish people have Jewish blood.

Towards the end of the Roman Empire and following its collapse, the Peninsula once again became a magnet for wandering peoples, this time a number of Germanic tribes, from the Vandals to the Suebi and finally the Goths. The Visigoths eventually dominated and managed to establish the first political entity which could be called 'Spain' – the kingdom of Hispania, which lasted until the Moorish invasion of the eighth century. Yet, as with the Greeks (and possibly the Romans), they left precious little in the way of genetic material. In the mid-twentieth century, during the Franco dictatorship, Spaniards were taught to view the Visigoths as their ancestors, rulers of a united, Christian nation which existed before Islam, yet Gothic DNA in the Spanish gene pool is noticeable for its absence.

The Visigothic kingdom was defeated by invading Muslims in AD 711, and within some ten years almost the entire Peninsula was under Moorish control. Given the various waves of peoples arriving from the eastern Mediterranean over the preceding millennia, this was nothing particularly new, although historically it has taken on enormous proportions. As for the Spanish gene pool, the invasion also brought fresh supplies. 'Moors' is an umbrella term to cover the numerous peoples who lived in Islamic Spain. The vast majority, genetically speaking, were locals who gradually adopted the ways of the new rulers. Arab and Berber blood predominated among the newcomers, but Persian and sub-Saharan African peoples also arrived in Spain in smaller numbers as part of a largely fluid culture that stretched from the Atlantic to the Hindu Kush. Today, some 10 per cent of modern Spaniards have 'Moorish' DNA. The fact that this is less than the amount of Jewish DNA underlies how most 'Moors' were actually local peoples – Spaniards.

The expulsion of the Moriscos – Spain's last remaining Muslims – in 1609 saw the forceful removal of some three hundred thousand people, but as with the expulsion of the Jews a century before, many managed to stay behind. Large numbers even slipped back unnoticed into Spain over the following years.

Peoples and cultures coming and going, fresh ingredients for the Spanish crucible . . . The trend continues throughout the country's history. In the early 1400s, the first Gypsies arrived, passing over the Pyrenees to travel to Santiago, and were given safe conduct by the king of Aragon. With the conquest of the New World, swathes of Spaniards left the Peninsula to seek adventure and fortune across the Atlantic. In turn, people from the other side started arriving in Spain, small in numbers initially, but increasing to their hundreds of thousands in only the past few years. Meanwhile, more waves of Spaniards have been leaving – around half a million forced into exile at the end of the Spanish Civil War in 1939; another million in recent years following the economic crisis of 2008: young people seeking work and a better life, not unlike their Conquistador ancestors four and five hundred years before.

And all the while, at the land borders between Spain's African exclaves of Ceuta and Melilla, thousands of young men and women throw themselves at the high fences and razor wire, dreaming of crossing to the First World.

For thousands of years these tides of humanity have swept across the Iberian Peninsula. And they still do.

TWO CAVES

Both lie in northern central Spain, no more than a two-hour drive from each other. They have – to a foreign ear – confusingly similar names. Both are hugely important archaeological sites which give important clues to, and raise fascinating questions about, our prehistoric ancestors. And the discoveries of both originate in the late nineteenth century. Chronologically speaking, however, they could hardly be further apart, one dating back some thirty-five thousand years, and the other around a million. Both, however, represent 'firsts' in their respective ways.

The Sierra of Atapuerca lies a few miles to the east of the city of Burgos, not far from the birthplace of El Cid, an important stop on the Camino de Santiago, home to one of the country's most magnificent Gothic cathedrals, and former capital, during the Spanish Civil War, of Franco's 'Nationalist' government. It was here, in the 1890s, that a British businessman trying to cash in on Spain's early industrialisation decided to build a railway line. Richard Preece Williams, head of the Sierra Company, Ltd, wanted to transport new sources of iron and coal to the Basque port city of

Bilbao, where Spain's early smelting factories were mostly centred. And so he created 40 miles of new track originating in the Sierra de la Demanda, to the south-east of Burgos, which would then link up with the existing network.

Preece Williams, however, did something odd when routing his new line, something which no one to date has been able to explain. Rather than following the River Pico, he made a detour to the north in order to go through the Atapuerca mountains. To do so slowed the project down and caused great expense, not least by having to blast a trench 800 metres long, 10 metres wide and up to 20 metres deep. Was he looking for limestone? Or perhaps phosphite, essential for producing fertilisers? Whatever it was, as a result the Sierra Company failed to prosper and went bankrupt in 1910, less than a decade after opening its new railway.

Thanks to Preece Williams's whim, however, we now have much greater knowledge – if not always answers – about the first proto-humans, or hominids, in Western Europe.

Admittedly, some basic excavations of the area had taken place in the years leading up to the Sierra Company's arrival, but it wasn't until the 1960s and '70s that studies began in earnest, taking advantage of the access to a complex and extremely ancient cave network which the railway had created.

As a result, the great findings of Atapuerca were made, and they caused a revolution in the study of early Man, one which continues to throw up new clues and puzzles almost every year.

The earliest signs of settlement in the complex are now thought to date to 1.2 million years ago, placing hominids in Europe many hundreds of thousands of years earlier than once thought. So old are these remains, and so recent their discovery, that they have yet to be identified: they show similarities with the earliest *Homo* remains from Africa and Georgia, yet have certain differences.

Other remains, found in a different cave, date to over eight hundred thousand years ago and have given rise to a new classification of early man – *Homo antecessor*. Both he and his predecessors are believed to have been involved in what is called Out of Africa I, the first theoretical movement of early peoples into the rest of the world starting roughly 1.8 million years ago. How these hominids reached Europe is unclear. Over the Sinai? Across the Mediterranean, then much lower than today? No one can say for sure. Even allowing for lower sea levels, the Strait of Gibraltar would still have been very deep and subject to strong currents.

Whatever their origins and routes taken, however, the Atapuerca mountains became a favoured spot. The area was used over many hundreds of thousands of years, with evidence of settlements there of *Homo heidelbergensis*, who lived between six hundred thousand and two hundred thousand years ago, and Neanderthals.

Elephants and rhinoceroses were some of the more exotic animals to have lived alongside early humans in these ancient times, and some of their bones show signs of having been cut into and scraped using stone tools. Atapuerca, with its sheltering caves and wealth of food supplies, was, in many ways, a desirable place to live.

But the living wasn't always easy. Bone remains of *Homo antecessor* show the same marks and cuts as animal ones, a clear sign that cannibalism was prevalent.

And then there is the curious case of Cranium 17 . . .

One of the caves at Atapuerca is called the Sima de los Huesos – the ditch of bones. In it have been found the remains of almost thirty people, over six and a half thousand bone fossils in total. All of them belong to *Homo heidelbergensis*, precursor of Neanderthals, and among them figure some of the best-conserved remains of ancient man, including Cranium 5, nicknamed 'Miguelón' in honour of champion Spanish cyclist and five-times winner of the Tour de France Miguel Indurain. Also a male pelvis (nicknamed 'Elvis'), considered the best example of the entire fossil record. Conclusions drawn from it suggest that Homo heidelbergensis was about the same size as us, if somewhat more robust.

All these bones lie at the bottom of a 13-metre-deep pit, and among them has also been found a stone axe (named 'Excalibur') made of red quartzite. Interestingly, the axe was never used, and was found in mint condition. Which raised the question, what was it doing there?

The conclusion is that the Sima de los Huesos was a primitive mortuary, a place where the dead were deliberately laid to rest. And the fact that Excalibur was thrown in there with them suggests an understanding of symbolism, of the concepts of 'life' and 'death'. Homo heidelbergensis weren't just human in the physical sense, they were also human spiritually as well.

The existence of Cranium 17 in the same pit, however, testifies to the fact that while our early Atapuerca ancestors may have conceptualised the other world, they were also prepared, on occasion, to hasten someone's passage there.

Cranium 17 was found in over fifty fragments. When it was pieced together, two holes above the left eyebrow became apparent. Subsequent analysis confirmed the scientists' suspicions: there was no sign of healing, so the cranial damage indicated the cause of death. Also, that the two holes had been made separately, with acute force acting downwards by a right-handed individual. In short, the original owner of Cranium 17 had been murdered.

Some half a million years old, and the mystery, only recently uncovered, now confronts us: why? Who was this person? Who killed him? (Or her; the gender is unclear.)

The only thing we do know is that the world's first-known murder took place in Spain.

If Atapuerca suggests an early – though not exclusive – tendency towards violence, the cave of Altamira clearly demonstrates its opposite, another side of the Spanish soul, capable of producing breathtaking works of art.

On visiting the caves and seeing their paintings, Picasso declared, 'After Altamira, everything seems decadent.' The most celebrated conjunction of paintings inside the cave is often described as 'the Sistine Chapel of the Palaeolithic'.

While Atapuerca is home to Western Europe's first-known hominids, Altamira is the site of the Continent's first identified Stone Age paintings. A local man named Modesto Cubillas found the cave in 1868 while looking for his lost dog. He told a local amateur archaeologist about it, but it took Marcelino Sanz de Sautuola two visits to discover the treasure on his doorstep. The first, in 1875, left him curious but unamazed. Only on a second visit, in 1879, did he understand, when his eight-year-old daughter accompanying him glanced up and exclaimed: 'Look, Daddy! Oxen!'

Sanz de Sautuola published his findings the following year, correctly identifying the cave paintings as being Palaeolithic. But such was the level of skill behind the artwork that his conclusions were rejected out of hand. The French in particular poo-pooed his arguments, even going so far as to claim that the Spaniard had hired a local artist to carry out a forgery. Nothing so beautiful or anatomically correct as the now-famous images of bison that decorate the Altamira cave could possibly be the work of primitive, ancient man . . .

The debate raged for several years, during which time Sanz de Sautuola died, a cloud still hanging over his name. It was not until the early twentieth century, when a host of other caves had been discovered in Spain and France with similar paintings, that his discovery was accepted as genuine.

And what had he found? Research to date the paintings continues, but what seems clear is that artworks were being produced in Altamira for some twenty thousand years. It is even possible that some of them – perhaps those found at similar sites – were the work of Neanderthals.

There are hand paintings, in which people would place a hand against the wall and spit over it a spray of paint made from natural pigments to create a negative effect. There are curious and unidentified abstract symbols. There are animals, such as deer and wild boar. And there are bison, lots of bison. What seems remarkable about them, apart from their spectacular artistic workmanship, is that many have been painted on to bulges in the rock to create a 3-D effect.

Altamira man – and his many cousins in northern Spain and south-eastern France – was clearly sophisticated, not only as a painter, but also as a thinker. If his ancestors at Atapuerca were capable of understanding the symbolism of throwing a stone axe into a pit full of the dead, then many hundreds of thousands of years later, at Altamira, symbols of extraordinary beauty and complexity were being fashioned on a regular basis.

And so what were the paintings for?

Theories, as you might imagine, abound. But magic and a spiritual element are often cited as being part of their meaning, which seems a safe bet. Perhaps an element of shamanism was involved, the invoking of spirits, communication with other worlds. In short, a kind of mysticism.

Two cave complexes, two very different atmospheres, which give a glimpse of two distinct sides of the character of early Spaniards.

MEN FROM THE EAST

Archaeological Spain flows into mythological Spain, which flows, gradually, into history.

Legends about the origins of human communities on the Peninsula have traditionally centred around two figures, both sons of the eastern Mediterranean brought to the west on their travels. As we shall see, their stories form a pattern which is repeated several times over Spanish history.

The first, the mythological founder of Iberia according to ancient sources, including St Isidore of Seville (d. 636 AD), was the biblical Tubal (not to be confused with Tubal Cain, who was a descendant of Cain). Tubal was the son of Japheth, son of Noah. At some point after the Flood, when Noah's offspring were repopulating the world, Tubal and his family landed on the north-west Spanish coast.[1]

Tubal established a dynasty of kings, naming the country after

---

[1] The stories of Santiago's body arriving in Spain have the Apostle's boat touching shore in a similar area: when the rest of the Peninsula was under Islamic control, it made sense for these stories to create a link between the Christian-controlled north and the biblical world.

his eldest son Ibero, who also gave his name to the River Ebro. He
in turn was followed by his descendants, including one Tago (after
whom the River Tagus is named) and Beto (from which came
Betis, the old name of the River Guadalquivir).

Tubal is curious for he appears to have established a new
community not only in Spain but also in Siberia (capital Tobolsk,
supposedly in his honour) and in the Caucasus. In an interesting
echo, ancient Georgia – or at least the eastern half of it – used to be
called Iberia, and the mythical character who established the
country was none other than Tubal. It seems far-fetched to put this
down to mere coincidence, as some insist. So what might be the
connection?

In a Georgian context, Tubal is often seen as synonymous with
a post-Hittite Anatolian state called Tabal. This area was populated
by, among others, a tribe known as the Tibareni, whose name may
derive from Noah's grandson. The Tibareni are thought to be one
of the peoples who founded metallurgy, which grew up on the
southern shores of the Black Sea during the Neolithic era. Did
these metalworkers then travel as far as ancient Iberia with their
new technology, perhaps in search of tin, an essential ingredient for
making bronze? That ancient peoples were quite mobile is now
more accepted than it once was, so early Georgians landing on the
shores of the far western Mediterranean, having first crossed
through the Bosphorus and down the Aegean Sea, is not so prepos-
terous a claim.

But back to Tubal in Iberia, who also, according to legend, put
his stamp on the place by founding the towns of Tafalla, Vélez-
Málaga, Tudela and Úbeda in Spain, and Setúbal in modern
Portugal, suggesting a wide extension over the Peninsula. His
descendants continued as kings for many generations, until we

reach the last two, Gárgoris and Hábis. Stories about these two kings are considered the first truly Spanish legends, as opposed to imports from other Mediterranean cultures.

Gárgoris introduced honey collecting to the peoples of ancient Iberia. He had a beautiful daughter and with her had a son, Hábis. Many attempts were made to do away with the child, fruit of an incestuous relationship, but to no avail – the baby refused to die, despite being exposed in the wild and even thrown out to sea. Eventually, sensing that there was something exceptional about the boy, Gárgoris accepted him, naming him his heir. In due course Hábis became king, introducing agriculture to the Peninsula through the use of yokes on oxen. He also divided society into seven social groups (or cities), and his line continued for many generations thereafter.

This first Spanish myth carries with it one of the main patterns running through the country's history, that of one version of the country trying to smother or annihilate the other: Gárgoris tries to rid himself of his son, Hábis. But the tale also holds the seed for the solution to this seemingly intractable problem: the 'other Spain' can never be got rid of, and so must be accepted; there must be mutual acknowledgement and toleration, and by doing this Spain can take great strides forward: Hábis as king goes on to bring new technologies and civilisation to the Peninsula. The structure of Spanish history is almost all there in this story, but the lesson from it has rarely been learned, as we shall see.

Hábis's Neolithic society has been linked with the historical culture, or city, of Tartessos.

Tartessos is Spain's Troy, existing in a twilight zone between myth and history. That a culture of this name existed in the late Bronze Age and early Iron Age in south-west Spain is not in doubt.

But its exact location is unknown: no city of that name has ever been discovered, leading some to argue that Tartessos described a civilisation rather than a specific place.

Archaeological evidence for the existence of Tartessos – either as a city or as an area – exists in abundance, including the remains of ancient settlements, pieces of gold jewellery, and scraps of a written language which was read from right to left (and which has yet to be deciphered). There are also references to Tartessos in ancient sources: it was mentioned by Herodotus and Pliny as well as many others. Ephorus of Cyme, a Greek historian and contemporary of Alexander the Great states clearly that the city of Tartessos lay between the two mouths of a river of the same name which had previously been called the Betis.

So the city of Tartessos, if it existed, probably lay near to where the Guadalquivir flows into the Atlantic, to the north of Cádiz, in what is today the National Park of Doñana, a wetland and protected nature reserve.

Which brings us to Atlantis, another lost city of the ancient world, located by Plato beyond the Strait of Gibraltar, not far from Cádiz . . .

Was Tartessos Atlantis – that is, if Atlantis existed at all? Some support this idea. An early proponent of the theory was Spanish seventeenth-century historian Juan Pellicer de Ossau. More recently, in the early twentieth century, German archaeologist Adolf Schulten suggested the same. The theory was taken up by several others in the early twenty-first century, but so far exploration of the Doñana area using modern archaeological techniques has revealed nothing.

It is possible, however, that stories linking the myth of Atlantis with ancient Iberia persisted for many centuries after Plato, possibly inspiring a new name for the Peninsula, as we shall see in a subsequent chapter.

But back to Tubal and his dynasty. Gárgoris and Hábis are the last mythological kings of Tartessos. The first was Gerion. And here is where a second, and hugely important, mythological character arrives on Spanish shores: Heracles/Hercules.

The parallels between Heracles and Tubal are striking: neither is a god or prophet in his own right, but both are connected to another greater than themselves – Heracles is a demigod, son of Zeus; Tubal the grandson of God's favourite, Noah. Both are characters belonging originally to traditions emerging from the eastern Mediterranean; and both reach Spain and leave an indelible mark, founding cities and civilisations in their wake. Heroes who connect the country with a powerful culture from the East and then change the course of Spanish history. The pattern is repeated several times.

Being a legend, Heracles steps in and out of the mythological 'chronology'. His first appearance is during the Tenth and Eleventh of his celebrated Tasks, when he tames Gerion's cattle, and then steals the prized apples from the Gardens of Hesperides. Both events take place, supposedly, in Spain.

Not only that, but Heracles created the very Strait between Spain and North Africa which for so long bore his name.

There are several versions of the tale:

The Ancient Greeks believed that the two continents were originally much further apart, and that Heracles brought them closer together, thereby making the passage narrower and shallower to prevent Atlantic sea monsters from entering the more placid waters of the Mediterranean.

The Romans told a story in which Africa and Europe were linked by a mountain during the hero's lifetime – there was no

Strait – and that their Hercules cut a way through it with his bare hands, thus opening the way for the Atlantic to flow into the Mediterranean. The remains of the mountain were left on either side of the newly created channel. These were the 'Pillars of Hercules' – known at the time as Calpe, to the north, and Abilyx, to the south.

But what really were the 'pillars' that Hercules left behind? The two peaks on either side of the Strait? Or actual columns that he himself constructed?

The ancient Iberians insisted that the real pillars were not mountains at all, but structures at the temple of Hercules in Cádiz.[2] According to legend, the real founder of Cádiz was this same Hercules. The temple marked his tomb (lying underneath today's cathedral). So important was this site that, despite its being at the far edge of the world, both Hannibal and Julius Caesar journeyed to visit it. Caesar broke down and wept with emotion on entering.

Along with Cádiz, legends also attribute the founding of Barcelona and Mérida to the demigod, along with a palace which bore his name in Toledo. In addition, a Roman lighthouse in La Coruña, on the far Galician coast, dating from at least the first century AD and measuring almost 60 metres high, is commonly known as the Tower of Hercules. As well as being the only functioning Roman lighthouse still in existence, it links Spanish mythology with the Irish, for it is said that from here Ith, son of the mythical King Breogan, first spotted distant Ireland, eventually sailing and settling there.

---

2 The two columns are part of the Spanish coat of arms to this day, and are the origin of the two vertical lines in the American dollar sign, having been borrowed from the Spanish 'pieces of eight', the common currency in the Atlantic following the discovery of the New World. They have subsequently been used in all major currency symbols.

Perhaps the most interesting stamp that Heracles made on the Peninsula lay in the ancient road that ran from Spain through southern France and into Italy, the Via Heraklea. The exact route this took is not known. Did it hug the Atlantic coast and end at Cartagena? Did it extend beyond and over towards Cádiz? Or was it, as author Graham Robb argues, a straight line which ran from the Cape of St Vincent at the far end of the Algarve to the Alps, following the course of the sun on the Summer Solstice? Whichever path it followed, it's interesting to note how closely Spain was associated with Heracles. A hero who originates in a different culture (or cultures: the Phoenicians had their own version of the demigod, Melkart) at the other end of the Mediterranean becomes synonymous with ancient Iberia. The Via Heraklea, an important route in ancient Europe, is so called precisely because it leads into Spain.

Which brings us to Santiago. Like Tubal and Heracles, St James originates in the eastern Mediterranean. Like them he is not a god or prophet in his own right, but very close to one (even being related to Jesus, as the various Jameses of the New Testament were frequently confused with one another by storytellers, St James the Great sometimes morphing with Jesus's brother of the same name). Like them, he brings change, ushering in a new age for the Peninsula. And like Heracles, he leaves behind a road which carries his name, a route which crosses the Pyrenees into France and thence to the heart of Europe.

Tubal–Heracles–Santiago – heroes from the East who shape and transform Spanish culture.

As we shall see, more like them are to come.

ITALIAN SPAIN

HISPANIAE – THE ROMAN SPAINS

The Romans' influence began to spread in Iberia – a land they called *Hispania* – as early as 281 BC. They understood the Peninsula as a geographical entity, not as a political whole. As with other lands which they conquered, during their seven-hundred-year presence they divided their territories there into a number of provinces.

During the earlier period, when Roman territory was limited to the eastern and southern coasts, the newcomers drew a line roughly where Murcia lies today. The northern part was referred to as 'this Spain' (*Hispania citerior*) and the southern as 'that Spain' (*Hispania ulterior* – the one further away from Rome).

As their control over the Peninsula slowly spread, so did the number of provinces.

By 27 BC, and with the conquest of Spain almost completed, the Emperor Augustus divided the Peninsula into three parts. 'This Spain' became *Hispania tarraconensis*, named after its main city,

Tarragona. 'That Spain' was subdivided: what is roughly today's Andalusia became *Hispania baetica*, while the western areas were known as *Hispania lusitania* (to this day, the Spanish sometimes use the word *luso* to describe things Portuguese).

But by the third century even three provinces were deemed insufficient, and a further two were added, with Tarraconensis split roughly north and south, the southern half named *Cartaginensis*, and northern Lusitania turned into its own province of *Gallaecia* – comprising what is roughly today's Galicia. Things continued in this way until the crumbling of the Roman Empire and the arrival of Germanic tribes in the fifth century.

Three, five, seven, nine . . . Over the centuries the Peninsula would unite and redivide into many different areas and 'countries'. But the final partition into five by the Romans is echoed today both in the number of official languages, and in the Spanish coat of arms, which combines the emblems of the five kingdoms that made up Spain during the High Middle Ages: the castle of Castile; the lion of León (named after the Roman VII *Legion* stationed there, not after any wild beast . . .); the chains of Navarre; the red and yellow stripes of Aragon; and the pomegranate of Moorish Granada (the English 'pomegranate' meaning 'fruit of Granada', hence 'grenade', 'grenadiers', etc.).

Five Spains . . . Roman rule over the Peninsula reflected its essentially fragmented nature. And it's interesting to note today how little the Roman part of Spanish history figures in the collective Spanish imagination. The Latin-based languages are the most significant legacy from the period, but the Romans are very much seen as 'them', not 'us'. And whereas the British will give a sense of how old something is by describing it as 'being there since the Romans', the equivalent phrase in Spanish evokes a later time: *desde los moros* – 'since the Moors'.

Roman Hispania is a key building block in the construction of Spain, giving the Peninsula the name by which it is known today – 'Hispania' – becoming, over time, 'España', Spain.[1] And yet the paradox is that at the same time it isn't, well, *Spain*.

Nonetheless, the Roman period is significant in that it sees the beginnings of both the Cassandra complex which becomes Spain's blessing and curse over the centuries, and of a pattern of forgetting the past in order to forge new ideas about national identity.

As elsewhere, the Roman Empire brought engineering, road-building, and the benefits of their advanced culture, as seen most magnificently at Segovia, whose aqueduct, built around 100 AD, still astounds today with its scale and ambition. The cities of Mérida and Tarragona are home to impressive Roman archaeological remains. In return, Spain gave to Rome some of its most important sons: the Emperors Trajan, Hadrian, Marcus Aurelius and Theodosius were all of Hispanic origin, as was Martial, and Seneca, who was born in Cordoba.

And yet this time in Spanish history is not a glorious example of the Pax Romana, of local peoples adapting to their new enlightened rulers after a period of token resistance. Nor particularly does it demonstrate the famed efficiency of the Roman military. For centuries, in fact, Hispania was a far-off western land which was essentially a theatre of war.

It took Julius Caesar eight years to conquer Gaul. Roman legions covered Britannia in about forty years. By comparison, Hispania

---

1 The etymology behind Hispania is unclear, with various suggestions ranging from 'land of rabbits' or 'far-away land' originating from Phoenician words, to 'last western land' via a garbling of the Greek word 'Hesperia'.

was not completely conquered by the empire for two hundred years. That it took so long can perhaps be explained by the difficult mountainous terrain, or perhaps by the warlike locals, referred to by Virgil as the 'restless Iberians', whose short swords, especially the *falcata*, were made with particularly strong steel and very much feared by Roman legionaries. But when you compare this with the ten years that it took the Moors to conquer the same territory in the eighth century, you begin to wonder.

Rome's initial contact with the Peninsula began in the context of the Punic Wars. Much of the southern and eastern coasts had been colonised by the Carthaginians (following in the footsteps of their predecessors, the Phoenicians). Once the Romans had pushed them out of Corsica, Sardinia and other territories closer to Rome, the Carthaginians saw Iberia as an important toehold on northern Mediterranean shores. The Greeks, however, fearful of further Carthaginian expansion northwards up the Iberian coastline towards their trading colonies, sought defensive alliances with Rome. The scene was set for further conflict, and the most celebrated of the Punic Wars, the Second, began over the town of Sagunto, a hilltop castle and natural defensive position just a mile inland from the sea[2] on Spain's eastern shore. The Carthaginians, now led by Hannibal, besieged and took it, slaughtering many of its inhabitants. The Romans, in turn, insisted their enemy had broken a treaty agreement, and war was declared.

Hannibal almost destroyed Rome in the subsequent campaign. But his eventual defeat in 206 BC opened the way for the Romans to become the dominant power in the Mediterranean. In her first Cassandra-like moment, Spain had therefore acted as the starting

---

2 The castle – much added to over the centuries, most recently by Napoleon – still stands today.

point for what would turn into six hundred years of an imposing empire and civilisation which shaped the Western world.

From a local point of view, Roman victory also opened up the Peninsula to further conquest. It was slow and very painful progress, however. Like other colonisers before them, the Romans concentrated their efforts in the south and east, particularly the fertile Guadalquivir basin. Forays were made to the interior, and a small number of towns and cities were founded or developed, but the full Romanisation of these areas was less intense than on the Mediterranean coast.

Part of this was thanks to the martial spirit of the native peoples they had to deal with. The eastern areas were populated by 'pure' Iberians, although quite who these were is debatable. Some Roman sources referred to these people as swarthy-skinned and with curly hair; others commented on their light skin and pale eyes. Meanwhile, in the far west lived Celtic peoples. And in the middle, sandwiched between them, were the 'Celtiberians' – so-named by the Romans – who supposedly shared characteristics of both Iberians and Celts. Beyond the fact that they spoke a Celtic language which was written using an Iberian script, descriptions of this nebulous culture are generally vague. (Perhaps for this very reason, they play a large role in contemporary concepts of Spanish collective identity as a loosely defined community existing before the foreign invasions of historical antiquity.)

Many Roman lives were lost trying to subdue them, for the warlike Celtiberians were damned if they were going to take Roman occupation lying down. In time they became highly skilled at defeating forces much larger than their own using guerrilla and raiding tactics.

One episode from this long and bloody period stands out,

defining as it does very Spanish traits of bellicosity, resistance, pride and a stubbornness of epic proportions. So emblematic has it become that it has entered the Spanish language, inspired Cervantes's most celebrated play, given the name to a football team and not one, but three, ships of the Spanish navy. The event in question is the Siege of Numantia.

Numantia – or Numancia, as the Spanish call it – was a hill fort in eastern central Spain, not far from the town of Soria, capital of the synonymous province. Today Soria is a weird and desolate place, one of the most sparsely inhabited areas in Europe. The joke goes that when, on the few occasions that the local football team plays away against Barcelona, the entire population of Soria could fit in Camp Nou (with seating for about ninety thousand) with room to spare. Sadly for local fans, however, the team rarely displays the doggedness shown by the Celtiberian inspiration for its name, Numancia, and tends to lag in the lower divisions.

Back in 133 BC, however, the name Numantia was on the lips of everyone in the Roman Empire.

After several humiliating defeats at the hands of the natives, the Roman Senate decided something had to be done about the Celtiberian tribes in the area. And the man they sent to do the job was none other than Scipio Africanus the Younger, the man who only a few years before had finally crushed Carthage, razed the enemy city to the ground and ploughed over it in a powerfully symbolic end to Rome's Punic difficulties. He was the ablest commander of his time, adopted grandson of Scipio Africanus the Elder, who had brought defeat on Hannibal back in 206 BC.

Scipio's first job when he arrived in Hispania was to beat the Roman army there into shape. A string of defeats had seriously lowered morale, and the troops languished, spending most of their time and money on prostitutes, soothsayers and the wares of local tradesmen. These undesirables were cleared out on Scipio's orders and the legionaries were ordered on forced marches, to build fortifications which they then had to pull down and rebuild, and to dig trenches which, likewise, they were ordered to refill before digging once more. There was to be no more lounging about: strict discipline and back-breaking work were the order of the day.

Scipio's forces were reinforced at this time by some fifteen thousand Nubians from North Africa, bringing with them archers, slingers and twelve war elephants, which could be used as mobile siege towers.

When his forces were ready, Scipio took all sixty thousand of his men and camped them near the rebel stronghold, Numantia, home to around two and a half thousand people. He avoided the shorter route, where Numantian guerrilla attacks were more likely, forcing his men to march a longer distance in an area with no sources of water. Wells were dug, but many pack animals died en route.

When they finally reached the town, Scipio had a siege wall built around it 9 kilometres long, 3 metres high and 2.5 metres thick. Cords were stretched across a nearby river with sharp blades attached, making escape – either by swimming or by boat – impossible.

The Numantians dug in their heels. The siege dragged on. Connections with friendly tribes and towns nearby were cut off. Hunger began to set in.

An embassy was sent asking for terms. Scipio's reply was cool. When the embassy returned, the Numantians killed its members, suspecting them of having made a private deal with the Romans.

The hunger worsened. The besieged townspeople resorted to cannibalism to survive.

After thirteen months, in the summer of 133 BC, and with disease rampant in the high heat, the Numantians made their fateful decision: rather than surrender to the hated Romans, they would commit suicide. After burning the town to the ground, the majority did so. The Romans picked up the few survivors and enslaved them. On his victorious return home, Scipio paraded through the streets of Rome with around fifty of them.

Numantia itself, meanwhile, had gone down in history as an example of heroic resistance which was admired by the Romans themselves, including Pliny. Like the Jewish resistance at Masada almost two hundred years later, it spoke of epic struggle and self-sacrifice, resonating down the centuries as something to be emulated and celebrated.

Over two thousand years on, and Numancia is still celebrated in contemporary Spain, the phrase *resistencia numantina* commonly used to describe bloody-minded stubbornness against the odds. As another Spanish saying goes, *Quien aguanta, gana* – 'He who resists, wins'. It's an attitude which can be seen today in modern Spanish politics, where holding on to power at any cost is often the only noticeable skill of many of those in office.

As recently as the Spanish Civil War, the spirit of Numancia was invoked during the siege of the Alcázar of Toledo. Inside the ancient city's historic castle some two thousand Franco supporters held out for almost ten weeks against everything Republican forces could throw at them, including heavy artillery and underground mines. Eventually the defenders were relieved, and the siege became a powerful symbol of resistance, Franco's Numancia, only victorious this time. 'Today we have won the war,' he said as he paced around the ruins of the castle for the news cameras. And in many ways he was right, although it would take him another two and a half years to complete the job.

The Siege of Numancia was not the end of Rome's Hispanic wars, which continued for almost another century. The Peninsula would, eventually, come under full Roman domination, at which point something of Roman influence began to penetrate the local culture. But ask modern Spaniards about the Roman period of their history, and while they will mention the remaining monuments and one or two other details, it is Numantia and the events there which dominate, which ring down through the centuries. We held out. We chose self-sacrifice over defeat.

Spain gave Rome war. In return, Rome gave Spain its name and language. But not its sense of self.

Numantia is the first example of a 'pact of forgetting' in Spanish history, drawing a veil over the past to create national myths about identity. While the siege of Numantia was an important episode of the Roman period, by concentrating on it at the expense of so much else that occurred, emphasis is placed on casting the invaders as mere foreigners who, despite a presence of several centuries in the country, and leaving behind a hugely significant legacy and some of the foundations of 'Spain', are viewed as never having fully integrated.

As we shall see, a similar pattern will play out over future invaders bringing advanced new cultures.

PRISCILLIAN

Ⓞne of the most interesting figures of Roman Spain was Priscillian, Bishop of Avila, the first person executed by the Church for heresy. Priscillian's life acts as a blueprint for one of the most prominent patterns in Spanish history; the dualistic conflict between light and dark, between free-thinking and violent authority. Interestingly, he is no mere shadowy character from ancient history, but quite possibly the man whose body lies at the holiest shrine in Christian Spain to this day.

Priscillian was born to a prosperous family somewhere in western Hispania in AD 340. He received a good, 'pagan' education in the traditional Roman style. As part of the empire, the Peninsula was officially Christian by this time, but the culture was still very Classical and built on centuries of continued occupation. Meanwhile, the Church, an underground movement until relatively recently, was in something of a state of flux: debates raged about its central beliefs, with heated arguments over fine details of doctrine. The result was that a movement officially considered heretical for over three hundred years now became obsessed with heresy inside its own ranks.

In this context, Priscillian began preaching in the Peninsula in the 370s. His beliefs and methods were notably different from those of his contemporaries. It is not always easy to piece together clearly what they were, but one of the central planks of his message was asceticism, particularly with regard to priests, who were expected to turn their backs on the world and practise strict celibacy and vegetarianism. This was at a time when sexual 'purity' was encouraged among members of the clergy, but not heavily policed.[1]

Other aspects of Priscillian's doctrine involved a numerical mysticism in which the number 14 was held to be particularly significant (2x7). Charismatic prophecy was also encouraged, and a link was argued between the Zodiac and parts of the body. Much of his evangelical preaching took place at night-time, when special gatherings were held in the countryside, and where – shockingly – not only did people congregate barefoot, but women were allowed to take part as well. Some of the prayers may even have been recited naked . . .

All this, not surprisingly, ruffled more conservative feathers, and Priscillian's many detractors were quick to accuse him of Gnosticism, specifically Manichaeism, the dualistic religious movement which had grown out of Persia some hundred years before and which had vied with Christianity at one point to become the official religion of the Roman Empire. Viewing the universe as being caught in an eternal struggle between the forces of dark and light, Manichees saw a clear distinction between the flesh and the spirit, between the dark, sullied world of materiality, and the purer world represented by Christ. From what we can tell, Priscillian's own ideas were not dissimilar (and

---

1 The early Spanish Church's views on crime and sin raise eyebrows today: sorcery brought immediate excommunication, according to a council held near Granada in the early fourth century, but a Christian woman who *wilfully* beat her slave to death only had to do seven years' penance, reduced to five years if death was not intentional.

were echoed, many centuries later, in Cathar beliefs), meaning that he came under suspicion within a Church hierarchy which, freed of its previous clandestinity, was beginning to test its strength.

But as well as enemies, Priscillian won over important supporters, including fellow Spaniards Bishops Instantius and Salvanius. And he appears to have attracted a large number of followers, particularly in the western half of the Peninsula: despite being found guilty of heresy at a special synod held at Saragossa in 380, the very next year Priscillian was named Bishop of Avila.

One of his enemies, however, was not prepared to let things stand. Ithacius was the Metropolitan Bishop of what is now Faro, on the Algarve (then known as Ossonuba), and as such, Priscillian's superior. A contemporary source described Ithacius as 'without any touch of holiness; rash, talkative, impudent, given to high living, much enjoying the pleasures of the stomach'. He was the polar opposite of the ascetic Priscillian, and the two men soon locked horns. Priscillian tried to get Ithacius ousted. Ithacius managed to hold on, and in return secured an order of exile against Priscillian from the Emperor Gratian, champion of 'orthodox' Christianity and the last Roman emperor to lead a successful campaign over the Rhine. Priscillian at this time was openly accused of Manichaeism, which had been officially banned.

Time passed. A direct appeal in Rome against the edict was eventually successful, but Priscillian's fate became entangled in the political infighting breaking out within a Roman Empire already entering its final days.

In 383, the governor of Britain, Magnus Maximus, rebelled against Gratian, who was subsequently murdered. Sadly for Priscillian, Ithacius was close to Maximus, who was proclaimed emperor of Britain and Gaul, making Trier, in what was then the

Roman province of Gallia Belgica, his capital. Ithacius had Priscillian condemned once more. Priscillian's response was to evoke his right to take his case to the emperor himself.

When he and his entourage arrived at Trier, however, they were quickly imprisoned and tortured. Barbed hooks were used to tear at their sides, their limbs pulled from their sockets on the rack. Priscillian 'confessed', admitting to the heresy he was accused of, as well as practising magic and holding nocturnal gatherings with loose women. Unbridled sexual passion and sorcery were two of the greatest fears of the early Church: Priscillian had signed his own death warrant. Ithacius led the case for the prosecution.

In 385, along with five other followers, Priscillian was beheaded. Officially his crime was the practice of witchcraft, but underpinning his final condemnation was the accusation of heterodox thought, essentially of daring to interpret the scriptures in his own way. Others of his followers received lesser sentences: Bishop Instantius was exiled to the Scilly Isles ('Sylinancis' – the first time they are mentioned in history). To all intents and purposes, it appeared that Priscillian's teachings had died with him.

But the story doesn't end there. Maximus himself died only three years later and Ithacius was ousted as Bishop of Faro and sent into exile, where he died (it is not known where). Priscillian's followers were able to take their master's remains from Trier back to Hispania, and almost certainly to the north-western province of Galicia, where his ideas were popular. Here, for several centuries, they were revered as holy relics, and Priscillian's final resting place turned into a shrine.

Things continued like this for some two hundred years. But eventually, by the sixth century, Priscillianism had all but disappeared. The bishop's tomb fell into disuse.

And then, one day in the early 800s (813 or 820, depending on whom you read) a Christian hermit wandering alone in the hills of Galicia, far from the power centres of the new Muslim masters of the Peninsula, hears mysterious music and sees a shower of stars. Investigating the source of his miraculous vision, he discovers an ancient tomb lost in the undergrowth, which includes bones and parchments. He travels to tell the local bishop about his discovery. On hearing the story, Bishop Teodomiro declares the remains to be those of St James the Great, one of Christ's closest disciples and the legendary evangeliser of Hispania. Word spreads, the tradition grows, the first pilgrims start arriving to worship at the saint's grave, and the town which grows up around it is named after him – Santiago de Compostela, the 'field of stars'.

Could the man venerated at the holiest site in Spanish Christendom, the headquarters of orthodoxy, actually not be St James but Priscillian, the first person to be executed by the Church for heresy? Many scholars, including Priscillian's biographer in English, Henry Chadwick, former Dean at Christ Church College, Oxford, believe it could be. An archaeological dig in the nineteenth century beneath Santiago Cathedral revealed an old Roman mausoleum. Further investigations between 1946 and 1959 uncovered a large necropolis from the fourth and fifth centuries with tombs facing east. The belief is that they were placed there, as was customary at the time, to be close to the last resting place of a holy man. Was that holy man Priscillian? Spanish author Fernando Sánchez Dragó recounts how a local aristocrat whose widow he spoke to once found a young boy from the town in tears. When asked to explain why he was crying, the boy said he had been ordered by the bishop to destroy a tombstone on which were carved the words: 'Here lie the remains of Priscillian.'

Priscillian, a free-thinker, a mystic, a nonconformist, exiled and eventually brought to a violent end by his orthodox and authoritarian compatriot. Priscillian killed by Ithacius: Santiago the Seeker murdered by Santiago the Slayer – as we shall see, it is a pattern that plays itself out over Spanish history many times.

Perhaps needless to say, the Church is not permitting any more archaeological research at Santiago (although, interestingly, the Vatican only officially identified the bones there as belonging to St James as recently as 1884). Why should they, when millions of pilgrims visit the shrine every year? An Ithacius of today would doubtless feel more at home there than Priscillian: as a stroll past Santiago gift shops indicates, St James is good business. He is also the country's patron saint, an honoured and much-loved face of Spanish national identity.

And playing with that can be dangerous.

GERMAN SPAIN

VISIGOTHIC SPAIN

'The only important event which occurred during the Visigothic era was the adoption of the Christian religion as the religion of the State.'

Writing in 1942, Spanish diplomat and historian Salvador de Madariaga[1] was harsh on the three-hundred-year period between the collapse of Roman rule in Hispania and the Moorish invasion of the eighth century. But he was not unfair. Other historians were even more damning; according to Ramón Menendez Pidal: 'The Visigoths left nothing, not one stone, one book, one memory.' The fact is that, beyond the establishment of Catholicism, there are really only a couple of other points to highlight from the Visigothic period of Spanish history. Both of them, however, are important: it marked the first systematic, State-sponsored persecution of the Jewish population; and second, it was the first time that the Peninsula became politically unified. Almost a thousand years later, these two developments would be mirrored during the reign

---

1 De Madariaga was Spain's ambassador to Washington and representative at the League of Nations in the 1930s.

of the Habsburgs, a dynasty, like the Visigoths, of Germanic origins.

The Visigoths were not the first 'Barbarians' to cross the Pyrenees in the wake of Rome's disintegration. In the early fifth century whole tribes of Vandals, Alans and Suebi had descended on to the Spanish tablelands through the pass at Roncesvalles.[2] The Vandals and Alans wandered around for a few years, formed short-lasting kingdoms in the face of weakened resistance by the Hispano–Roman inhabitants, before finally deciding that Spain was not for them: in 629 they jointly crossed the Strait of Gibraltar and headed for modern-day Tunisia, where they eventually settled. The Suebi, however, found Spain more agreeable, particularly the lush, wet, north-western areas, where they bedded in for the long term.

Meanwhile, fresh from sacking Rome itself in 410, the Visigoths passed into Spain at the eastern end of the Pyrenees, taking Barcelona in 415 (founded centuries before by Hannibal's father, Barca). In time they would become masters of the whole Peninsula.

As de Madariaga's comment suggests, the importance of the Visigothic period of Spanish history exists mostly on a symbolic level. Largely Romanised themselves by this point, the Germanic tribe brought little in the way of new culture to the Peninsula, ruling as a military elite distant from the local population. For centuries this division was established in law, with different legal codes applicable to either group. Linguistically, the Visigoths brought almost nothing, eventually dropping their own language in favour of the vulgar forms of Latin then developing in the

---

2 This gateway near the western end of the mountain chain later became the setting for the *Chanson de Roland* – the twelfth-century cornerstone of Western literature – and remains the starting point for many embarking on the Camino de Santiago.

Peninsula. (Interestingly, the handful of Spanish words of Visigothic origin almost all have military connotations, denoting where this Germanic people concentrated its energies; for example: *hacha* – 'axe', *estribo* – 'stirrup', and *varón* – 'male'.) Even religiously, they abandoned their preference for the Arian interpretation of Christianity – which saw Christ as subordinate to God the Father rather than his equal – adopting, in 589, the Catholic line. And in three centuries they only founded three cities: Vitoria – today the administrative capital of the Basque Country; Olite, a small town in Navarre; and Recópolis, in Guadalajara province, which was later abandoned. When it comes to the legacy of the Visigoths in Spain, any statement has to be heavily qualified.

Let's take, for example, their unification of the Peninsula under one rule. From their arrival in the early fifth century, various groups stood in the Visigoths' way: the Vandals and Alans were quickly heading south towards North Africa, but the Suebi were entrenched in the north-west. Meanwhile along the northern coastal areas, groups such as the Basques were continuing a long-standing tradition – alive to this day – of giving new rulers an awkward reception. Finally, in the south and east, the Byzantines invaded and were creating the province of *Spania*, stretching from Lucentum (modern-day Alicante) all the way to the Algarve. It would take the Visigoths two hundred years – the same time that it took the Romans – to conquer and subdue all these enemies, finally becoming lords of the entire Peninsula in the early seventh century.

That they did so was close to a miracle given the near-permanent infighting among themselves. This was caused in large part by having an elective monarchy, which meant much energy was lost in civil wars. If the Visigoths were good at one thing, however, it was fighting. King Suinthila was the man who finally pushed out the last Byzantine forces and became the first monarch of all of Spain in the 620s – *rex totius spaniae*, in the words of a contemporary historian. Not that it did him much good: following a pattern typical of the Visigothic period, his rule was short-lived. In 631 he was ousted by a rival, excommunicated by the Church, and exiled.

But why isn't he better known today? A very small street is named after him in a leafy suburb of Madrid. There's also a statue of him . . . somewhere. The point is that today, as with the Romans and most other invaders, many Spaniards, again, view the Visigoths as outsiders.[3] Admittedly this time with more justification: the Visigoths unified the country and established Catholicism as the State religion, but out of a total population at the time of around six or seven million people, this military elite of around two hundred thousand never became fully integrated with the local population. Perhaps it had something to do with their unpronounceable names: Chindasuinth? Recceswinth?

Nor were the Visigoths ever really in complete authority. Shortly before completing their conquest of the Peninsula, they passed laws against the Jews. These included banning them from marrying Christians, and ordering the execution of Jews who converted Christians to their own faith. In addition, forced conversions were carried out, and a large number of Jews left Spain as a result, heading for France.

Yet despite their draconian nature, and the furore that surrounded their initial passing, these laws were not fully implemented, and many local authorities turned a blind eye to them. Such a state of affairs was even expected by the king who introduced them,

---

3 An exception to this is to be found among some right-wingers and Francoist diehards who cling to the Dictatorship's attempted co-opting of the Visigoths as a heroic Spanish people of the past.

Sisebut, who placed a curse on his successors if they failed to impose his anti-Jewish measures. To a large degree, in fact, Visigothic kings were only in nominal control. The Church was an equal, even more powerful, authority during the period, which effectively held the country together.

The fact is that, unlike their descendants of the fifteenth and sixteenth centuries, the Jewish community of Visigothic Spain was able to survive thanks in large part to the instability of the governing elite. The Visigoths may have eventually managed to rule over the entire Peninsula, but infighting, civil wars and rebellions continued apace for the next hundred years, meaning that the Germanic kings had little time to devote to matters beyond their power struggles.

If anything, the importance of the Visigothic period for Spanish history lies less in what it was and more in the patterns which were laid down during the time: struggles to unify the country, persecution, and perpetual civil conflict. These play out time and again over the centuries to come.

A SEVILLIAN SAINT

One individual stands out from the three hundred years of Visigothic Spain: Isidore of Seville, scholar, polymath, archbishop, saint and the last Father of the Church.

Sainthood was something of a family business for Isidore: his brothers Leander and Fulgentius, as well as sister Florentina, all managed to obtain the title as well. Probably born in Cartagena around 560 to a wealthy family, Isidore was educated in Seville, later becoming the city's archbishop. He helped restructure and strengthen the Church, fighting off new heresies in the wake of the defeat of Arianism.

What Isidore is best known for, however, and the reason for his continued fame, is his writing of the *Etymologiae*.

Later, the idea of writing an encyclopedia containing all world knowledge would become more widespread: the *Ikhwan al-Safa* – the 'Brethren of Sincerity' – undertook a similar exercise in tenth-century Baghdad, as did Roger Bacon in the thirteenth century with his *Opus Maius*. But Isidore was one of the earliest people in the post-Classical world to come up with the idea,[1] a beacon of light aware, perhaps, that he was living in an age which later generations would qualify as 'Dark', and that therefore it was necessary to compile and summarise as much knowledge as he could before it was lost for ever.

Interestingly, he was not alone: Eastern Christians had had a similar idea. Around 600, Nestorian scholars in what is now south-eastern Turkey were hailing the combined works of the scholar Theodore of Mopsuestia – leader of the School of Antioch who died in 428 – as the sum total of all knowledge. Whether Isidore was inspired by this is not known, but his work makes a tantalising fit to a common trend in Spanish history of picking up an intellectual or cultural baton from further east before passing it on to the rest of Western Europe.

And thank goodness he did, for large numbers of Classical texts are only known to us today thanks to their inclusion in Isidore's magnum opus, which stretched to twenty volumes, and took some twenty-five years to write. Predictably, given the author's Classical education, it contains material on the standard *Trivium* (grammar, logic and rhetoric) and *Quadrivium* (arithmetic, geometry, astronomy and music). Further volumes dealt with the law, the structure of Heaven and Hell and the hierarchies therein. But then Isidore started branching out, covering subjects as varied as the nature of oracles, agriculture, the different metals and stones and their qualities, the Animal Kingdom, roads and their construction, food, heretical beliefs, clothes and furniture. The work contained maps of the known world, as well as a whole volume on, not surprisingly given its title, etymology.

---

1 Roman authors Marcus Terentius Varro and Pliny the Elder both wrote works considered encyclopedias several centuries before.

The *Etymologiae* – or *Origenes* as it's sometimes called – was a hit. Published by Isidore's disciples after his death in 636, copies quickly found their way over the Pyrenees to Christian communities hungry for the lost knowledge and wisdom to be found in its pages. Irish clerics in particular clung to it, naming it the *Culmen*, the summit of all learning. Isidore's book was, in effect, all that any intellectually curious person would ever need, being a summation of everything held both in the Christian and Pagan scholarly traditions. All over Europe this Spanish-born work was used as a single reference – no other was required. The beacon which was lit in Seville spread its light throughout the Continent.

Centuries later, Dante was so impressed by Isidore that he honoured him and his work by placing him firmly in the sphere of the Sun next to Bede in his *Paradiso*. The eleventh-century Christian King Ferdinand of León so respected Isidore's memory that he struck a deal with the then Muslim ruler of Seville to have the saint's remains transferred to a basilica in the northern capital (these remains have been scattered since, with some now in Murcia and more in Almería . . .).

Isidore is one of the first of many Spaniards who, over the course of history, nurture and promote knowledge which subsequently goes on to illuminate the rest of the Western world. We shall come across several others in subsequent chapters, but for centuries, all the way through the Middle Ages and up to the Renaissance, the *Etymologiae* was a must-have tome for any self-respecting library in Europe, the first thing anyone would reach for when starting research on practically any subject. Does that sound familiar? Well, it will come as little surprise to hear that thanks to his efforts, St Isidore has been proposed as patron saint of the Internet. Spain

– a Spaniard – in this instance was almost fifteen hundred years ahead of its time. At the time of writing, the Vatican is still pondering the matter . . .

THE LAST GOTH

Visigothic Spain came to an end when the Moors invaded Hispania in 711, sweeping away the old order in about a decade and conquering the Peninsula for Islam. That much is fairly well known. What is less well known, however, is that by the early eighth century the Spanish kingdom which the Muslim warriors conquered was no longer unified: for a short period beforehand it had been divided in two.

Many theories try to explain how Visigothic Spain collapsed so quickly when it did. It may have been partly thanks to the persecuted Jewish population welcoming and assisting the Arab newcomers as fellow Semites. In addition there was a notable drop in morale around this time within the Visigothic armies. But this is a period where it's hard to rely on the scarce historical sources that exist, not least because they were mostly written at best decades – and more usually centuries – after the events. What *is* clear, however, is that civil conflict among the Visigoths was a decisive factor in their defeat. True to a repeated pattern throughout its history, Spain, having been unified for a time, had broken apart. And it would take a new violent force to put it back together again.

Internal warfare had been a theme throughout the Visigothic period, and few kings made it to the throne without a palace coup at the very least along the way. But since the early 600s these conflicts hadn't caused an actual rupture within the kingdom itself. Until some time around 710. What actually happened at this time is uncertain, but the key person is a man called Roderic, who appears to have taken the throne by force. Later legends talk of him actually grabbing the crown in the capital, Toledo, and placing it on his own head, an act which caused alarm among the Visigothic aristocracy.

Did Roderic assassinate King Wittiza to reach the top? Again, it's unclear, but Roderic was not a popular man, for his coup led to a 'tumult'. Visigothic Spain, quite suddenly, was divided.

That Roderic ruled from Toledo is confirmed by a handful of coins which have been recovered from the time, showing the correct dates and his name in Latin, *Rodericus*. However, coins from the same period show that there was now a new king in the north-east of the Peninsula, minting his own gold coins – a man called Achila. Even less is known about him than about Roderic, but the coins and their location indicate a kingdom at war with itself.

And civil conflict was breaking out just as a new, vibrant force in the shape of Muslim armies arrived from the Middle East and conquered North Africa, a mere eight miles away across the Strait of Gibraltar.

To be 'the last king' of somewhere is generally a guarantee that history will judge you harshly. Boabdil, the last king of Moorish Spain, was widely depicted as an effeminate fool after losing Granada to Ferdinand and Isabella in 1492. Although he has been cast in a more favourable light more recently by modern historians. His Visigothic counterpart, Roderic, eight hundred years earlier, may have been more manly, according to legend, but equally responsible for what happened to his realm owing to deep character flaws.

Two stories depict him as a hothead who flagrantly broke sacred taboos.

The first, later mentioned by both Christian and Moorish chroniclers, tells of a palace in Toledo, the House of Hercules, which had been sealed up for centuries. On his coronation, each Visigothic king would visit the palace and put a new lock on the door as part of a long-standing tradition. But when Roderic seized the crown, he charged over to the building and had the locks smashed. Inside, however, instead of great treasure, he found a simple box. Opening it, Roderic pulled out a piece of cloth with pictures painted on it, and writing, which said: 'If this building is ever broken into, and this box opened, let it be known that the people whose pictures are drawn on this cloth will invade and conquer Spain.' The king looked at the images and saw armies of men on horseback carrying great swords, with turbans on their heads. Men from the East. Frightened, Roderic closed the box and had the building sealed once more, but, of course, it was too late. The 'genie' was out of the bottle.

The second story recounts how Roderic took a fancy to the daughter of a man called Julian. Julian may have been the Visigothic governor of Ceuta – what to this day is still a Spanish exclave on the North African coast. Or he may have been a wealthy merchant based in the same area. What the stories agree on, however, is that having laid eyes on Julian's daughter (named as Cava in one source), Roderic tricked the family to come to the mainland, where he raped the girl. Horrified, Julian smuggled himself back to North Africa (leaving poor Cava behind . . .) in order to plot his revenge. And to do so he turned to the Muslim armies that had only recently arrived in the area. He struck a deal: he would help them cross the Strait, showing them the best sea routes and landing places, and in return they would exact revenge on Roderic for him. The Muslims, led by their governor Musa, agreed.

Freudian echoes between a 'locked box' and a maiden's virginity apart, the two stories agree that Roderic's downfall was due to his breaking a sacred bond or taboo. Perhaps it is just a storytelling technique, a way of tarnishing his name and making him responsible for subsequent events – a bad guy who got what was coming to him. Or perhaps what these stories refer to on one level is how Roderic had broken the unity of the Spanish kingdom, only a hundred years after it had finally and painstakingly been forged – something precious, delicate, and easily lost, as was about to be proven. That was his sin – and for that he would never be forgiven.

Whatever the case, Visigothic Spain was now doomed, about to be replaced by Moorish Al-Andalus. And Roderic himself would be dead, slain on the battlefield as his men – once proud Visigothic warriors, conquerors of Rome itself – were crushed by the Muslims.

PART TWO

ARABIAN SPAIN

VIEWS OF
MOORISH HISTORY

The word 'Moorish' comes from the term *mauri*, which early Christian chroniclers used to describe the Muslim invaders who invaded the Peninsula in 711, drawing on the Latin name for western North Africa, *Mauretania*. The name is vague but has stuck, and is useful as an umbrella term for all the areas of Spain which were politically or culturally under Muslim control for the next nine hundred years. This is because all manner of peoples lived there during that time. Three religious groups dominated: Muslims, Christians and Jews (with a handful of animists surviving in isolated mountainous regions). Racially, however, there was even more of a mixed bag: indigenous Spaniards had a largely Iberian, Celtic and Semitic genetic make-up, as we've seen, but to this were now added new arrivals from all over the Islamic Empire, including Arabs, Berbers and Persians. In addition, slaves were imported from Sub-Saharan Africa and Slavic regions of Europe. When we include the long-established Jewish community on the Peninsula, the term 'melting pot' could well have been coined to describe medieval Spanish society. Which is why 'Moorish' is so useful a term: it encapsulates the crossroads nature of the Peninsula during this period.

Yet this very usefulness can also cause problems. Because it fits so well, 'Moorish Spain' is generally seen somehow as an entity, as a single, coherent whole, clearly delineated, as though a pair of brackets could be put around it to isolate it from the rest of the country's past. Older books on Spanish history (particularly ones written by Spaniards) often deal with the Moorish period in a single chapter, treating it as a curious anomaly, a pause before normal Christian service resumed with the completion of the 'Reconquest' in 1492.

Generally speaking – and there are exceptions – this is how many Spaniards think of it today. Yes, the Moors were around for many centuries, and yes, they left behind a not insignificant legacy (the Alhambra in Granada, for example), but it was all a very long time ago and mostly concentrated in the south, in today's Andalusia. This same Spaniard will be able to name the country's cultural giants, such as Cervantes (*hombre, ¡por supuesto!*) and Picasso, but will almost certainly give a blank stare when told that the first novel in European history was written four hundred years before Cervantes by a man from Guadix (Ibn Tufayl), that the most authoritative medieval map of the world was compiled by a Ceutan (Al-Idrisi), or that arguably the most influential Spaniard who ever lived was born in twelfth-century Cordoba (Averroes). These people, and many, many others from the Moorish period, have been all but airbrushed from the national story. Lack of awareness of how deep the Moorish influence still runs in Spanish life is the norm. As with the Romans, a 'pact of forgetting' has been followed to disassociate 'Spain' from much of its rich historical heritage in an attempt to find a common national identity.

But the Moorish period is too long and important simply to be ignored. Following Napoleon's invasion of Egypt, Europeans as a whole became increasingly interested in the Middle East, and nineteenth-century travellers to Spain saw echoes there of the rich cultures they were beginning to discover at the eastern end of the Mediterranean. Spain's Moorish past became an integral part of the country's exoticism, seen, for example, in Washington Irving's *Tales of the Alhambra* (and rooms where the American writer stayed at the then crumbling old palace form part of the modern visit around the highly restored structure of today).

The Spanish themselves, however, remained less enamoured of their Moorish past. Following the war with the US in 1898 and the loss of the country's last colonies (Cuba, Puerto Rico and the Philippines) Spain fell into a moral slump known as *el Desastre*, with much navel-gazing on how from being the world's most powerful nation they had fallen so far behind. A scapegoat was needed, and so the Moorish period – the one thing which clearly differentiated Spain from the rest of Europe – was dragged out for a beating. Much of the country's perceived backwardness was laid at its door, and a movement even began to eschew Spanish words of Arabic origin in favour of Latin-based counterparts, further attempting to eradicate an unwanted period of history, as though it could somehow be made to disappear altogether.

This in turn brought about something of a reaction, in which the Moorish past became more celebrated and its cultural and scientific achievements – far in advance of the rest of medieval Europe – were highlighted for the first time. But the debate shifted from understanding and correctly interpreting a crucial period in the country's past to become part of the perpetual debate about what Spain and Spanishness actually is. Was the Moorish period generally 'good', or 'bad'? One view still sees the Moors as an essentially foreign invasion force which, in turn, 'the Spanish' eventually pushed out; the other views them as having been so integrated into the local population that the very idea that the Moors invaded in the first place has been challenged. According to this theory, Spain was culturally absorbed into the Islamic world in a much more peaceful fashion, and the invasion and conquest narrative was fashioned centuries later to justify the 'Reconquest'.

What the various interpretations boil down to is the question of identity: are the Moors 'Spanish' or 'foreign'? If seen as 'us' they are viewed with sympathetic eyes. If 'them' then, generally, the opposite.

All of this has greater emphasis today given the more intense relations between the Western and Islamic worlds. There are a million Muslims living in Spain today, mostly concentrated in and around large cities. Terrorist attacks carried out in the name of specific interpretations of Islam have left scars, with an ever-present threat of more to come. How Spain views its Moorish past is directly relevant to how it manages its relations with Muslim communities living in the country today. An enormous precedent exists in its own history waiting to be examined – a period marked by spectacular cultural achievements, but also by the worst inter-communal violence.

The lessons are there to be found. But can they be learned?

WHAT'S IN A NAME?

For the Greeks it had been Iberia. For the Romans and Visigoths, it was Hispania, and Spania for the brief Byzantine interlude in the south. But then Muslims invaded in 711 and named the Peninsula Al-Andalus, which bears no relation to any previous names. Why?

In 711, Islam was still less than a hundred years old. The death

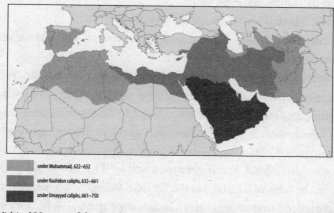

under Muhammad, 622–632

under Rashidun caliphs, 632–661

under Umayyad caliphs, 661–750

Within 100 years of the Prophet Muhammad's death in 632, the Islamic Empire stretched from the Himalayas to the Iberian Peninsula

of the Prophet Muhammad in 632 had heralded the beginning of a period of military expansion out of Arabia in which Muslim armies very quickly pushed north-east to conquer the old Sassanian Empire, northwards into Byzantine territories of the Levant, and north-west across the Sinai and into Africa. Victories came rapidly, a wave of conquests the like of which hadn't been seen since Alexander the Great. Aware of their 'difference' from the peoples they defeated – possibly through a combination of their faith, traditions and race – Muslims often (but not always) founded new cities rather than settling in old ones, establishing, for example, Kufa and Cairo. Giving their conquered territories new names followed a similar pattern, so Mesopotamia became 'Al-Iraq', and Egypt 'Al-Misr'. Spreading ever westwards, the Muslim forces reached the end of the North African coast, naming the land they found there 'Al-Maghreb', 'the western area' (hence 'Morocco'). Gazing across the Strait of Gibraltar towards the Spanish Peninsula, they likely followed their now established pattern of coming up with their own name for it.

But where does 'Al-Andalus' come from?

The short answer is that no one really knows. There are several theories, nonetheless.

For a long time the accepted version was that 'Al-Andalus' was a mispronunciation of 'Vandals'. According to this idea, somewhere around modern Tunisia the spreading Muslim armies came across the descendants of the Vandals, who, in some après-battle fraternisation, described how they had originally crossed over into North Africa from Spain centuries before. The image stuck, and when the Muslims arrived at the Strait of Gibraltar a few years later and glanced northwards, they remembered the Vandals' story and named the land on the other side after them.

That the Vandals had been in Spain for only a few decades back in the early fifth century – three hundred years before – might raise doubts about this theory. And while not impossible, it has its detractors. So others have been suggested.

One is that the Muslims decided to name Spain after a system of land distribution used by the Visigoths, who parcelled their country up by 'lots'. So *landalauhts* – 'the place where land is distributed by lots' – became 'Al-Andalus' . . . The idea that Muslims were so stretched to come up with a new name that they had to seek inspiration in local land distribution methods makes little intuitive sense. So let's move on.

A third theory suggests that Al-Andalus was derived from 'Atlantis'. Which may not be as crazy as it first sounds. A suggested origin for the Islamic name 'Iraq' (or 'El-Iraq' in Arabic) is that it came from Uruk, the ancient Sumerian city (possibly the first true city in the world) founded around 4500 BC and one-time home of King Gilgamesh, hero of the eponymous Babylonian epic. For a largely oral culture, which Islam was in the seventh and early eighth centuries, myth and legend would have figured greatly in Arab imagination. And just as tales of ancient Uruk would have been part of the storytelling tradition, so were accounts of a mythical city in the far western Mediterranean: Atlantis was named in pre-Islamic Arabian poetry, and Plato made it clear that it lay beyond the Pillars of Hercules – today's Strait of Gibraltar. Arriving there, it may well have made complete sense from their own storytelling tradition for Muslim soldiers to associate Spain with the Atlantis tales. Only they mispronounced it, turning it into 'Al-Andalus'.

The problem with this theory is that so much guff has been written about Atlantis in general that even mention of the name can cause a rolling of the eyes. The point is, however, to try to think like Muslims in the eighth century. For them, the existence of Atlantis, and its position at the far end of the Mediterranean, may have been taken very seriously indeed.

Which brings us to the most recent theory about Al-Andalus and its origins. According to this idea, it comes from the original, pre-Moorish name for the Tarifa peninsula, right at the southern tip of the Spanish mainland. Landing there in 711 and adopting it, the Muslim forces used the same denomination for the entire Peninsula, as far as the Pyrenees, as they pushed further north and defeated the Visigoths. According to this idea, the original name was pre-Indo-European, coming from some indigenous people who were possibly related to the Basques . . .

This raises the question: why name a place only *after* you've invaded it? Surely those same Muslims looking longingly across the Strait had come up with something before they boarded their landing vessels?

As mentioned at the start, the origins of 'Al-Andalus' are anything but clear. For the time being, however, my money's on Atlantis.

CIVIL CONFLICT IN
AL-ANDALUS

We shall come to the cultural achievements of Moorish Spain, to how scientifically and artistically it shone a light in Europe, providing an intellectual foundation from which the Renaissance could eventually emerge. But if there is one thing which characterises the Moorish period as a whole, it is internal conflict and warfare. As with all other civilisations throughout Spanish history, the dominant theme was violent struggle against itself. Not for being 'Moorish' was it any different in this regard, and as such it followed a set pattern which the Visigoths – the creators of the first political Spain – would have recognised.

In fact, Al-Andalus was divided against itself from the very beginning of its existence. After a few raids on the southern Spanish coast in 710, the full invasion was launched in 711 under a commander called Tariq. The chronicles tell how his force landed at Gibraltar, still known then by its old Greek name, Calpe. Following a custom of renaming places they conquered, the

Muslims called the Rock after their leader: *Jabal Tariq*, the 'Mountain of Tariq' morphed centuries later into 'Gibraltar'. Tariq and his army had great initial success on the Peninsula. An Arab chronicler tells how he sowed terror among the local inhabitants by capturing some of them, chopping them up and boiling their remains. Other captives were set free and quickly spread word about the horrors of the new invaders.[1] Having done this, Tariq then defeated King Roderic in battle and moved swiftly towards the heart of the country, the Visigothic capital, Toledo.

Meanwhile, back on the southern side of the Strait, the Muslim governor – the man who had sent Tariq out in the first place – was becoming jealous of his commander's increasing glory. So he gathered his own army and launched a second invasion of the Peninsula. Driven, as most of the early conquests of the Islamic Empire were, by religious fervour combined with lust for booty, both men were keen to get rich, and the most sought-after object for both was King Solomon's Table. The belief was that after many adventures this treasure had crossed the old Roman Empire in the wake of the Jewish Diaspora, eventually ending up in Visigothic Hispania. Tariq found the table first, in a castle not far from Toledo. But he knew that Musa, his superior, would claim it for himself. When the two men met, having already conquered great swathes of the Peninsula between them, this is precisely what happened. But Tariq had previously cut off one of the table's legs, encrusted with gold and jewels, and had it replaced. In time, both men were recalled to the Islamic capital at Damascus to report on their

---

1 There is an interesting parallel here with Franco's army in the Spanish Civil War. Landing from Morocco on the Spanish mainland in 1936, his troops – many of whom were Muslim Berber warriors – were encouraged to perform acts of barbarism on captured civilians, including women, tales of which then caused panic among the defending Republican forces.

conquest. In an attempt to ingratiate himself with the caliph, Musa presented him with Solomon's Table, claiming to have found it himself. At which point Tariq pulled out the original leg he had sawn off, proving that he had got it first.

The story may seem petty, even childish, but it holds important elements which would characterise the many centuries of Moorish rule now beginning in Spain: division, rivalry, lack of singular purpose, and squabbling. In the end they would cause the very downfall of Al-Andalus.

Unlike the Roman or Visigothic invasions of the Peninsula, which had taken two hundred years apiece, the Moorish conquest was achieved in about a decade. The Pyrenees initially provided little protection for southern France, and the Muslim forces carried on into Visigothic Septimania (capital, Narbonne) and up towards the Loire. It was only here, in 732, that they were stopped by the army of Charles Martel, the Battle of Poitiers marking the furthest extent of Muslim penetration into north-western Europe. From this point on, Moorish energies would largely be concentrated in the Iberian Peninsula.

Immediately, however, civil conflict within Muslim-held areas began. The armies that had crossed with Tariq and Musa were largely Berber in origin. Having been conquered themselves by Muslims only shortly before, the Berbers had converted to Islam but felt poorly treated by the Arab elite controlling the Islamic Empire. There were many grievances over distribution of booty and land. As early as 739 this anger came to a head in the shape of a Berber revolt in Morocco which spread over to Al-Andalus. This racial divide was exacerbated by long-standing inter-Arab disputes between Yemenis and Qaysis, splitting Moorish Spain along tribal lines. Less than twenty years after the initial invasion, and ten years after completing the conquest of the Peninsula, Al-Andalus was at war with itself.

The conflict seriously destabilised the new province of the Islamic Empire, and might well have led to its early demise. But instead, a curious development ensued, one which probably secured Moorish civilisation in the Peninsula, and which, following a pattern in Spanish history, involved the arrival of another man of destiny from the East.

Tubal, Heracles and Santiago are all very closely related to a powerful religious figure – Tubal is the grandson of Noah; Heracles is the son of Zeus and a demigod; Santiago (St James the Apostle) is one of Christ's closest disciples. After a disaster or setback, each one has to abandon his homeland and head westwards along the Mediterranean: Tubal in the wake of the Flood; Heracles after being sent mad by Hera and murdering his wife and children; and Santiago following the Crucifixion and Pentecost. On arriving in Spain, each figure then succeeds in establishing a new order – Tubal with the country's first peoples and kings; Heracles founding cities and civilisations; and Santiago bringing Christianity.

The story of Abd al-Rahman, founder of the Umayyad dynasty in Al-Andalus, follows the same structure.

Born in Palmyra in 731, Abd al-Rahman was the grandson of the Islamic Caliph Hisham. The caliph (from the Arabic *khalifa*, meaning 'successor' or 'deputy') was both the spiritual and political head of the Islamic Empire. In the late 740s, a rebellion brought down Abd al-Rahman's family (the Umayyads), establishing in their wake the Abbasid dynasty, which went on to build a new capital, Baghdad. The Abbasids relentlessly hunted down members of the old dynasty and killed them, even slaughtering some after a promise of clemency. Of them all, the young Abd al-Rahman was the only one to escape. Son of a Berber mother, he spent several years travelling across North Africa in disguise to find refuge among relatives. Arriving in Morocco, he saw the political turmoil gripping Moorish Spain and seized his chance. Through skilful negotiation he managed to have himself proclaimed *emir*, or prince, of Al-Andalus. He had royal blood; the Umayyads hailed originally from Mecca, the Prophet Muhammad's home town. And now that Islamic political power was shifting further eastwards from Syria to Iraq, Al-Andalus felt more of a provincial backwater than before. Abd al-Rahman brought a much needed touch of glamour and royal charm.

The establishment of the Umayyad emirate in Al-Andalus in 756 meant that politically Spain was no longer within the Islamic Empire. Culturally and religiously, however, it was still very much a part of it. The Umayyad dynasty would go on to form the bedrock of the Andalusi Golden Age of the tenth century. Like Tubal, Heracles and Santiago before him, Abd al-Rahman had arrived under a cloud from the East and managed to establish a new order which would dominate the Peninsula for the next few centuries.

Yet as the pattern of Spanish history dictates, it would only be able to do so against a backdrop of perennial efforts from within and without to break the country apart.

A SONG FROM THE EAST

One figure more than any other captures the movement of ideas from East to West which helped to turn Al-Andalus into the most advanced country in Europe, and its capital, Cordoba, into 'the ornament of the world'. That man was a ninth-century musician, astronomer, and perhaps the single most important trendsetter in history: Ziryab, the 'Blackbird'. He is a second Man from the East during the Moorish period, a cultural ambassador cementing the political work begun by the Umayyad Emir Abd al-Rahman.

Ziryab was born Abu al-Hassan Ali bin Nafi in 789, although exactly where is not known. Some sources say he was Persian, others that he was Kurdish, while others again claim that he was African, his nickname – 'blackbird' – referring not only to his beautiful singing voice but to the colour of his skin.

What is known was that he was a freed slave who spent the first period of his life in Baghdad, the capital of the Abbasid caliphate. There he studied music under Ishaq al-Mawsili, court musician to the Caliph Harun al-Rashid. Ziryab was more talented than his master, however, a fact he kept secret until the day the caliph himself asked Ziryab to perform for him.

'I can sing what the other singers know,' said Ziryab when he appeared at court, 'but my own repertory is made up of songs suitable only to be performed before a caliph like Your Majesty. The other singers don't know those pieces. If Your Majesty would allow, I shall sing for you what human ears have never heard before.'

Ziryab went on to perform his own elaborate and novel compositions, making his master, Ishaq, look a fool in the process. Ishaq vowed revenge, and Ziryab had to flee Baghdad with his family in fear for his life.

He headed west, soon arriving in Kairouan. From there he wrote to the Emir of Al-Andalus, offering his services to the royal court in Cordoba. At the time the Moorish leader, Al-Hakam, was trying to introduce a level of sophistication to what was still, at that point, a distant and rather backward outpost of the Islamic Empire. He leapt at the chance to have a musician from Baghdad at his court.

Ziryab crossed the Strait to Al-Andalus, landing at the port of Algeciras in the Bay of Gibraltar. The year was 822. Just over a hundred years before, Tariq had made the same crossing, marking the start of the military invasion of Iberia. Now, as Ziryab sailed the few miles from south to north, the cultural conquest of the Peninsula could begin.

Al-Hakam had died during the interim, but Ziryab was warmly welcomed by his son, Abd al-Rahman II, great-grandson of the Abd al-Rahman who established the Umayyad dynasty in Al-Andalus. The musician was given a large salary and lands around Cordoba, and very quickly established himself as a leading light at court and confidant of the emir, discussing poetry, music, history and the arts and sciences.

Before long, Ziryab was acting like a 'minister of culture' in the Andalusi capital. He set up a music school, where his compositions were handed down and experimentalism was encouraged. He introduced the innovations he had made with the lute: while the normal instrument had four pairs of strings – said to represent Aristotle's four humours: bile, blood, phlegm and melancholy – he had added a fifth to represent the soul.

Ziryab knew as many as ten thousand songs by heart, and his radical musical style was very influential, spreading not only through Moorish Spain, but centuries later inspiring the songs of the European Troubadours. Today the music of northern Morocco is a direct descendant of his repertoire.

Yet his cultural significance went far beyond music. Everything in Moorish Spain from food to clothes to pastimes and fashion was revolutionised by the new man from Baghdad.

Before Ziryab, meals in Al-Andalus were eaten from bare wooden tables, with the dishes served all at once. Now the concept of tablecloths was introduced, and the food was presented in a series of courses, starting with the soup, moving on to meat and fish, and finishing with fruit, desserts and nuts. The American expression 'from soup to nuts' – from beginning to end – echoes this ninth-century novelty even today.

Then there were new foods to be enjoyed. Asparagus had previously been considered nothing more than a weed. Now it became a delicacy. Other new dishes included a plate of meatballs with pieces of dough fried in coriander oil, sweets made of honey and walnuts – still made today in Saragossa – and spiral pastries soaked in saffron syrup. Meanwhile, replacing heavy metal goblets for wine (Andalusi Muslims were not strict when it came to religious injunctions against alcohol), came fine crystal glasses.

Beyond the dinner table, Ziryab's influence was felt in personal grooming and fashion. He stressed the need for personal hygiene and frequent bathing, introducing deodorants and toothpaste. Men and women alike were encouraged to wear bright colours in the spring, white clothes in summer, and long cloaks trimmed with fur in the winter. Short hairstyles, leaving the neck, ears and eyebrows free, were also introduced. Previously everyone at court had worn their hair long, parted in the middle.

Ziryab had Jewish doctors brought to Al-Andalus from North Africa and Iraq, and astrologers from India. These men introduced the game of chess to the royal court, which quickly spread and centuries later reached the Christian world. Around the same time, certain superstitions also entered Andalusian culture, including a nervousness over the number 13, or broken mirrors.

In almost every aspect of life, this one man had a tremendous impact, transforming the Cordoban court, and beyond it the rest of Al-Andalus, creating cultural gold in the crucible of Moorish Spain. And in time, his innovations spread into Christian Europe. Subsequently they became so engrained in Western culture that today we are mostly ignorant of their Eastern origins.

DEATH IN CORDOBA

Much of the political history of Arabian Spain centres around the Umayyad's bloody suppression of rebellions by disgruntled Berbers, local governors, and rival power groups. But one much smaller episode stands out, if only because the violence was willingly brought upon the victims themselves. It went on to become an important and celebrated incident within Christian Spain.

The name 'Cordoba Martyrs' is used to describe a group of around fifty Christians living in the Moorish capital in the mid-ninth century. All of them died at the hands of the Muslim authorities for deliberately committing crimes which they knew would bring the death penalty, including blasphemy and apostasy.

The conquest of the Peninsula had brought many native non-Muslim communities under the control of the Islamic authorities. Once peace had been established, these groups were generally allowed to live normal lives, as long as they were either Christian or Jewish – which most of them were. These religions were officially tolerated because, like Islam, they were based on holy scripture, on a book. The only concerted hardship they faced was having to pay a special tax, called a *jizya*. Barriers to social mobility were more to do with not being of Arab descent (the Berbers' constant gripe) than with religion.

Life for a Christian in ninth-century Al-Andalus, in fact, was quite good, as the early biography of one of the first Cordoba 'Martyrs' shows. His name was Isaac. He spoke fluent Arabic and had risen fairly high in the city administration, probably reaching the position of *katib*, or secretary. Interestingly, his biographer – Eulogius, a fellow Christian writing at the time who would later go on to be martyred himself – mentions this in a matter-of-fact way: speaking Arabic and working in the Muslim administration was clearly quite normal by this point, less than one hundred and fifty years after the Moorish invasion. What happened next, however, was different.

Isaac left his post and retired to a monastery not far from Cordoba (again, the fact that this monastery continued to exist at all is further testament to a relatively tolerant attitude to non-Muslims at this time). Three years later he returned to the capital, apparently having undergone something of a character change. He went to the office of the *qadi* – the chief religious judge – and asked to convert to Islam. But when the *qadi* appeared, Isaac launched into an attack on Islam and the Prophet, and called on the judge to convert to Christianity instead. Somewhat taken aback, the *qadi* assumed the poor man was drunk, or out of his mind. But Isaac insisted, continuing his verbal attack and making it clear that he was prepared to die for his beliefs. The judge became inflamed, struck him and had him arrested.

And so, after a brief spell in prison (during which time he was well treated), on 3 June 851 Isaac was executed. In the words of Eulogius:

> *This servant of God bent his head under sentence of*
> *death: he was hanged head downwards on the gallows*
> *. . . His body was cremated after a few days and the*
> *ashes were scattered in the river.*

It is probable that while at the monastery Isaac had been inspired by tales of the early Christians martyred by the Romans. Living himself as a subject of a non-Christian authority, he may have felt a need to follow in their footsteps. But there was a problem: how could he be persecuted in a largely non-persecuting society? Christians were generally left in peace in mid-ninth-century Al-Andalus. In fact, the *qadi* who struck Isaac was restrained and chastised by other Muslim officials for his actions; Isaac's biographer virtually lamented the fact that Isaac and those who followed his path were not tortured while in jail. The answer, of course, was deliberately to commit an act which would guarantee execution and the much desired 'martyrdom': blasphemy.

Isaac's example caught the imagination of a small number of his fellow Christians, and over the next five years around fifty more committed similar acts of deliberate offence to the authorities in order to be judicially killed. It is likely, however, that most Christians in Al-Andalus at the time were scandalised by this curious, extremist movement. The Bishop of Seville was very vocal in his condemnation of the 'Martyrs'. Maintaining a generally harmonious status quo was almost certainly uppermost in his mind. Most Christians preferred a low-key approach in order to carry on with their lives.

So why did Isaac and the others choose to bring this violence upon themselves? The answer may lie in the increasing numbers of Christians who by this point were converting to Islam. What is known of the Cordoba Martyrs reflects something of the mixed racial make-up of Andalusi society: most of them were of indigenous stock, but Arabs, Berbers, Syrians, perhaps even a Greek numbered among them as well. After almost one hundred and fifty years of Muslim domination, Islamic culture was in the ascendency. And, as occurs in any part of the world at any time, people were attracted to the ways of the most powerful and advanced culture of their period. Christians and Jews who adopted Muslim dress and customs were known as 'Mozarabs', from the Arabic *musta'rib*, meaning 'one who adopts Arab ways'. In fact, Paul Alvarus, a close friend of Eulogius, complained that young Christians in Cordoba were speaking Arabic so much that they could barely remember their own native tongue and traditions:

> The Christians love to read the poems and romances of
> the Arabs. They study Arab theologians and
> philosophers, not to refute them but to form an elegant
> and correct Arabic . . . They have forgotten their own
> language. For every one who can write a letter in Latin
> to a friend, there are a thousand who can express
> themselves in Arabic with elegance and write better
> poems in this language than the Arabs themselves.

With a growing economy and a fiscal incentive to conform with the ruling class, the ninth century was a time of increasing assimilation by Spaniards into Islamic culture. Christian, pre-Islamic Spanish identity was therefore coming under threat. And

Isaac's response was to resort to the one tool that has been used extensively throughout Spanish history in such circumstances: extreme violence. Not against the ruling authorities. As one individual there was little he could do. Instead he brought the violence upon himself. And just as tales of early Christian martyrs inspired later believers, so his sacrifice would become a rallying cry for his co-religionists.

The martyr movement itself was short-lived and limited to a small number of people, but word of it soon spread to the northern parts of the Peninsula, where tiny Christian statelets had managed to establish themselves after the Moorish conquest. Taking advantage of the natural fortifications provided by the landscape, and often walled in by mountain ranges, centuries later these tiny warrior nations would go on to form the founding kingdoms of modern Spain. For the time being, however, they were cowed and subdued, still licking their wounds and living at a far remove from the rest of Christian Europe. News from Cordoba in the mid-ninth century, however, had a galvanising effect. The executed Christians of Cordoba were immediately hailed as heroes. Within thirty years, the king of Asturias had bought the remains of one – Eulogius, Isaac's biographer – from the ruler of Al-Andalus and set up a cult of worship centred on them at Oviedo.

With time, these men and women would become cornerstones of the mythology which fired the 'Reconquest', Spain's cultural and military expunging of its Moorish self. Meanwhile, back in Cordoba, the Muslim rulers responded to the increasing numbers of Christians seeking martyrdom by reinforcing long-lapsed restrictions against their community, for example by banning them from administrative posts. In a complex environment, with many racial and religious textures and variations, stories of the Martyrs and the violence surrounding them helped to boil things down to simple terms of 'us' and 'them'.

Isaac's plan eventually worked, perhaps to an even greater extent than he had ever imagined. His legacy resonates to this day: at the time of writing a dozen Catalan independence activists are on trial in Madrid on charges of rebellion. They will be hoping that their own 'martyrdom' will have as powerful a boost for their cause as Isaac's did for his.

SPANISH MEDICINE

In the tenth century, medical knowledge and practice in Moorish Cordoba was so advanced that kings of northern Christian lands travelled to the enemy capital in search of cures for their ailments. Muslim Spaniards of the Middle Ages were carrying out pioneering work, establishing a tradition of medical innovation which is alive to this day.

The most outstanding physician of the Moorish period is a man called Al-Zahrawi. Known in the Latin-speaking world as Abulcasis, al-Zahrawi is renowned as the 'father of surgery', a branch of medicine which he considered the highest form of his art and which he developed almost single-handedly. The last volume of his magnum opus – *Kitab al-Tasrif* – is an illustrated guide to surgical techniques and was the very first such book ever to be written. A hundred and fifty years after his death (1031) it was translated into Latin in Toledo and became the standard textbook on the subject in Western universities and hospitals for five centuries. Even today modern surgeons still use the instruments which al-Zahrawi invented, among them the scalpel, the forceps, the surgical needle and retractor, and the speculum. In all he designed some two hundred surgical tools, each described in detail in his book.

Many of al-Zahrawi's breakthroughs came from observation of nature. One day his pet monkey ate some spare strings for his master's oud, made out of cat gut. When al-Zahrawi noticed that the strings appeared to cause the animal no harm and were in fact absorbed into his body, he started to think how he could use his discovery for medical purposes. His answer was to employ cat gut for sutures in operations on humans, a technique which is still used today.

Another advancement came when he was called to treat a slave girl who had tried to commit suicide by stabbing herself in the throat. Al-Zahrawi noticed that she hadn't managed to sever any arteries and that in fact the bleeding was quite mild. In addition, air was passing in and out of the wound while she breathed. This observation later formed the basis of tracheotomies.

Al-Zahrawi was a master of his art: he developed neurosurgical methods to cure head injuries and migraines, he was an accomplished dentist, and made important advancements in childbirth techniques. He was also the first person to recognise haemophilia as a hereditary disease. A thousand years later, the Spanish royal family still hadn't learned this important lesson, with two of Alfonso XIII's sons suffering from the disease as a result.

A hundred and fifty years after Al-Zahrawi died, another giant of medicine was working in Cordoba: Abu Marwan ibn Zuhr, who insisted on a purely rational approach to medicine, and who also wrote books on his art which were later translated into Latin and had a huge influence on Western medicinal thinking. Ibn Zuhr was a pioneer of dissection, using animals to learn about internal organs. Dissection of humans was forbidden under Islamic law, but it is possible, given the accuracy of some of his observations, that Ibn Zuhr secretly performed this procedure, possibly introducing into the corpse a substance made of cinnabar and vegetable oils, a rich red liquid which helped to identify blood vessels. The oldest known example of a dissected human body dates from the thirteenth century, just a hundred years after Ibn Zuhr's death, and shows signs of this technique being used in Europe at the time.

Ibn Zuhr also developed Al-Zahrawi's ideas about the tracheotomy, carrying out the procedure on goats before putting it into practice on his patients.

With the translation movement in Toledo of the twelfth and thirteenth centuries,[1] Moorish medicinal knowledge started to seep into Christian Spain, establishing a tradition which thrives to this day. In Valencia a number of medicinal herbal gardens were set up in the Middle Ages, later being absorbed into the *Jardí Botànic*, which was created in the 1500s. Around a hundred years before, the same city had seen the establishment of the first psychiatric hospital in Christian Europe, setting a trend which was quickly followed in other Spanish cities.

Fast-forward to the early nineteenth century and it was the Spanish who set up the world's first international healthcare programme. The Englishman Jenner invented vaccination in 1797, but it was a Spanish doctor, Francisco Javier de Balmís, who decided to use the technique to carry out the first vaccination mission, travelling to Latin America and Asia. The plan was given royal approval, and in 1803 Balmís set sail on a three-year voyage around the globe, accompanied by twenty-two orphans as live carriers of the virus, which could then be passed on to others in the

---

1 Covered in a later chapter.

ports and cities they visited along the way. Jenner himself wrote of the Balmís expedition:

I don't imagine the annals of history furnish an
example of philanthropy so noble, so extensive as this.

Further medical advances followed. In the 1920s a Spanish military surgeon, Fidel Pagés, invented epidural anaesthetics, while during the Spanish Civil War, the first blood transfusions were carried out – developed by a Canadian, Dr Bethune (who later became a friend of Chairman Mao) – during the battle for Madrid in 1936.

And this trend continues. Today, despite deep cuts in government spending on research, Spanish investigators (and Cubans, who have picked up the baton from their former colonial masters) are at the forefront of many medical innovations. Behind them stretches a tradition laid down over a thousand years before. Al-Zahrawi would be proud of his descendants.

RISE AND FALL

As with every regime in Spanish history, from the Visigoths to the Second Republic, the collapse of Arabian Spain came about through civil war. And, as happens on other occasions, the demise of the Umayyad regime in Al-Andalus followed very quickly on the heels of its greatest and most celebrated period. The 'Golden Age' of Moorish Spain was the tenth century, during the reigns first of Abd al-Rahman III and then his son Al-Hakam II. Politically, Al-Andalus showed greater confidence during this time. For a brief pause, the internal disputes and rebellions which had so dogged it from the beginning were subdued. This coincided with its elevation on the international stage: from being simply an 'emir', or prince, in 929 Abd al-Rahman declared himself 'caliph', or leader of the Islamic community, in a direct challenge both to the recognised caliph in Baghdad and the rival Fatimid caliphate which had been established in North Africa. Abd al-Rahman III was a direct descendant of his namesake who had established Umayyad rule in Al-Andalus in the eighth century, and there was a family link to the early rulers of the Islamic world. Ethnically, by this point the Arabian lineage had been watered down: the fruit of many generations of marriages with local women, Abd al-Rahman III, the greatest ruler of 'Moorish' Spain, had red hair and blue eyes and possibly lighter skin than many Spaniards of today.

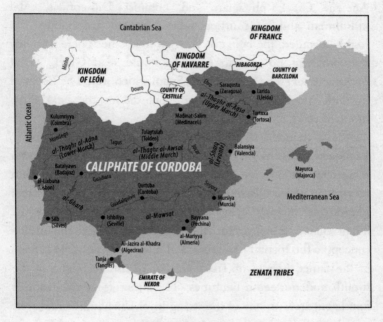

Umayyad Spain at its height (c. 1000)

This period is celebrated now for its extraordinary cultural achievements. Cordoba became the epicentre of a spectacular flourishing of the arts and sciences which converted the city into a bright intellectual light in the relative darkness of Europe at the time. Much of the groundwork for this had already been laid thanks to the efforts of Ziryab, but we can date the start of this development to the arrival, in 949, of another Man from the East who would change the history of Spain. This time, however, it wasn't the person himself who arrived, but his written words. In that year an embassy arrived in Cordoba from the emperor in Byzantium, and among the gifts brought were the works of the Ancient Greek physician and botanist Dioscorides. Abd al-Rahman and his courtiers were delighted: Dioscorides was highly regarded, the father of Western medicine. There was only one problem: no one in Cordoba could read Greek. What happened next set a precedent in Spain which would be followed in both Moorish and Christian contexts for the next three hundred years.

Abd al-Rahman III didn't invent the school of translators – Baghdad's House of Wisdom had been the centre of a translation movement almost since the city's founding in the mid-eighth century, in which Classical Greek and other texts were translated into Arabic, thereby laying the intellectual foundations for the infant Islamic Empire. But Abd al-Rahman III did import the concept to the Iberian Peninsula, and it would go on to be echoed in the famed School of Translators in Christian Toledo of the twelfth and thirteenth centuries. The structure of the team of translators drew on one of the strengths of Umayyad Cordoba: its mixed population and policy of relative tolerance to non-Muslims. Members included the Christian Bishop Recemund, the Muslim scholar Ibn Juljul, and a leading member of the Jewish community Hasday ibn Shaprut. Further testament to the openness of the period lies in the fact that Ibn Shaprut was also personal physician to the caliph and a trusted palace official. Not only that, in a further example of the slightly blurred lines between the various religious and political communities on the Peninsula in the tenth century, he also cured the king of Navarre of obesity in 964 when he came to visit Cordoba.[1]

This tolerant and intellectually curious atmosphere made Cordoba the greatest city in the western Mediterranean, second only to Constantinople in terms of splendour and population (estimates vary between anything from one hundred thousand to half a million people living in and around the city at this time). In fact, Byzantium acted as a kind of midwife for Cordoba's blossoming, not only sending the texts of Dioscorides (and, eventually, a Greek-speaking monk to help with the translating) but also artists and artisans to decorate the new buildings that were springing up in the Moorish capital: Al-Hakam II's extension of the Great Mosque has exquisite Byzantine mosaic work around the Mihrab niche which is still visible today.

During its Golden Age, Cordoba was said to be home to eighty schools, six hundred mosques, fifty residences for the poor and orphans, and as many as nine hundred bathhouses. One of its many new libraries claimed to have up to four hundred thousand books. The streets were paved, there was an extensive underground sewerage system, and lamps at street corners and above the entrances to most houses meant there was, in effect, street lighting – seven hundred years before such a system was set up in London.

Women also enjoyed greater freedoms: one of the brightest lights of the time was Lubna, poetess, mathematician, grammarian and private secretary to the Caliph Al-Hakam II. Other women exceeding in their fields included the poetess and historian Radiya, and Maryam of Seville, who taught literature to the daughters of Cordoba's elite.

---

1 Perhaps not surprisingly, back home Sancho was nicknamed 'the Fat'.

In an atmosphere of expansion and increased possibilities, a brand new palatial city was built just three miles to the west of Cordoba: Medina Azahara (*Medinat al-Zahra* in Arabic) became the physical expression of the new glory of Moorish Spain, an architectural wonder designed to enrapture and impress: mirrors of liquid mercury casting lights on the ceiling of the reception hall left foreign visitors speechless, while two hundred thousand loaves every day were needed just to feed the fish in the caliph's fish ponds.

Confident and vibrant, this culture didn't escape the attention of Christian Europe, and it became a magnet for adventurous and inquisitive types who sought more intellectual stimulation than their own countries could provide at the time. According to some sources, the future Pope Sylvester II – then known as Gerbert – even made it as far as Cordoba 'in search of knowledge' (some say he never made it beyond Barcelona). Such was Cordoba's fame that in the 950s a Christian nun from Saxony wrote about it:

> *The brilliant ornament of the world shone in the west,*
> *a noble city newly known for the military prowess that*
> *its Hispanic colonisers had brought. Cordoba was its*
> *name and it was wealthy and famous and known for*
> *its pleasures and resplendent in all things, and*
> *especially for its seven streams of wisdom* [the Classical
> Trivium and Quadrivium] *as much as for its constant*
> *victories.*

What tells us more about Cordoba's increasing reputation at this time is that the author of this eulogy, Hroswitha, never even went there.

Yet even as this great flourishing was reaching its highest and greatest achievements, few at the time could imagine that within a mere generation it would all lie in ruins. The light of Cordoba, like so many in Spanish history, shone very brightly, but all too briefly.

The rot set in shortly after the death of Al-Hakam II in 976. The caliph's successor, Hisham II, was only eleven. A triumvirate was set up to rule as regent, but within a few years one of these three had despatched the other two and taken over as dictator. This man was Al-Mansur, a former high-ranking and ambitious civil servant who effectively ruled Al-Andalus until 1002. Acting in caliphal fashion, he expanded the Great Mosque, virtually doubling it in size, and built another palatial city near Cordoba to rival Abd al-Rahman's Medina Azahara, confusingly with almost the same name – *Medinat al-Zahira*. In Spain today, however, he is still remembered as the terrible 'Almanzor' for his repeated campaigns to subdue the small Christian kingdoms to the north: on one occasion he even reached as far as Santiago and stole the bells from the cathedral tower.

Yet despite these feats, Al-Mansur sowed the seeds which would eventually bring about the rapid destruction of Umayyad Al-Andalus. By acting as dictator he effectively reduced the caliph to a puppet figure whose prestige could never be restored. And to bolster the army he brought in thousands of troops, or mercenaries, from Berber tribes in North Africa. As long as these men were busy fighting Christians, all was fine. But they became a large and powerful presence in a society with a long history of divisions between Arabs and Berbers, the latter very much looked down upon by the former as being culturally and racially inferior.

Al-Mansur's successor carried on in much the same vein as his father. But when he died, still quite young, in 1008, real problems began.

What followed was later termed by Arab chroniclers as the *Fitna* – the great strife or rebellion. Lasting from 1008 to 1031, it was, in essence, a string of civil wars with frequent and sometimes rapid changes of government, assassinations, plundering and massacres of civilian populations. The details are messy and often confusing, but as an example of the chaos that reigned at the time, one of the puppet caliphs put on the throne at one stage 'ruled' for less than three months before being deposed and replaced.[2]

Importantly, Christian rulers became involved for the first time in Andalusi politics: different kings supported different Moorish factions at various moments during the complex and very violent shifts in power. This set a precedent which would then be followed over the next five centuries.

Disaster came in 1013. For two years, Berber mercenaries fighting for one faction had been established at Medina Azahara, from whence they blockaded Cordoba. Having thoroughly looted the palatial city, they finally took the capital after an outbreak of the plague had seriously reduced the inhabitants' resolve. On breaching the city's defences, the Berbers continued as they had previously done across much of the Andalusi countryside: the libraries were sacked and the city denuded of its wealth. Many civilians were cut down in a frenzied massacre. One eyewitness later named as many as sixty of the city's intellectuals who had been murdered at the time, their bodies left to rot in the street for days afterwards.

Umayyad Spain never recovered from this blow, and although it managed to stagger on for several more years, in 1031 it finally

---

2 There are very powerful echoes from this period in the nineteenth century, a time of great upheaval and many hundreds of rebellions and coups. These are dealt with in a later chapter.

collapsed when the last caliph, Hisham III, was deposed and not replaced. Cordoba itself, its once glorious capital, lay in ruins. Despite a brief renaissance a hundred and fifty years later, it would never again be the great cultural centre it had once been.

Civil war brought Arabian Spain to an end, and with it the strong political force which had only briefly held the country together. For the next seven hundred years, Spain would exist once more only as a geographical concept, with the Peninsula breaking up into a patchwork of warring mini-states. The creation of a new political Spain would eventually require many wars, foreign intervention, and much Spanish blood.

HEROIC SPAIN

FITTING IN

Barring a handful of small Christian statelets to the north, the Arabian Spain of the Umayyads had encompassed most of the Iberian Peninsula, drawing it together as the Visigoths had done before. With the collapse of the Cordoba caliphate in the *Fitna* civil wars, however, the Peninsula became a patchwork of mini-kingdoms and principalities, some Muslim, some Christian, with shifting and often ill-defined borders, highly complicated alliances and rivalries between them, and always fighting among themselves. Into this state of endemic civil war – which lasted around five hundred years – entered foreign powers on all sides, both from North Africa and from Europe, intervening as they saw fit and often imposing harsher, more 'fundamentalist' beliefs as the price for their involvement.[1] This period, often referred to as the 'Reconquest', would see the eventual disappearance of Moorish Spain as a political entity.

---

1 Something similar occurred during the Civil War of the twentieth century, when the Republic paid a very high price for Stalin's support. Imported Soviet-style paranoia and purges form the backdrop to the left-wing repression George Orwell chronicles in his *Homage to Catalonia*.

It is not common to regard the 'Reconquest' as a 'civil' war. In general, the view in Spain today is that the Moors invaded and conquered the Peninsula in the eighth century, and then over several centuries were pushed back and eventually driven out with the conquest of Granada. In this vision, the Moors are clearly 'foreign', and the Christians, led by the country's Moor-Slaying patron saint, 'Spanish'. The 'Reconquest' is as much to do with ethnicity as it is with religion.

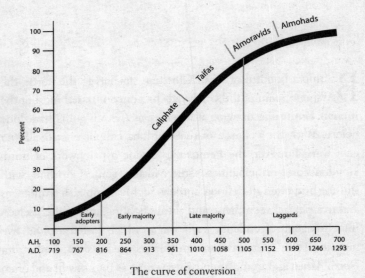

The curve of conversion

It's a convenient image which flies in the face of both historical research and common sense: two communities living side by side for almost a millennium were only ever going to integrate – at least to some degree.

The US historian Richard W. Bulliet studied the question of integration and conversion to Islam in the 1970s. Basing his research on medieval biographical records, he noticed something interesting: as a person's lineage was traced back through the generations, at some point Islamic names gave way to non-Islamic, or pre-Islamic, ones – for example, Ali son of Muhammad, son of Ahmad, son of Umar, son of Alvaro . . . Collecting the data from these documents and extrapolating from them, he concluded that in the century between 900 and 1000 – coinciding with the Umayyad Golden Age – the number of Spanish converts to Islam leapt from around 25 per cent to 75 per cent. And while his findings were based on a relatively small number of records, they are corroborated by the various expansions carried out over roughly the same period to the main mosque in Cordoba: as the number of Muslim faithful grew, so they needed more space in which to pray.

By the twelfth century, as Bulliet's research indicates, the vast majority of people south of the Peninsula's religious divide were Muslims – or in other words, 'Moors'. They were local people who spoke Arabic and prayed to Allah, yet nonetheless were Spanish. The 'Reconquest', therefore, if it can be seen as a whole at all, should be viewed as the slow and very staggered process of northern Spain militarily dominating the south – a civil conflict driven more by ideology than ethnicity. There were as many cultural differences between the various northern kingdoms chipping away at Al-Andalus (including linguistic ones: Basque is no closer to Latin-based Iberian languages than Arabic is) as there were separating them from their Muslim enemies.

In this light, the fall of Granada in 1492 is less the completion of the 'Reconquest', and more an expression of a refrain running through the history of the Peninsula in which one 'Spain' fights to dominate and ultimately annihilate another 'Spain' (in the twentieth century, Franco fitted this pattern neatly when he labelled his Republican enemies the 'anti-Spain'). The conquest of Granada may have been seen as a triumph at the time and the culmination of the 're-Christianisation' of the Peninsula, but as in the tale of Heracles – that other Spanish patron saint – and the Hydra, the severing of one head only produced others: as the history of the country shows, the 'other Spain', however it is defined, can never be definitively killed off and always rises again in some form or another.

Yet despite being a period of constant warfare and violence, the crucible that is Spain continues to bubble, and the 'Reconquest' also sees some of the greatest cultural achievements in the whole of Spanish history. This is a time of heroes, some Christian, others Moorish. All of them will have an enormous impact not only on Spain itself, but also on the rest of the world.

PARTY TIME

Minutes before I started writing these words, a new prime minister was installed in Spain – Pedro Sánchez, a man accustomed to fighting many political battles, despite his youthful appearance. Spain is going through turbulent times; its very existence as a nation is under threat. And as it does so, parallels are naturally drawn with a period in the distant past, one which continues to resonate many hundreds of years on. This is the period of the *taifas* and the complex and often chaotic events of the eleventh century.

Less than half an hour into office, and Pedro Sánchez has been compared to El Cid, the most renowned figure from the period (thanks, not least, to Charlton Heston and Sofia Loren). We'll come back to the Cid and his story. For now, let's concentrate on the *taifas*.

Like the *Fitna* which led to the breakdown of central Umayyad authority, *taifa* is an Arabic word. It is used to describe the many different mini-kingdoms into which Al-Andalus broke up in the 1000s. The fact that journalists and others still use the word today is testament to the fact that this was no isolated period in Spanish history, but rather a tendency, an ever-present threat to the political unity of the country.

The Umayyads had lost power long before the last of them was overthrown. But even stripped of real authority, their mere presence as caliphs could act as a unifying idea: they formed a blood link to Mecca and the Umayyad caliphs of Damascus, a lineage of legitimacy which served as a symbolic reminder of national unity. But with the last of them gone, and no strongman or dictator like Al-Mansur capable of holding the centre, Moorish Spain inevitably splintered into its constituent parts. The reality of the nation – a conglomeration of regions both connected and divided by geography – asserted itself. And from a society which had grown comfortable and even 'soft' with its high cultural achievements, it was impossible to find the necessary martial will or energy to pull it back together.

This is how the *taifas* were born – the small, petty kingdoms, or 'party kings', as the word translates into English. 'Party' as in political faction, but the play on words is fortuitous, for despite being a period of constant internal warfare, this was also a hedonistic age – at least on the Moorish side. With central authority gone, the *taifas* sprang up in different ways. In some cases local bosses simply carried on as before, but no longer answering to Cordoba. In other places, military factions took over, their commanders hailing from Berber families or, in some instances, having Slavic origins, former slaves now becoming rulers in spectacular feats of social climbing. Not all of them were created at once – the process took time. And although as many as two dozen or more existed at one time or another, their numbers waxed and waned as they engaged in near permanent warfare among themselves, smaller kingdoms often being absorbed into larger ones in a scrabble for power and land.

The picture is complicated, not least because while the Moorish states were fighting among themselves, they were often also engaged in battles with the Christian states to the north, creating a multi-dimensional chessboard in which allegiances often crossed religious lines, and Moors and Christians regularly fought side by side against common foes with a similarly mixed religious make-up. As the eleventh century progressed, religious differences did to a degree become more important, particularly as the concept of 'holy war' – long established in the Islamic world – began to take hold within Christendom. But far from being black or white, the situation was generally both black *and* white at the same time – as things in Spain tend to be. This was the world in which men like El Cid – adventurers and chancers – were able to flourish.

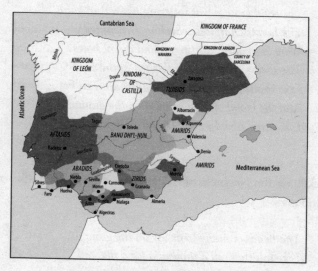

The Taifas, a constant Spanish refrain

Some of the *taifas* were more successful than others. The kingdom of Denia on the eastern coast started essentially as a pirate state which preyed on shipping off the coast. Expanding into the Balearic Islands, it eventually spread as far as Sardinia, becoming a powerful player in the western Mediterranean. A *taifa* was also established at this time at Granada; previously the main city in the area had been at Elvira in the fertile plains of the Vega, but the *taifa* rulers founded their new home in the foothills of the Sierra Nevada, a much more easily defendable location in the more warlike environment. A leading vizier at the Granadan court was the Jewish rabbi and poet Samuel ibn Naghrela. This is how he describes a battle between the Granadans and the *taifa* of Almería in 1038:

> *At sunrise all the earth appeared to melt;*
> *The solid ground was tottering like a drunkard.*
> *The horses charging, wheeling, backing off,*
> *Were like snakes darting in and out of holes.*
> *The spears, as they flew, flashed in the sun*
> *Like shafts of lightning, filling the air with fire . . .*
> *And the blood of men coursed on the ground*
> *Like rams' blood in the Temple of the Lord.*

Luckily for Ibn Naghrela, the Granadans emerged from the battle victorious:

> *The heads of many lords lay on the ground*
> *Like figs that sell a thousand for a fils.*
> *The bloated corpses of fallen princes lay*

'Santiago the Apostle'
(© Museum of Fine Arts,
Houston, Texas, USA/
Bridgeman Images)

'Santiago the Pilgrim'
(Jason Webster)

'Santiago the Slayer'
(Shutterstock)

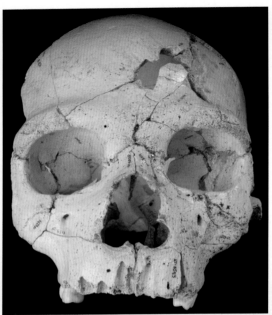

The Altamira cave paintings, the 'Sistine Chapel of Paleolithic art'.

The mythical Pillars of Hercules across the Strait of Gibraltar are an essential element of Spanish national identity. *(Wikipedia)*

The Pillars of Hercules on Spanish 'pieces of eight' later transformed into the American dollar sign, with the two stripes becoming the universal symbol of currency.
(© Julia Kanivets/iStock)

Ziryab, the 'blackbird' from the East, brought the latest fashions from ninth-century Baghdad to Europe. *(Wikipedia)*

The rule of Abd al-Rahman III was the high point of the Moorish Golden Age. *(© Heritage Image Partnership Ltd/Alamy Stock Photo)*

The ceiling of the Mihrab in the great Mosque of Cordoba shares the same symbolism as Christian Spain's Pilgrimage to Santiago. *(Wikimedia)*

The Arabian hero Antar predated his European chivalric counterparts by several centuries. *(Wikipedia)*

The city of Játiva, where, in the eleventh century, Ibn Hazm wrote the *Ring of the Dove*, a key text in the development of European ideas about romantic and courtly love. *(Jason Webster)*

El Cid is the quintessential Spanish hero: brave, violent and very hard to pin down. *(© Stephen Bay/Alamy Stock Photo)*

Just who exactly is buried at Santiago? St James? Or Priscillian, the first heretic to be executed by the Church? *(Shutterstock)*

(above) Arab scholars were fascinated by the works of Aristotle and went to great lengths to translate and understand them. *(Wikipedia)*

(left) Thomas Aquinas built much of his ideas on the work of the great Spanish philosopher Averroes, as represented visually in this Florentine mural from the fourteenth century. *(© Santa Maria Novella, Florence, Italy/ Bridgeman Images)*

Alfonso 'the Wise' not only built much of the Spanish state, but also actively imported learning from his neighbours, the Moors. (© *Book of Games,1282, by Alfonso X of Castile (1224–1284)/ Tarker/Bridgeman Images*)

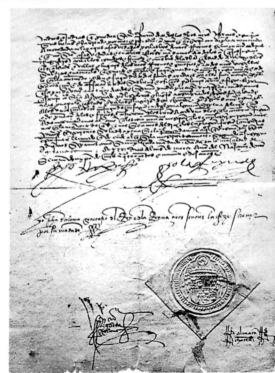

The end of Jewish Spain: the Alhambra Decree ordering the expulsion of the Sephardic community. *(Wikipedia)*

A sixteenth-century illustration of an *auto da fé*. (*Wikipedia*)

The Inquisition's last victim: Cayetano Ripoll.

Bartolomé de las Casas, the first advocate of human rights. (*© Hilary Morgan/Bridgeman Images*)

Like swollen wine-skins or heavily pregnant women.
Slaves lay beside their masters, beggars
Next to kings, all one rank,
All turned to dung.

The battle was personal: a vizier on the opposing side had previously called for Ibn Naghrela to be executed. Now the Jewish vizier took his revenge, imprisoning his foe and having him executed:

. . . my enemy
Died like a dog on the festival of the Torah.

Vivid and emotionally honest, Ibn Naghrela's poem is an example of a Golden Age for Hebrew letters at this time, in which Jewish writers composed verse in Hebrew, rather than Arabic, for the first time. It is also indicative of the cultural flourishing throughout Moorish Spain that existed side by side with the constant civil wars. Ceramics, ivory work, music and the decorative arts all blossomed. But following a long-established tradition dating back to pre-Islamic days, poetry was held as the highest form of artistic expression.

One of the most celebrated poets of the day was Al-Mu'tamid, who as well as being an accomplished writer was also king of the *taifa* of Seville.

Many a night I spent enjoying their shadows
With maidens round-hipped and slim of waist;
Their white and brown beauty pierced my heart
Like white blood-spilling swords and points of brown lances.
And those nights spent playfully on the river dam

With a girl whose arm bracelet was like the crescent moon.
She would pour me wine with bewitching glances,
At times in a cup, at others in her kisses.
The tunes played on her lute stirred me, as though
I heard in her chords the clash of sword blades.
Then she let her robe fall, her magnificent figure like
A bud unfolding from a cluster of blossoms.

Scimitars and seduction, sex and violence – Al-Mu'tamid's poetry encapsulates the mood of the time, its hedonism, admiration for high culture, and constant threat of a gruesome end. When not fighting his neighbours, Al-Mu'tamid would hold night-time poetry and music contests on the Guadalquivir on boats illuminated with torches. Extravagance was the keynote to his rule: when his favourite wife – a Christian girl from the north – cried that she would never see the snows of her native land again, Al-Mu'tamid had an entire grove of almond trees planted outside her bedroom window one night. 'There!' he proclaimed, pointing to their bright blossom the following morning. 'There is your snow!'

Seville was not alone in becoming a cultural centre at this time. Like the city states of medieval and Renaissance Italy three and four centuries later, the *taifa* kingdoms expressed their rivalry through the achievements of artistic and intellectual lights at their respective courts. The pirate kings of Denia surrounded themselves with Quranic scholars; the king of Badajoz compiled (or, more probably, had compiled for him) an encyclopedia fifty volumes long; an astronomer at Toledo built a water clock which became famous throughout the Peninsula; while the ruler of Zaragoza was an accomplished astrologer, geometrist and philosopher.

Culturally and politically, Seville was the leading *taifa* state, yet its power was never such that it could reunite Moorish Spain under one rule. As often in Spanish history, it would require a greater force, one from outside the Peninsula, to achieve that.

Christian Spain at this time was equally divided, and the *taifas* on the Moorish side were reflected almost perfectly by the myriad counties and kingdoms in which Christianity was the official faith. And during a period of such political complexity, raw military might became the single most important factor for success. Not surprisingly then, the eleventh century saw the rise of Castile, a region which would go on to stamp its mark on the Peninsula like no other. Born as a small county on the fringes of the kingdom of León, it was the martial spirit of the Castilians – men originally from the mountains around Oña to the north of Burgos – which marked them out; while the Leónese preferred a more peaceful life, the Castilians were warriors willing to take the fight to the Muslims. As a result, their county expanded and their power increased. In 1065, Castile became a kingdom in its own right.

Yet there is an interesting difference between the *taifas* and the Christian kingdoms: while lack of unity led Moorish territory to shrink in size, division on the Christian side was no barrier to expansion and conquest. From being the undisputed supremo of the Peninsula in the tenth century, in only a hundred years Al-Andalus as a whole was placed on the back foot as Christian lords started taking larger nibbles out of the Moorish lands on their southern borders.

The advance effectively caught the Moors napping.

'Because the rays of the sun do not fall perpendicularly upon their heads, their climate is cold and the atmosphere cloudy. For that reason their temperament has become cold and their humour uncouth. Their bodies have stretched, their complexion has become light and their hair long. They lack, moreover, acuteness and intellectual penetration, for indeed there is great foolishness and madness among them.'

So wrote a Moorish judge in Toledo about the northerners at this time, and his opinion was most likely shared by other inhabitants of Al-Andalus. But this lack of respect for the enemy brought danger. In a surprise move which shook Moorish Spain, Toledo fell into Christian hands in 1085, only fifteen years after the judge's death. Despite many counter-attacks, the city would never be ruled by Muslims again.

The old Visigothic capital was once more under the Cross. For Christian Spaniards – and indeed around Christian Europe as a whole – it was a cause for great celebration, the first major victory against the Moors since the invasion of 711.

For the Moors, it was a disaster. Down in Seville, the poet–king Al-Mu'tamid was about to make a very difficult decision.

MOORISH VIEWS OF
CHRISTIANS

Moorish attitudes towards Christians were varied, and shifted over the many centuries of Al-Andalus. One constant, however, and a view which echoed throughout the Mediterranean following the arrival of the Crusades, was a combination of disgust and bemusement at Christian washing habits – or rather their lack of them.

In the eleventh century the Moorish chronicler Al-Bakri quoted an earlier Jewish traveller, Yaqub of Tortosa, as saying this about the Christians living in the northern parts of the Peninsula:

> *The whole area is flat and most of the land is covered in sand* [while this doesn't sound like the green and lush coastal areas, it is a fair description of the high tablelands of León and Castile]. *Their food consists mostly of millet and sorghum, and they drink cider and 'bushka', which is made with flour. The inhabitants are*

treacherous and morally depraved. They do not keep
themselves clean and only wash once or twice a year –
and then in cold water. They never wash their clothes,
wearing them until they fall to pieces, and insist that
the dirt on them mixed with their sweat is actually
good for them and keeps them healthy. Their clothes
are very tight-fitting with wide openings through which
most of their bodies can be seen. They are brave and
never entertain ideas of retreat from battle, considering
death a lesser evil.

Compare that with this portrayal of the Moorish forces who conquered the Peninsula in the eighth century – written five hundred years later and probably reflecting contemporary ideas about the Muslim soldiers who Christians regularly met on the battlefields of the time:

The Moors . . . wore silks and colourful clothes . . .
The reins on their horses were like fire; their faces were
as black as pitch – the handsomest of them was as
black as a cooking pot – their eyes blazing like torches.
Their horses ran as fast as leopards and their knights
were far more cruel and hurtful than a wolf among a
flock of sheep at night. The vile Africans . . . praise
neither strength nor goodness, and achieve everything
through artfulness and deceit, and never help each
other except by paying over large amounts of wealth.

CHIVALRY

Military ranks in different countries mirror one another to a large degree: the various grades within individual armed forces are largely the same, from 'private' to 'general'. The military in Spain and several Latin American countries, however, have a rank which is unique. This is an *alférez*, sometimes translated as 'second lieutenant'.

As the word itself suggests, *alférez* has an Arabic origin, coming from *al-faris*, meaning horseman, or knight. In medieval Spanish courts, the *alférez* was a powerful man in charge of the king's personal retinue of knights. This borrowing of an Arabic term highlights a curious quality to relations between Islam and Christendom at the time: that while they were often at war, there existed a simultaneous interchange of cultures and ideas – a social contact – between the two communities. A clear example of this is the area of horsemanship and knightly behaviour – activities of the medieval *alférez*.

We usually think of chivalry as a native Western concept, embedded in our culture since the tales of Roland and King

Arthur, books and stories of knightly deeds which laid the foundations of European literature. Yet the *Chanson de Roland*, written in the eleventh century and one of the cornerstones of the chivalric movement, gives a clue, as does the word *alférez*, to the origins of the code. The historical Roland was killed at Roncesvalles by Basques; the author of the *Chanson*, however, turns the enemies of the literary Roland into Moors: the hero's acts of selfless valour are carried out against a Muslim force.

The Arabic word for knight – *al-faris* – is derived from the word for horse, *al-faras*, and linked to *al-furisiyya*, the Arabic tradition of horsemanship and chivalry, also known as *futuwwa*, with strong ideas about honour and bravery, and a gallant and even romantic attitude to women involving the revolutionary concept of unrequited love.[1] These were not new ideas in medieval Islam, however. In fact, by the Middle Ages they were already centuries old, having originated in Pre-Islamic times with the legends of Antar and Abla.

Virtually unknown to this day in the West, Antar is the Arab national hero, a warrior–poet of the sixth century and prototype for European knights. A King Arthur of the desert, he fights for justice and honour throughout Arabia and the Middle East, subduing the wicked and defending the weak with the aid of his magical sword and his fleet-footed jet-black steed Abjer. In all his exploits he is inspired to feats of incredible strength and daring by his love for the beautiful Abla, whose hand he seeks in marriage. Many are set against this match, however, for Antar, though fathered by a tribal

---

1 The master horsemen of Moorish Spain belonged to the Zanata tribe, who in turn gave the Spanish language its word for horseman, *jinete*. This Spanish culture travelled across the Atlantic in the wake of Columbus's discovery, and formed the basis of the traditions of the Mexican and Californian cowboys, known as 'buckaroos' from the Spanish *vaquero* meaning 'cowboy'.

nobleman, is also the son of a black slave woman, and as such can aspire to little more than the life of a camel-herder under the constraints of the strict desert hierarchy. He must pass through a lifetime of trials to prove his worth before Abla can be his.

Like Roland and Arthur, Antar is both mythological and historical. The historical Antar had the honour of seeing the best of his *qasidas*, or odes, chosen to feature among the *mu'allaqat*, seven poems that were embroidered and then 'hung' from the Kaaba in Mecca. He died as an old man in battle fighting the Tayy tribe.

The mythological Antar extends beyond this story, the various strands and tales about his exploits first being collected and compiled in Baghdad in the ninth century at the time of Harun al-Rashid. The *Sirat Antar*, the *Romance of Antar*, is one of the best-loved and most re-told epics of the Arab world, and was almost certainly among the Arabic 'romances' read by Christians in Cordoba which Paul Alvarus took such offence at in the 800s.

That Western Chivalry is inspired by Islamic *futuwwa* traditions is conceivable given the close contact between Christians and Muslims throughout the medieval period in Spain, the Holy Land and Sicily. Knights from all over Europe – from France, England, Scotland, Germany and Italy – were involved in these encounters, taking the ideas they found abroad back home to the far corners of the Continent. The echoes between Arthur and Antar are obvious, from his noble yet complicated origins to his magical sword and final demise through treachery and poison (and here there is an additional echo of the Norse myth of Balder, Antar being killed by a javelin thrown by a blind man). Even as he is dying, Antar never ceases to be chivalrous, protecting his beloved Abla and their retinue and allowing them to escape while he holds back his enemies through a combination of strength and subterfuge.

It is interesting that just at the time when ideas of chivalry are seeping into Western consciousness from the Islamic world, the Courtly Love movement is also developing in southern France, likewise deriving inspiration from Islamic sources, not least the *Ring of the Dove,* a treatise on romantic love written in the Spanish city of Játiva during the eleventh century by author and legal scholar Ibn Hazm. The musicians associated with the movement – the troubadours – derived their name, according to some authorities, from the Arabic word *tariba* – 'to make music, to sing, to delight'.[2]

And into this world step new figures who stand astride the myth–history division. In Spain, the most famous of these is El Cid.

It would be impossible to write a book on Spanish history without mentioning El Cid. No figure from the Spanish Middle Ages enjoys such public recognition as the great Castilian warrior and conqueror of Valencia. He inspired the first major work of poetry in Castilian Spanish, became the subject of plays and books, had three operas written about him (by Bizet, Debussy and Massenet, although only Massenet's was finished), and, of course, provided the story for the classic Hollywood epic.

El Cid has become Spain's national hero, as much a symbol of the country as Santiago. But just as the Christian saint came to have at least three conflicting guises – Apostle, Pilgrim and Moor-Slayer – so El Cid shifts from being a simple hero at first glance to a more ambiguous figure full of contradictions. Not unlike Spain herself.

First, a few facts. El Cid was born Rodrigo Díaz near Burgos around 1043. By this time the northern reaches of the central

---

2 Other etymologies point to the word *trovar,* from which comes the French *trouver,* 'to find'; this draws an interesting parallel with the English word for street musician, 'busker' – a kind of modern troubadour – which comes from the Spanish *buscar,* 'to seek'.

Spanish tablelands were in Christian control, with Burgos as the capital of the fledgling Castilian kingdom. The Díaz family belonged to the lower nobility and as a teenager Rodrigo was sent to the court of Fernando I to be trained as a warrior. Although not exactly of humble origins, his rise from the lower ranks of the ruling class to become a king in all but name is part of the appeal of his story.

This is the time of the *taifas*, when Moorish Spain shattered into a multitude of city-states and kingdoms after the collapse of the Cordoba caliphate. Christian Spain was likewise divided, and the frontier between Muslim and Christian areas was blurred and porous. No central power existed; authority was won through sheer military might. It was a time of rivalries and fluid alliances, of warfare, plunder, and glorious opportunities for ambitious men. The Wild West of America is not a bad comparison to get a sense of the period.

In this environment, Rodrigo became the most respected and feared warrior of his age, fighting his way through danger and betrayal to be hailed Lord of Valencia in 1094. En route he became the closest ally and greatest foe of kings, fought for both Christians and Muslims, made himself enormously rich by robbing his enemies, and was turned into a legend. A Moorish contemporary writer, while condemning him, recognised him as 'one of the miracles of God'. He was never once defeated in battle, and, according to legend, was even victorious over his enemies from beyond the grave: after his death in 1099, his widow, Jimena, managed to rally the troops one last time by putting armour on her husband's corpse and propping him up on his horse to charge the enemy lines. El Cid is Spain's Achilles, a mythical warrior gifted with near superhuman power.

So much for the story. The first thing to emphasise is El Cid's prowess as a soldier. Fighting was the dominant activity of his age, and El Cid was very good at it, as his other nickname – *El Campeador*, 'the hero of the battlefield' – testifies. In hand-to-hand combat he was once said to have taken on fifteen knights simultaneously, killing one, wounding another and sending the others off in flight. And he was also an excellent commander, understanding the need for meticulous planning and highly trained soldiers. In addition, he was lucky, and by never suffering a defeat, even in engagements in which he was seriously outnumbered, he gained a reputation for invincibility.

All of which are noble and much-needed qualities for an old-school hero. But dig a little deeper and El Cid often appears to have been anything but noble. To begin with, who was he fighting for? The simple answer appears to be: for himself. Over his lifetime he served several masters, most controversially Muslim as well as Christian kings. The *Poema del mio Cid*, the poem written about him roughly a hundred years after his death, makes no mention of this. But El Cid spent much of his life soldiering on behalf of the ruler of Zaragoza, Al-Mu'taman. Indeed, it appears to have been the Zaragozan who gave him the name by which he is known to this day: 'El Cid' comes from the Arabic *Al-Sayyid* which means 'lord', a rough equivalent of the title 'sir'.

It is interesting at this point to contrast El Cid with Santiago Matamoros. Both are emblematic Spanish heroes, both are warriors, both have the power to turn battles against the odds; and yet while Matamoros knows very much which side he's on in the Moor–Christian divide, El Cid is a much fuzzier character, his very nickname derived from Arabic.

Morally, El Cid is equally hard to define. Under him, Valencia had both Moors and Christians working in the city administration. Yet his treatment of a Moorish judge who had helped overthrow the previous ruler suggests a far less tolerant man: after confiscating his property and having him tortured, El Cid had the man dragged out, buried in a pit up to his waist, and burnt alive. His wives and children were only spared the same fate after an outcry from the public. According to a Muslim source, the persecution didn't end there, and he subjected the Muslim population to an 'inquisition':

> He seized them and extracted fines from them until he
> had rooted out everything they possessed . . . Many of
> them died during this treatment.

Compare this with how Christian sources reported a speech he made to the Muslims of Valencia after conquering the city:

> 'I wish to hear about all your affairs, and to become a
> sort of companion to you, behaving to you as friend to
> friend, or relative to relative.' . . . After he had said all
> this to them, he ordered them to go about their
> business. The Moors left well content with the Cid,
> marvelling at the promises he had made to them and
> at the kindness he had shown them.

Given the times, the treatment of the Moorish judge was not, perhaps, extraordinarily cruel. But another anecdote quoted in more than one source gives a further sense of El Cid's moral ambiguity. Needing cash, El Cid went to a pair of Jewish moneylenders, presenting them with treasure chests as security for the loan they would give him. Bizarrely, but perhaps thinking they could trust El

Cid, the moneylenders agreed not to look inside the chests for a year. When they did so, they found they were filled not with jewels, but with sand . . . When they appealed to El Cid for justice, they were brushed aside. Perhaps not surprisingly, according to Moorish sources, El Cid's favourite stories were those of the famous liar of Arabian tales, Al-Muhallab of Basra.

Warlike, mercenary, heroic, tolerant, cruel, rapacious, morally ambiguous, noble . . . and a rogue. Were it not for the more romantic portrayals of him in poems and on film, El Cid might almost be a character from the Picaresque style of literature which flourished in Spain in the sixteenth and seventeenth centuries, in which craftiness, guile and the ability to slip through the illogical ups and downs of fortune are celebrated.

In this, he is quintessentially Spanish, combining military skill and prowess with stubbornness and wiliness that enable him not only to survive, but also to become a proud and magnificent hero, a man whose name continues to resonate to this day.

PILGRIMAGE AND
MOOR-SLAYING

The Middle Ages sees both the high point of the pilgrimage to Santiago, and the final development of Spain's patron saint as a 'Moor-Slayer'. That these happen during the most intense years of the 'Reconquest' is not accidental.

Pilgrims began travelling to Compostela to venerate the supposed remains of St James shortly after they were discovered in the early ninth century. But it wasn't until the eleventh century that large numbers began to arrive from all over Europe. The city had been sacked by the Moorish dictator Al-Mansur in 997 (and the cathedral bells stolen and taken back to Cordoba, where they were turned upside down and converted into flaming torches for the main mosque). But by 1003 a new cathedral was being built in the saint's honour to accommodate the growing number of visitors. Political upheaval within Al-Andalus meant that raids from the south were becoming less common, making the pilgrimage a little safer.[1] By the early twelfth century, Compostela's position and strength were such that the now hundred-year-old cathedral was pulled down and a larger structure put up in its place. This is the one that stands to this day, consecrated in 1105.

The rising popularity of the route to Santiago led to the compilation of the first tourist guide in Western history – Book V of the *Codex Calixtinus*. Probably written by a French monk in the twelfth century, the *Codex* is a long work which describes the history of Santiago, miracles associated with the saint, and the liturgical texts used at Compostela, among other things. But Book V is designed to be a functioning travel guide for the average French pilgrim setting out for the holy Spanish city. Advice given includes which churches to visit along the way, which relics to venerate, and details about the various stages of the route. But it also gives practical advice, such as how to avoid the 'huge flies' which infest certain areas, or the best way to deal with untrustworthy boatmen when trying to cross a river: *'Whatever you do, don't get into an overloaded boat, which can capsize.'*

Descriptions of the various peoples living along the Camino are colourful, to say the least.

Here's what the author of the *Codex* has to say about the Navarrese:

> *These are an undeveloped people, with different*
> *customs and characteristics to other races. They're*
> *malicious, dark, hostile-looking types, crooked,*
> *perverse, treacherous, corrupt and untrustworthy,*

---

1 It's worth pointing out that the Moors were not the only people threatening Compostela: Norman Vikings had sacked the city in 968 as well. Meanwhile, pilgrims had to face all manner of dangers, from bandits on the open road to predatory animals, and unscrupulous and sometimes inhospitable locals along the route.

obsessed with sex and booze, very violent, wild, savage,
condemned and rejected, sour, horrible, and
squabbling. They are badness and nastiness
personified, utterly lacking in any good qualities.
They're as bad as the Getes and the Saracens, and
they despise us French. If they could, a Basque or
Navarrese would kill a Frenchman for a mere cent.

In some places, like Vizcaya and Alava, when they get
warmed up, the men and women show their private
parts to each other. The Navarrese also have sex with
their farm animals. And it's said that they put a lock
on the backsides of their mules and horses so that
nobody except themselves can have at them. Moreover,
they kiss lasciviously the vaginas of women and of
mules.

Given that Navarre was the main gateway into the Peninsula for most pilgrims, you wonder how any of them made it to Compostela at all . . . But such was the importance of the Santiago pilgrimage that by the thirteenth century Dante was insisting that 'in the narrow sense, none is called a pilgrim save he who is journeying towards the sanctuary of St James at Compostela'. Within the spiritual hierarchy, the route to Santiago was more sacred than a voyage to Rome or even to Jerusalem.

The main promoters of the Camino were the Cluniacs, keen to bring their reforming zeal over the Pyrenees into the Christian areas of Spain. The Spanish Church had been using a different liturgy until this point, known as the Mozarabic Rite. But the Cluniacs introduced the Latin Rite, which was formally adopted by

El Cid's contemporary King Alfonso VI, who did most to welcome the Cluniacs, and offered them the highest positions in the Spanish Church.

Religious fervour wasn't the only draw for the French reformers: many of the Moorish *taifa* kingdoms were paying tribute – a polite term for 'protection money' – to Spanish Christian kings, who then passed large quantities of this wealth to the Cluniacs. In fact, it is said that without the Moorish gold reaching their coffers, the great Abbey at Cluny itself could never have been built. The same source of treasure also helped build the Cluniacs' Spanish headquarters at Sahagún, near León, once a cosmopolitan metropolis and the most powerful religious centre in Christian Spain, but today a dusty and rather pathetic one-horse town with only a few scraps of ruins to remind locals of their glorious past. Religion and wealth, as ever, were making cosy bedfellows.

And to this was added a third element: military force. The end of the eleventh century sees the development of the pan-European Crusader movement and the marriage of faith with organised violence, out of which come the knightly orders and the conquest of the Holy Land. But this strange partnership between a fighting culture and a religion predicated on 'love' had been developing for some time before Pope Urban's rallying speech at Clermont in 1095. In fact Urban himself had used similar rhetoric to urge Christians to capture the Spanish city Tarragona from the Moors in 1089. And over twenty years before, Pope Alexander II had helped rally an international Christian force to capture the Aragonese fortress town of Barbastro in 1064, a campaign which a leading twentieth-century Spanish historian has described as 'a crusade before the Crusades'. As the Catholic world began to reinvigorate itself and test its strength, the obvious battle front was the Peninsula, the Saracen enemy never more than a few miles away. The Norman conquest of Muslim Sicily in 1091 and the European invasion of the Levant should be seen in this context, born out of the military testing ground that was Spain at the time.[2]

And the figure who symbolises this transformation is Santiago, no longer simply an Apostle of Jesus, but now a warrior astride a white steed, dressed in contemporary armour, sword raised high to lop off the heads of the dastardly Moors cowering on the ground beneath him. His shape-shift into man of violence began as early as the tenth century, but it is in the twelfth century that he emerges fully fledged as 'Matamoros'. In 1150 an account was written of a battle which had taken place three hundred years previously at a small hill fortress in La Rioja known as Clavijo. Although earlier accounts of the battle existed, it was in this twelfth-century version that King Ramiro I was said to have been visited the night before the battle by a vision of Santiago himself, who urged the desperate monarch to fight on against the odds, promising him victory.

And so it turned out, for during the next day's fighting:

> . . . *the holy Apostle of God appeared, as he had*
> *promised, raising the morale of our men and urging*
> *them into battle, striking and immobilising the*
> *Saracen hordes.*

Not surprisingly, only a few years after these lines were written, in 1158 Spain's own knightly order was established along the lines of the Templars and Hospitallers. Its name? The Order of Santiago.

---

2 In similar fashion, new military techniques, such as Blitzkrieg, were tested in Spain during the Civil War before being applied during the Second World War.

From Apostle and Pilgrim, Spain's patron saint had been transformed by the bellicose environment of his adopted homeland into a man of the sword, forever fighting unwanted versions of himself. He had, in a sense, been 'Iberianised'.

Yet there is a twist in this tale. The symbol of the pilgrimage to Compostela, and of Santiago himself, is the scallop shell, often seen attached to the front of the saint's hat, and nowadays tied to the top of a pilgrim's staff. The French dish *Coquilles Saint-Jacques* is so called precisely because it is made with sea scallops, and scallop souvenirs can be bought by the bucketload from Compostela tourist shops. Theories abound as to why this particular shell should have been elevated to such a position. Do its various lines echo the many different routes to Santiago? Is it because Compostela is near the Atlantic coast, where scallops can easily be found? None really have the ring of truth about them. But here's a funny coincidence: the symbol of the shell can not only be found at Christian Spain's most important centre, but also inside the most sacred spot in Islamic Spain, the Great Mosque at Cordoba. If you visit the mosque, don't look for the shell because it's safely hidden from view. But if – as I have been – you are lucky enough one day to get right inside the Mihrab niche built by Abd al-Rahman II in the ninth century, look upwards. There you will find a magnificent ceiling in the shape of a scallop, made from a single piece of stone. The Mihrab is the holiest site within a mosque, so to place that there in the most important mosque in the whole of Al-Andalus was certainly significant. And the Moors did so in the ninth century, when the remains of Santiago (or Priscillian . . .) had only recently been discovered in distant Galicia. Indeed, the shell as a decorative form in religious architecture can be found throughout Al-Andalus, and is also an important feature in the synagogue of

Santa María la Blanca in Toledo, the most important Jewish building in the Peninsula during the Middle Ages.

So who was copying whom? Perhaps no one was. Perhaps the shell has a religious significance deeper than more superficial definitions of 'us' and 'them'. Perhaps it represents a common ground between all religions. For cannot a shell also produce a pearl? It may be no accident or coincidence, then, that the most important temples of the three great religions in Spain – whose adherents were for centuries at each other's throats and yet at times could live in harmony – all have the symbol of a scallop shell at their heart.

PEOPLES OF THE VEIL

The development of Santiago into nation-building man of violence was not happening within a vacuum. In a curious echo, a similar marriage between faith and military might was developing in Moorish Spain at the same time.

The *taifa* kingdoms managed to survive for some fifty years. The high culture of the Cordoba caliphate continued among them in scattered form, but their lack of unity and frequent wars among themselves made them an easy target for northerners. At the beginning this was expressed in the payment of protection money by the Moors to the Christians to keep them at bay. But the flow of gold simply made the rulers of countries like Castile and Aragon stronger, more confident, and greedy for more. In 1085 the decisive moment came, when Castile's Alfonso VI captured Toledo, the ancient Visigothic capital.

For centuries Christian Spaniards had felt inferior towards their Muslim compatriots. Militarily and culturally, the Moors were far advanced – a fact which, grudgingly, the northerners accepted. The capture of Toledo, however, was a turning point, and a huge fillip for the Christians: for the first time they had taken an important city from the Moors, and a doorway into the advanced culture of Islam had been opened. Suddenly Christians didn't feel so inferior any more.

On the Moorish side, meanwhile, the fall of Toledo was a disaster. Militarily, the Christians were clearly becoming a more dangerous enemy. But unable to unite to defend themselves, and more enamoured of artistic than warrior culture, the *taifa* kingdoms understood that their very existence was at stake. Drastic measures were needed if the Christian momentum was to be halted.

The solution was obvious, but fraught with its own difficulties. Over the Strait, in Morocco, a new power had emerged: Berber tribesmen from the far southern deserts had taken over the country. Preaching a message of asceticism and religious purity, they had imposed a harsh, intolerant regime, with strict – if not always properly understood – interpretations of Islamic law. Holy warfare – *jihad* – was celebrated; the Berbers organised themselves around monasteries where faith and fighting skills were combined. Known as *murabits*, these institutions gave the warrior monks their name – *Al-Murabitun*, Latinised into 'Almoravids'.

The Almoravids were the polar opposites of the *taifa* rulers in Spain, whose love of wine and astrology was abhorrent to these illiterate but energetic new fundamentalists. Yet the Berbers' military skills were only too evident. As fellow Muslims they would be more than willing to fight alongside their Spanish co-religionists against the Christians, but as hardliners, they would make an uncomfortable fit in Al-Andalus. The *taifa* rulers sweated over the decision, but in the end the most powerful of them, the poet–king Al-Mu'tamid of Seville, made the decision. 'I would rather die a camel-herder in Africa,' he said, 'than a swine-herd in Castile.'

His words were prophetic, as he would later die in exile near Marrakech. But for now he needed the Almoravids to fight the Christians, and so the invitation was sent.

The Almoravids duly arrived and did everything that was expected – and predicted – of them. In a series of campaigns they helped push back the Christians and halted their advance. They failed to retake Toledo, and El Cid's Valencia held out against them, only falling, in 1102, shortly after the great warrior's death. But within less than twenty years, Al-Andalus was under their control: brought in as friends to help against a common enemy, they were quickly seduced by the charms of Spain and decided to stay.

What followed for ordinary people in Al-Andalus, however, were very difficult years. Their terrain may have been united under one leadership again, but the Almoravids were anything but benevolent rulers. Despite preaching religious purity, they saw Spain as little more than a land for raiding, and plundered and pillaged their way across the southern Peninsula into the early decades of the twelfth century. In addition, they brought with them far less tolerant attitudes to non-Muslims, and for the first time Christian and Jewish communities living under Moorish rule were subject to systematic persecution.[1]

It didn't take long, however, for these ascetic Berber warriors to become fond of the more sophisticated life they encountered north of the Strait, and within a generation or so they had effectively gone 'soft'. So soft, indeed, that by the 1140s the indigenous Moorish populations – who had never taken to them – began to rebel and overthrow them.

---

[1] Previous incidents of persecution had occurred, for example the massacre of Jews at Granada in 1066, in which poet and vizier Joseph ben Naghrela was killed, but these had fallen short of becoming official policy; with the arrival of the Almoravids, that changed.

But if the Almoravids had one redeeming quality, it was that they had managed to bring unity to Al-Andalus. Once their power was broken, a key pattern of Spanish history played out again, and once more the Moorish lands shattered into separate parts, in what has been called the 'second *taifa*' period.

And as before, the Christians took advantage of the situation. Alfonso VII of Castile, grandson of the Alfonso VI who had taken Toledo in 1085, even struck as far south as Cordoba, briefly taking the former caliphal capital in 1146.

In an extraordinary example of history repeating itself, however, Muslim Spain was once again saved by the arrival of a second group of Berber fundamentalists from Morocco.

Since the early twelfth century, the Almoravids had been challenged in their own heartlands by a group that emerged from the Atlas mountains. With a new message of purity, these people were equally vigorous and warlike, but had a more solid religious grounding and possibly a better understanding of Islamic teaching than their rivals. Their founder, a man called Ibn Tumart, claimed to have travelled east to the Muslim heartlands and to have studied under the great Al-Ghazali (d. 1111), a leading expert on Islamic law who had reconciled Sufi mysticism with mainstream religious doctrine. These new Moroccans have been described as 'unitarians' who stressed the singularity of God and His attributes, hence their name, *al-Muwahhidun*, which was Latinised into 'Almohads'.

To Western ears the name is confusingly similar to 'Almoravids', and both groups emerged from a similar part of Morocco within less than one hundred years of each other, and went on to rule Moorish Spain. But an easy way to distinguish them is this: the Almoravids veiled their men; the Almohads veiled their women.

As part of their efforts to overthrow the now decadent Almoravids, the Almohads sailed over to Spain to occupy their Peninsular lands, arriving just as the Christians were making inroads into Moorish territory once more. The Almohads retook Cordoba for Islam in 1148. Within a few short years the new *taifa* kingdoms were defeated and Al-Andalus reunited (although Valencia remained independent until 1172 under the 'Wolf King' Ibn Mardanish).

The Almohads brought new unity to Moorish Spain, this time in a far more settled form than under the Almoravids. They were more accepted by the locals, and for a brief time Al-Andalus prospered. Cordoba, which had never fully recovered after the *Fitna* civil wars of the early eleventh century, now enjoyed something of a renaissance, with new building projects designed to restore some of its previous glory. This was the period of Averroes, the great Spanish thinker, who as a religious judge and personal physician to the Almohad rulers, enjoyed certain protection for the development of his 'philosophical' ideas. Yet the religious intolerance towards minorities as practised by the Almoravids continued, with Jewish communities in particular suffering at their hands, especially Jews who had previously been forced to convert to Islam. One Almohad ruler stated that he would happily massacre all of them were it not for the fear that some might have genuinely become Muslims in their hearts.

Militarily, the Almohads gave Al-Andalus greater protection against the Christians, launching summer campaigns against them on a common, if irregular, basis. Their greatest triumph came at the Battle of Alarcos in 1195. At a site not far from Ciudad Real, on the southern fringes of Spain's central Tableland, the Almohads routed the Castilian forces, pushing them back to Toledo and recapturing several towns along the way.

It was a huge victory, celebrated throughout Al-Andalus. But it was short-lived. The defeated Castilians rallied themselves and managed to forge an alliance with other Christian kingdoms – Aragon, Navarre and Galicia – to stage a comeback. The result was a second battle, in 1212, not far from Alarcos, near the gorge of Despeñaperros at a place known as las Navas de Tolosa. It proved to be the single most important battle in the history of the 'Reconquest', resulting in a collapse of the Almohads and the near capture of their caliph on the battlefield. Protective chains used by his personal bodyguard were captured by Navarrese forces during the fight, and to this day can be seen decorating the walls of the monastery at Roncesvalles: they still form the design, in a circled eight-star cross, of the Navarrese flag and form part of the contemporary Spanish coat of arms.

The Almohads were unable to recover after defeat at Las Navas de Tolosa, and over the following three decades Christian kingdoms captured Moorish territory at a faster rate than ever before. Cordoba fell – definitively this time – in 1236, Valencia in 1238 and Seville, the Almohad capital, in 1248. The capture of Cordoba meant that the bells of Santiago, seized by the Moorish dictator Al-Mansur in 997, could finally be regained, and were ceremoniously reinstalled at Compostela shortly afterwards.

Christian Spain was victorious and Moorish Spain was finished . . . except for one small rump kingdom in Granada. Curiously, this would hold out for another two hundred and fifty years, helped by old Spanish standards: difficult mountainous terrain, and infighting among its opponents.

A DESERT ISLAND STORY

At the eastern end of the Sierra Nevada, not far from Granada, there is a small town tucked away in the dusty hillsides, almost forgotten amid the dry, desert-like landscape. Tourists who stray here will find an imposing cathedral, half-empty streets and a vast number of caves in the surrounding area, homes to the large Gypsy community who settled centuries ago in this part of Andalusia. Guadix has a special and rather quiet charm, but its most important gift to humanity – a metaphor that one of its greatest sons developed almost a thousand years ago – is hardly mentioned today, despite forming such an integral part of our culture that it is used constantly in literature, in jokes, and even in Hollywood films.

The name of a small street and a hotel are the only reminders now that Guadix was the birthplace of Ibn Tufayl (or 'Abentofail' as the locals prefer). If he is referred to at all, it is simply as a writer of the twelfth century whose greatest achievement was to have been the mentor of the philosopher Ibn Rushd, or Averroes. Nonetheless, Abu Bakr Muhammad ibn Tufayl was and is a great figure in the history of ideas. Poet, physician, mystic, mathematician, astronomer and philosopher, he was, like so many others of his time, a polymath, and wrote what is arguably the first European novel.

Hayy bin Yaqzan can be translated as 'Alive son of Awake', and is his only prose work that has survived to the present day. Based on an earlier tale by the Persian philosopher Ibn Sina, it is the first desert island story, and has been the inspiration for many other better-known versions, from Daniel Defoe's *Robinson Crusoe* to the Tom Hanks film *Cast Away*.

Hayy bin Yaqzan tells the story of a baby – Hayy – the son of a princess, whose birth must be concealed. He is abandoned on an equatorial island, where a doe suckles and looks after him. The baby becomes a child, then a youth, and finally a man. He is possessed of great intelligence, and spends his days studying the world around him. Like a good scientist, he observes natural phenomena, develops theories to explain them, and then returns to his observations to see if his ideas stand up. In this way he discovers such things as the circulation of the blood, the effect and use of fire, and the movement of the heavens. Each phase of his learning lasts seven years and his knowledge grows until he becomes aware of the soul and the Creator. Finally, in a vivid and transcendental moment, he passes from an intellectual understanding of such things to an intuitive and direct experience of Reality.

Shortly afterwards, a second person arrives on the island by boat. His name is Asal, a devout man seeking a place of quiet contemplation. When they meet, Hayy and Asal realise they share the same ideas – one through direct experience, the other through reasoning – and decide to travel together to Asal's home town in order to communicate what they know. Once they reach the city, however, they discover that few people there can or want to understand their message, and in the end the two men return to the island.

After *A Thousand and One Nights*, Ibn Tufayl's story of *Hayy* is said to be the most translated work of Arabic literature in the world. A Hebrew version already existed in the fourteenth century with a commentary by the Jewish philosopher Moses ben Joshua of Narbonne. This was later translated into Latin in Florence in the fifteenth century. In England there were various translations from 1671 onwards, both into Latin and English. One of these, carried out by Simon Ockley, was published in 1708. Only a decade later, Defoe brought out *Robinson Crusoe*, widely regarded as the first modern novel in English.

At the time it was believed that Defoe had been inspired by the story of Alexander Selkirk, a Scottish sailor who had survived four years alone on a remote island off the coast of Chile, and it is likely that Selkirk's experiences did influence the writing of *Crusoe*. Yet there are many echoes of *Hayy bin Yaqzan* in Defoe's story, partly in the appearance of a second character on the island (Man Friday), but particularly in the third volume, in which Crusoe tells of his vision of the 'angelic world' – an unmistakable parallel with Hayy's experiences.

With the publication of *Crusoe*, the powerful metaphor of a person living on a desert island, alone and forced to survive and reflect, fully entered Western culture. As a reflection of human life itself, it is so common today that we have largely forgotten where it came from or who introduced it. But the influence of Ibn Tufayl, a Spaniard from Guadix, continues nonetheless, and will doubtless carry on inspiring as it has done for the last nine centuries.

STRAIGHT THINKING

A Spaniard – a Cordoban – is widely credited with being the father of Western rational thought.

'Rationalism was born in Spain in the mind of an Arabian philosopher as a conscious reaction against the Arabian divines,' wrote the French historian Etienne Gilson in 1938.

This view was echoed more recently in the 1990s by the Spanish Arabist Joan Vernet, who described the man in question as 'possibly the Spaniard who has exercised the greatest influence on human thought throughout history'.

Yet mention his name to Spanish people today and you will generally receive a quizzical look. As an Arabic-speaking Muslim of the twelfth century, he is rejected as belonging to the 'anti-Spain' which the warrior Santiago busies himself slaughtering.

Abu al-Walid Muhammad Ibn Rushd was an astronomer, physician, courtier, lawyer, poet and philosopher. Latin-speaking contemporaries referred to him as Averroes.

Averroes was a hugely influential figure in late twelfth-century Cordoba. He was friend and personal physician to the Almohad caliphs, and rose to high rank by becoming chief *qadi* – the leading authority in religious law, a position held by previous members of his family. As a young man he met Ibn Tufayl, author of *Hayy bin Yaqzan*, and was introduced at court. After a philosophical discussion, the caliph complained about the obscurity of Aristotle's writings. Averroes was subsequently given the task of explaining them.

The result was his writing of three Commentaries on Aristotle's work, which became the basis of his fame and philosophical importance for centuries to come. An obsession of the times was the apparent contradiction between two different ways of under-standing the world and the universe; either through the revealed word of the prophets, or, following Aristotle's methods, via the intellect.

The intuitive was at loggerheads with the rational, the holistic with the sequential – 'faith' with 'reason'.

Averroes was living in a superstitious age in which, for example, a leading rebel of the time could escape capture by 'transforming himself into a cat' (leading to the slaughter of many strays), or the destruction of a statue of the Madonna at Medina Azahara could lead to howling winds which caused much structural damage throughout Cordoba. 'Reason' was a novel idea, and seen as highly dangerous by religious authorities who recognised the threat it posed. What if ordinary people applied 'rational thought' to the religious teachings which formed the basis of society?[1]

Averroes's achievement lay not only in his explanation of Aristotle's often dense and unclear texts, however, but in his reconciliation of these two modes of thought. In a world created by God, Averroes argued, there could be no contradiction between

---

1 Averroes's reply was to insist that philosophy was a reserve of the social and intellectual elite, and not for the masses.

what our own observation told us and what He Himself had revealed in holy scripture. Analysing the universe could only ever confirm religious truths.

It was by squaring this circle that Averroes earned his high place in the history of philosophy. What's extraordinary is that within a very few years of his death in 1198 his teachings were translated into Latin at Toledo.[2] These texts had an enormous influence on medieval Christian thinkers, not least St Thomas Aquinas, who had been grappling with the same question. Aquinas went on to quote Averroes over five hundred times in his own writings on the subject. Dante honoured 'The Commentator' – as Averroes became known in Europe – by placing him in Limbo among other virtuous non-Christians such as Homer, Ovid and Saladin.

But Averroes's work wasn't limited to analysis of Aristotle. He also developed ideas about the 'universal mind', a vision of God as a 'universal intelligence', an 'ocean of spirits shared by each man', not dissimilar to Jung's concept of the 'collective unconscious'.

In addition, he found inspiration in the work of the Baghdadi group the *Ikhwan al-Safa* – the Brethren of Sincerity, who, among other things, evolved highly influential musical theories. Most historians of music insist that the note names *do, re, mi* come from Italy, but an alternative suggestion points out their marked similarity with the Arabic letters *dad, ra, mim, fa, sad*.

Averroes had his critics, however. Ibn Saba'in of Ceuta, a contemporary, was scathing about the Cordoban: 'If he had heard the Philosopher (Aristotle) saying that whoever is standing is at the same time sitting, he would have professed and believed this.'

And Averroes was accused of being too close to the Jewish

---

2 Some of them by Michael Scot, who spent time in Toledo before moving to Italy and the court of Frederick II.

community, at a time when they were being systematically persecuted by the Almohad authorities. From his high position, he fell from grace in 1195 and was exiled. He died in Marrakech in 1198, but his body was transferred back to his native Cordoba, where he was later buried.

His influence, however, lived on. Averroes's writings were standard texts at European universities well into the eighteenth century, and Columbus himself mentioned him as one of his inspirations for his world-changing journey across the Atlantic . . .

But more on that later.

CROSSOVER

Ibn Tufayl and Averroes are key elements in the Spanish crucible of the Middle Ages, producing new gold. But the alchemy of the time isn't limited to Al-Andalus: Christian Spain has an equally important role to play, nurturing the refined precious metal and, crucially, helping to pass it on to its Western European neighbours. Although divided politically and religiously, the Peninsula as a whole transmits the fruits of its more advanced civilisation, and in so doing lays the groundwork for the Renaissance, Europe's most celebrated re-engagement with its Classical heritage. And the most significant channel through which this lost learning reached the rest of the Continent was the School of Translators in Christian Toledo.

Before its capture by Alfonso VI in 1085, Toledo had been a *taifa* kingdom where a mixed community of Muslims, Jews and Arabised Christians ('Mozarabs') lived in relative harmony. And following the example of the other Islamic statelets, its rulers had placed great emphasis on cultural achievement. The groundwork for an intellectual blossoming had therefore already been laid when, in a surprise move, the city fell into Christian hands.

The fall of Toledo led directly to the arrival of the fundamentalist Almoravids in Al-Andalus and a partial eclipse of Moorish culture. Yet it also meant that the torch of inquisitiveness and brilliance which had so characterised the Andalusi Golden Age passed to Christian Spain, with Toledo as its new heart.

The School of Translators is an umbrella term used to describe a movement which began in Toledo in the early twelfth century and continued for some one hundred and fifty years, developing and changing in complexion until it was brought to an end by King Sancho IV in the thirteenth century. Its objectives and methods were not unique: it echoed the translation 'school' which had been established in Cordoba under Abd al-Rahman III in the mid-tenth century, which in turn had mirrored similar movements in the central lands of the Islamic Empire of the ninth century. But it was the first time that anything on such a scale had been set up within Christian Europe.

As with Cordoba and the arrival there of the works of Dioscorides in 949, the Toledo translation movement was born out of intellectual curiosity and openness mixed with an underlying sense of (at least partial) inferiority: Christians understood that the Moors were significantly more advanced in certain areas, and wished to catch up with them as quickly as possible. A similar spirit had infused the mass translation of Greek knowledge into Arabic centred around Baghdad from the eighth century. The capture of a sophisticated Moorish capital like Toledo only underlined their cultural deficiencies to eleventh-century Spanish Christians, despite following, in their own eyes, the true faith. And the respect which they had for their Muslim contemporaries can be seen in an anecdote concerning the main mosque in the newly captured city:

On taking possession of his new prize, King Alfonso, who termed himself 'Emperor of the two religions', swore to protect the Muslim population, in particular not to touch the main mosque. Shortly afterwards, however, he was called away to Sahagún, the Cluniacs' Spanish headquarters. In his absence, Alfonso's queen – Constanza, a Frenchwoman – connived with the new archbishop, Bernard, also from France – to take the mosque and turn it into a cathedral. In the words of a later chronicler:

> The Christian troops entered the main mosque of
> Toledo and, having purged it of the filth of
> Muhammad, set up a Christian altar and placed bells
> in the minaret so the Christians could be called to
> worship.

Up in Sahagún, Alfonso heard of what had happened and rushed back to Toledo, a journey of three days. He was so furious that his agreement with the city's Muslims had been broken that he was determined to burn the archbishop and his own queen at the stake as punishment. The Muslims, however, were the ones who restored peace. Such an action, they pleaded with Alfonso, would only bring more violence on their own heads in revenge, and so they begged him to be lenient. Alfonso agreed, and the mosque continued to function as a cathedral.

What's interesting to compare here is the tolerance of the Spanish Alfonso with the more aggressive attitude of the French queen and archbishop. The Muslim and Christian communities may have been at war for much of the time (as well as between themselves), but organised persecution was still in its infancy. It would develop quickly within Al-Andalus with the arrival of the

Berber fundamentalists, and would eventually become a dominant trend within Christian Spain. Before it did, however, a brief window of relevant tolerance allowed the creation of a world-changing movement.

The School of Translators began under a later archbishop – Raymond, another Frenchman, this time a Benedictine from Gascony. Some time after taking up his position in 1126, Raymond started to bring together Muslim, Jewish, Mozarab and Cluniac scholars with the intention of translating texts from Arabic via Castilian into Latin. The centre of this activity was the library at the cathedral, now housed in what had been the main mosque and containing many books which had been collected during the Muslim period. It was an obvious step to start translating them in order to unlock their secrets. The process was haphazard and anything but systematic, but in general the Arabic speakers would perform an oral translation of a book into Castilian which was then retranslated into Latin and written down. Jewish members of the teams often acted as linguistic intermediaries.

The school had a tremendous impact within Christian Europe. Combined with a similar movement developing in Sicily and southern Italy in the wake of the Norman conquests there, it suddenly opened up a whole wealth of knowledge which had been lost or out of reach to Latin-speaking communities for centuries. As at Cordoba in the 940s, knowledge of Greek had all but vanished. Now the works of the great minds of the Classical past were once again becoming available via earlier translations of them into Arabic.

It didn't take long for news to spread throughout Europe, and soon scholars were arriving at Toledo from around the Continent, eager to be involved in this new and very exciting project. The most celebrated of them was Gerard of Cremona, who came from

Italy in around 1140, remaining in Toledo until his death in 1187. He was originally drawn by hearing that in Spain he could find a copy of a book he longed to read: Ptolemy's great astronomical work, the *Mathematika Syntaxis*. This had been translated previously into Arabic, with the title *Al-Majisti*, which in turn gave it the new name under which it became known in Europe, the *Almagest*.

An obituary of Gerard, written by one of his pupils, explains:

> For love of the Almagest, which he could not find at all
> among the Latins, [Gerard] went to Toledo. There,
> seeing the abundance of books in Arabic on every
> subject, and regretting the poverty of the Latins in
> these things, he learned the Arabic language in order
> to be able to translate. In this way he passed on the
> Arabic literature in the manner of the wise man who,
> wandering through a green field, links up a crown of
> flowers, made not just from any, but from the prettiest.
> To the end of his life he continued to transmit to the
> Latin world (as if to his own beloved heir) whatever
> books he thought finest, in many subjects, as
> accurately and as plainly as he could.

In total, Gerard alone translated seventy books into Latin, including twenty-four on medicine, eighteen on the stars and alchemy, seventeen on various areas of mathematics, eleven on philosophy and three on logic. And he was not alone: Toledo at this period became a magnet for other brilliant people from around Europe who thirsted after the knowledge available there. Another celebrated example is Michael Scot, who arrived around 1215 after leaving Oxford. A leading astrologer and alchemist, Scot eventually established himself at the Sicilian court of Frederick II (with whom he supposedly had an affair), but not before translating several books by Averroes, particularly the Cordoban philosopher's commentaries on Aristotle. What makes this even more remarkable is that Averroes himself had only died in 1198: the flow of knowledge from Muslim to Christian orbits was unhindered and almost immediate.

Much of the knowledge which reached Europe via Toledo at this time has had a powerful effect – and continues to do so – on our modern world. For example, algorithms govern much of our daily lives, and the name for them derives from the Persian mathematician of the ninth century Al-Khwarizmi. His works, which also give us the word 'algebra', were translated by Gerard and others and subsequently found their way across Europe, making Al-Khwarizmi – or Algoritmi, in the Latinised version – the most widely read mathematician on the Continent in the Middle Ages.

The Toledo translation movement went through various stages. After intense activity through the twelfth century, it entered a transitional phase before being reinvigorated under Alfonso X in the thirteenth century.

Alfonso, known as *el Sabio*, 'the Wise', is one of the most important figures to emerge from this period. Politically, he wasted vast amounts of money and energy on an unsuccessful attempt to be crowned Holy Roman Emperor, but culturally he placed his stamp on Christian Spain through his promotion of numerous writing projects. As well as reviving the School of Translators in Toledo, he commissioned (and even helped to write) several important books. These included: *Las Siete Partidas*, an attempt to synchronise the country's laws; and the *Estoria de España*, a history of the Iberian

Peninsula. In what was in effect a mini-renaissance before the Renaissance, Alfonso revived an ancient Spanish tradition dating back to the Golden Age of Umayyad Cordoba and St Isidore's Seville of turning his country into a powerful cultural centre. And as at Cordoba in the ninth and tenth centuries, now Christians, Muslims and Jews were drawn together to collaborate in the enterprise, not only at Toledo but also at newly conquered cities such as Murcia, where Alfonso established a university run by the mathematician and physician Muhammad al-Ricotí, and Seville, where he set up a school of Arabic studies. Salamanca and Palencia also became university cities during his reign.

Alfonso also did his best to establish what might be considered the beginnings of a modern state, with the monarch holding supreme power at the centre. He introduced a basic justice system, put governors responsible to him in positions of authority in the various provinces of his kingdom, and established a cabinet in the shape of a Royal Council. In addition he created La Mesta, an organisation controlling the sheep and wool industry, which became Castile's biggest cash earner for centuries to come. This was based on merino wool[1], which was in high demand in Europe thanks to its exceptional thermal qualities. Moneys brought in from the trade helped to pay for the construction of the cathedrals of Burgos and León, both jewels of Spanish Gothic architecture.

The School of Translators in Toledo was reinvigorated under Alfonso, who brought in several changes. This time books in Arabic were translated directly into the local vernacular, laying the foundations of modern Castilian Spanish as it is spoken and written today. The texts were largely mathematical and scientific works as before, but this time also included stories and fiction, such as the

---

1 The name derives from the Berber Merinid tribe.

classic ancient Indian collection of animal fables *Kalila and Dimna* (or *Panchatantra*), a guide to precious stones and their medical properties known as the *Lapidario*, and books on chess and other games. Jewish translators became very prominent at this time, assisting with the translations of many astronomical and astrological books, and in drawing up the Alfonsine Tables, a highly important work which compiled observational data allowing the computation of the Sun, Moon and planets based on the position of the fixed stars. Copernicus later owned a copy of these, and in conjunction with his study of the Toledo translation of the *Almagest* he later developed his revolutionary theories about a heliocentric universe.

The impact of the School of Translators cannot be overstated, introducing both Greek and Oriental science, philosophy and culture to Europe and eventually inspiring the revival of Greek scholarship which was one of the principal drivers of the Renaissance, and later of the Reformation. Despite being wracked by civil wars, through the twelfth and thirteenth centuries the Peninsula became the key link in a chain of knowledge running from East to West, not least the works of Aristotle, travelling from Athens to Averroes's Cordoba and thence to Toledo and the rest of Christian Europe. In the process, it changed the intellectual foundations of the West. The works which emerged from the school provided the raw material for the Continent's great minds of the later Middle Ages, from Albertus Magnus to Thomas Aquinas and Roger Bacon, who even wondered around Oxford dressed in Arab robes in a symbolic act denoting the origin of much of his inspiration, namely the learning arriving from the Islamic world via Toledo.

The Toledo of the translators was another of Spain's many beacons of light which shine brightly for limited periods of time in the country's history. Umayyad Cordoba had been one before, as

...d the Seville of St Isidore in the sixth century. But as with *its* predecessors, Toledo's time was short: Alfonso's successor, his son Sancho IV, was at war with his father, and following a pattern the forces of light were brought into violent civil conflict with those who would extinguish them. When Sancho finally emerged victorious, he quickly dismantled the School of Translators, and many of the scholars who were involved left the city. Toledo would never regain its position as a European cultural hub. Santiago the Slayer had once again defeated his more inquisitive pilgrim self. Indebted to his supporters, Sancho's reign also saw supreme royal power ebb away, flowing back into the hands of aristocrats and local magnates. It would take two hundred years for the crown to claw it back.

The openness which had characterised Toledo had come to an end, replaced by an intolerant and persecuting culture which seized the entire Peninsula, and which would go on to create one of its most lasting and infamous legacies.

PART THREE

1492

THE ROAD TO
1492

Events in Spain in the year 1492 seem to hint at the existence of a 'hidden hand' moving history in a certain direction. This is the country's pivotal moment, the year in which modern 'Spain' is conceived, when many defining and revolutionary developments occur in a startlingly concentrated period of time. The suddenness of change is an essential part of the patterns of Spanish history: an explosive reaction within the crucible after years of increasing agitation. The year 1492 is one of the most significant of these moments, and it changed not only Spain, but the rest of the world.

Moorish-controlled territory shrank rapidly following the Almohad rout at las Navas de Tolosa. For Castile, Fernando III captured Cordoba and Seville, while in the east Jaime I of Aragon simultaneously pushed southwards, taking Valencia and the Balearic Islands. Christian Spaniards had the momentum, and were in a position to conquer all remaining Muslim lands in the Peninsula. But instead, after making huge advances, they stopped. Skirmishing would continue and a few towns and cities would exchange hands, but effectively from 1250 to the late 1400s the borders remained static between the Christians and a last rump of Al-Andalus clinging on around the Sierra Nevada mountains in the kingdom of Granada.

As mentioned earlier, this period is known in Spanish history as *los cinco reinos* – 'the Five Kingdoms', these being: Castile, Leon, Portugal, Navarre and Aragon. It's a curious term, as in fact there were several more, and the number had a tendency to change. Granada was a kingdom, and the 'kingdom' of Aragon was actually a confederation made up of the kingdom of Valencia, the county of Barcelona and the kingdom of Aragon proper (as well as other territories in the Mediterranean, including Sardinia, Sicily, Naples and, for about a hundred years, Athens). Meanwhile, Castilla and Leon would form a single kingdom from 1230. So in fact we should be talking about the period of the 'Six to Seven Kingdoms, Depending', although that doesn't have quite the same ring to it.

Following the culturally enlightened reign of Alfonso X, multiple civil wars marked the fourteenth and fifteenth centuries. The most important took place during the reign of Pedro 'the Cruel'. As well as being a homicidal maniac, Pedro was friends with the Nasrid kings of Granada, and it was thanks to this not unusual alliance that the Alcázar palace at Seville was built during his reign in Moorish style by artisans lent by the Muslim monarch. While happily swapping interior design tips with his neighbours, however, Pedro was at war with his half-brother, who claimed the crown for himself. The conflict was complicated by Europe's

Hundred Years' War, and for a time England's Black Prince journeyed to the Peninsula to fight alongside Pedro.[1]

English support notwithstanding, Pedro eventually came to a sticky end when he was ambushed in his own tent during the siege of Montiel. His half-brother, Enrique, finished the job.

Enrique's reign brought the Trastámara family to the throne. It was they, in conjunction with another line of the same family, who would bring about the famed union, almost a century later, of the crowns of Castile and Aragon which would lay the foundations of the modern Spanish state.

But before that could take place, many more civil wars were to come.

---

1 According to some theories, as a result of his Spanish sojourn, the Black Prince took back home with him Morris Dancing, 'Morris' originating from 'Moorish'. My own observation of traditional dances at the Valencian town of Algemesí would support this view: in dress as in choreography, the similarities with English Morris dances are striking, although the Spanish version is more vigorous and passionate than its English counterpart.

NO MOOR

On 2 January, the second day of the fateful year 1492, Queen Isabella of Castile and her husband King Ferdinand of Aragon arrived in Granada as conquerors. The defeated Moorish King Boabdil had handed over the keys to the city and prepared to leave with his family, now protected against his own people by Christian troops. After eight hundred mixed but often glorious years, Moorish Spain had come to an end. As he departed into exile, Boabdil looked back at the jewel he had lost – the city and its magnificent Alhambra fort – and wept. And coining a phrase which Spanish parents repeat to their blubbing offspring to this day, his mother Fatima rubbed salt into his open wound: 'Cry like a woman,' she said, 'for what you were unable to defend like a man.' Thereby sealing Boabdil's public image as one of the greatest wimps in history. For the Moors, it was over. Christian Spain was finally triumphant. The 'Reconquest' – a centuries-long Spanish civil war – was complete.

Over the next few months, things were going to move very quickly. But before we go forward, we must rewind a little to see how we got here. How did this momentous event come about?

Remarkably, Granada had existed as an independent state for some two hundred and fifty years. That it withstood Christian assault for so long was due in part to the very mountainous terrain of its kingdom, home to the highest peak on the Peninsula, Mulhacén[1], which reaches over 3,200 metres. Granadan survival was also thanks partly to divisions on the Christian side: hostilities between the various kingdoms were added to by repeated civil wars within their respective boundaries. In addition, large bribes in the shape of tributes of gold brought in from across the Sahara helped keep the Christians at bay. Nasrid Granada was a cash cow, and no one in Christian Spain was in a hurry to see it disappear.

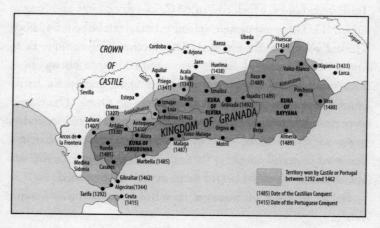

The Nasrid Kingdom of Granada

The balance was uneasy and fragile, but while it lasted, Granadan culture shone. In the fourteenth century the Nasrids build the most luxurious sections of their Red Fort – *Al-Qasr*

---

1 Named after one of the last Granadan kings, Muley Hasan, who, legend says, is buried at the summit.

al-Hamra – a wonder of the world and today one of the most visited tourist sites in Spain (second only to Gaudí's Sagrada Familia in Barcelona). Around the same time, as mentioned earlier, Muhammad V loaned his artisans and builders to his friend, Pedro the Cruel. Moors and Christians settled into a kind of cohabitation which had marked much of the past several centuries.

All this changed, however, in the final decade of the fifteenth century. And what precipitated the change was a marriage.

Ferdinand, heir to the Aragonese crown and later the model for Machiavelli's 'Prince', married Isabella, heir to the Castilian crown, at Valladolid in 1469. Both were members of different lines of the Trastámara family, which had ruled Castile since 1369, and Aragon since 1412. The nuptials were celebrated in secret; Isabella had been whisked away from the clutches of her brother King Enrique IV to find refuge with friends, while Ferdinand had made his way from Zaragoza by night in disguise, narrowly escaping death at the hands of an overzealous guard en route at Burgo de Osma. The couple were penniless and had to borrow money from Jewish moneylenders to pay for the wedding. With time they would become the richest and most powerful couple in the world and force into exile the very Jewish friends who had helped them in their time of need.

Before they did so, however, they had to fight and win many battles.

Powerful figures within Castile, headed by King Enrique himself, were lined up against Isabella and Ferdinand and were prepared to go to war. The couple's marriage, followed by a successful accession to their respective thrones, would create a union of the Castilian and Aragonese crowns. This was something which their enemies were keen to prevent, preferring to bring about a union of the Castilian and Portuguese crowns through a proposed marriage between Isabella and the Portuguese king. Isabella, however, was strong-willed and independent and had her own ideas. Unlike the ageing Portuguese monarch, Ferdinand was only one year younger than herself and a far more attractive proposition. Meanwhile Ferdinand had come under the influence of Catalan intellectuals who for some time had been advocating the creation of a political 'Spain' – as opposed to a merely geographical one – through the union of Aragon and Castile.

The irony that the impulse behind what would eventually turn into a unified Spanish state largely originated in Catalonia will not be lost to contemporary readers. It will come as little surprise, however, to see how a country forever racked by civil war could only be forged through yet more civil war. Ferdinand's father, King Juan II of Aragon, was fighting within his own lands against much of the Aragonese nobility over the succession to the throne and how to deal with a deep economic crisis. Lasting ten years, the war only ended in 1472, shortly before Juan died and Ferdinand became king. Meanwhile in Castile, King Enrique's death in 1474 sparked a full-blooded civil war over who should succeed him: his half-sister Isabella, wife of the new Aragonese king, or Enrique's daughter Juana, engaged to be married to the same king of Portugal whom Isabella had rejected. The conflict would last for four years, and Isabella emerged victorious thanks largely to Ferdinand bringing his Aragonese forces (and his own skill as a military commander) into the fight. By 1479 the war was over, but tensions within Castile still remained; the union of the Aragonese and Castilian crowns was anything but secure.

What helped to cement their power and the joining of the two kingdoms, however, was another civil war – this time the reigniting and completion of the 'Reconquest'.

As discussed earlier, the 'Reconquest' should be seen as a long series of civil wars in the same way that the myriad wars between Christian Spaniards are. Civil conflict is a common denominator of Spanish history and the differences between the various sides can be cultural, ideological, religious or any number of identifiers. Not because the 'Reconquest' wars are nominally between Muslims and Christians should they be seen as any different from the other civil wars throughout Spain's complex national story (in some of which, for example the Spanish Civil War of the twentieth century, religion also played a pivotal role).

Christian Spain in the run-up to 1492 was far from being a unified nation: Portugal and Navarre were independent kingdoms, while Isabella's rule in Castile was still shaky following the war which broke out on her accession to the throne. Nonetheless, the joining of the Castilian and Aragonese crowns brought about by Ferdinand and Isabella's marriage gave the Christian side an advantage over Muslim Granada, whose downfall was largely brought about by its own internal divisions. In the 1480s, dynastic struggles among the ruling Nasrid family led to a full-blown inter-Muslim civil war which saw the kingdom split in two for several years. Christian Spain took its chance and leapt.

What followed was a ten-year war in which the borders of the last Moorish kingdom were gradually whittled away until all that remained was the city of Granada itself. Ferdinand skilfully used the infighting among the Nasrids to his own advantage, as well as employing gunpowder to great effect with the use of cannon during the long sieges, and primitive handguns among his infantry. This gave his forces a technological advantage which the Granadans, still fighting a more medieval style of warfare, couldn't match. And with his navy blockading the Granadan ports, no Muslim army from North Africa could be called upon to relieve the struggling Moors. Defeat was inevitable, and on 2 January 1492, Ferdinand and Isabella took their prize. The final campaign of a civil war, itself born out of other civil wars, had come to an end.

The conquest of Granada had huge ramifications, leading directly to the other momentous events of that fateful year. Ferdinand and Isabella had made history, and victory sealed their joint rule of the greater part of the Peninsula. 'Spain' as a political project was no longer an idea, but on its way to becoming a reality as a (largely) united, Catholic state. The king and queen's energies were now free to turn to other projects.

One man who had witnessed events in Granada was riding away from the city as it was falling. He was distraught: his plan for a revolutionary naval expedition had been rejected once more by the court. But as he wearily made his way, he was overtaken by a royal messenger calling him back for an audience; in the wake of victory, Ferdinand and Isabella were reconsidering their decision.

The man, a Genovese merchant and sailor, pulled on his horse's reins and retraced his steps with renewed hope. In so doing, he changed the world for ever.

NO JEW

The expulsion of the Jews from Spain in 1492 did not occur in a vacuum: anti-Jewish sentiment in Castile and Aragon had been peaking for at least a hundred years before. But it did come as a surprise, particularly to Spanish Jews themselves.

Ferdinand and Isabella's wedding in 1469 was cause for celebration among the Jewish community. Jewish advisors to Ferdinand had counselled him to go ahead with the marriage and even lent the impoverished prince the money for the moderate ceremonies. The heir to the Aragonese crown had Jewish blood on his grandmother's side. But more importantly, a strong and stable state was generally considered a better environment for Jews in Spain, with royal protection given to a minority increasingly subject to violent persecution.

As elsewhere in Europe, the fourteenth century had been particularly bad for Jews in Spain, not least in the wake of the Black Death of the 1340s, for which they were widely blamed. Growing hostility within Christian Spain to the 'killers of Christ' culminated in 1391 with a series of pogroms which began in Seville and spread into Castile and Aragon. Jewish quarters were ransacked and burnt, and many hundreds, possibly thousands, of Jews were murdered. Large numbers of the community converted to Christianity in order to save their skins.

Things continued in a similar vein into the fifteenth century. One particularly zealous converter of Jews at this time was the Valencian 'Saint' Vicente Ferrer. Ferrer's method was simple: first he sent his thugs into a town or village to stir up anti-Jewish feelings, while he waited at a distance. As the violence escalated and the Jews began to fear for their lives, Ferrer would make his move and ride into town, 'miraculously' bringing the violence to a halt. The grateful Jews, amazed by his special powers and thankful for being saved (while, presumably, still scared out of their wits) then converted to Christianity en masse, becoming known as *conversos*, or 'new Christians'.

This gave the authorities a new, self-created difficulty, however, one which the Almohads had struggled with two hundred years before: how to tell if the conversions were genuine. While tempted to slaughter the converts, the Almohad caliphs had stopped short for fear of killing people who had truly become Muslims. The Catholic solution to the problem was to set up the Spanish Inquisition.

We shall explore the Inquisition in greater depth in a later chapter. For now it needs to be understood as an important step on the road towards the final expulsion of the Jews. At the beginning at least, its target was the *converso* community.

From being pro-Jewish at the start of their reign, by 1478 Ferdinand and Isabella's ears had been turned by growing rumours about 'false' *conversos* – converts to Christianity who were secretly true to their Jewish faith. In that year a Papal Bull gave them permission to set up their inquisition. By 1481 the new persecuting organisation had established its first office in Seville, where the pogroms of 1391 had begun. That same year, dozens of *conversos* from prominent families were burnt alive in *autos da fé* – 'acts of faith'.

For the time being, however, Jews who had not converted still enjoyed royal protection. But powerful figures within the Church were already planning their eventual expulsion from the Peninsula. Chief among them was a *converso* himself, the notorious Grand Inquisitor and Isabella's confessor, Tomás de Torquemada. As the conquest of Granada neared its conclusion, Torquemada seized his chance: in the town of La Guardia, near Toledo, a sixty-year-old *converso* named Benito Garcia was accused of crucifying a Christian child. Under torture, Garcia named several other *conversos* and, importantly, Jews as being involved as well. Torquemada set up a special commission to investigate. Not surprisingly, the accused were found guilty and later executed at Avila.

The case became well known, inflaming anti-Jewish anger even further. And it had the desired effect: a sixteenth-century inquisitor later wrote that the La Guardia 'murder' was the decisive factor in swaying Ferdinand and Isabella to sign the expulsion decree.

The monarchs didn't waste their time. The exact date is unclear, but by the end of January 1492, only weeks after taking possession of Granada and signing a peace accord in which the Jews were specifically given protection, the royal signatures were on the infamous 'Alhambra Decree', the order for all Jews in their kingdoms either to convert or to leave the country. At the end of March the edict was formally issued, being sent to city and regional authorities with the order that it should be kept secret until a formal announcement in May. Jews were given until the end of July to pack and go. Anyone staying after that date who had not converted to Christianity would be subject to summary execution.

While an estimated one hundred thousand converted and remained, as many as one hundred and seventy thousand people fled Spain over the summer of 1492 (the figures are anything but certain; it is still not known exactly how many were involved). Jewish leaders, some of them close to the royal couple, begged for the decision to be reversed. But to no avail: Ferdinand and Isabella remained firm. The Jews had to go.

After a presence of over fifteen hundred years, another bright Spanish light was, once again, simply extinguished. Jews had seen Spain – *Sefarad* – as a promised land in its own right, yet now, forced into exile, they were forbidden from carrying gold, silver or jewels with them, and had to sell their possessions at give-away prices before making their way out of the country. Many fled to Portugal, where, for a hefty price, they were given only temporary refuge. Others went to Navarre, still an independent kingdom – although not for long. Meanwhile, thousands of others made their way to ports where they sought passage across the pirate-infested Mediterranean at the hands of unscrupulous and greedy captains, only to find their entry often blocked on the other side. Many, however, did make it, spreading across the Ottoman Empire, forming the basis of the Sephardic Jewish community, and speaking a fifteenth-century form of Spanish still in existence to this day known as 'Ladino'.

They were the lucky ones, however. One particularly tragic outcome lay in wait for a number of Jewish children who were forcefully separated from their parents. A Portuguese Jewish chronicler tells the story:

> *Mothers scratched their faces in grief as their babies,*
> *less than three years old, were taken from their arms.*
> *Honoured elders tore their beards when the fruit of*

their bodies was snatched before their eyes . . . Several
women threw themselves at the king's feet, begging for
permission to accompany their children, but not even
this moved the king's pity. One mother, distraught by
this horrible unexplained cruelty, lifted her baby in her
arms, and paying no heed to its cries, threw herself
from the ship into the sea and drowned, embracing her
only child.

At Ferdinand's orders, the children were put on board a ship bound for the newly discovered island of Sao Tomé, off the West African coast, 'inhabited by lizards, snakes and other venomous reptiles, and devoid of rational beings'.

Finally, when those innocent children arrived at the
wilderness of Sao Tomé, which was to be their grave,
they were thrown ashore and mercilessly left there.
Almost all were swallowed up by the huge lizards on
the island and the remainder who escaped these
reptiles wasted away from hunger and abandonment.

Meanwhile, back in Spain, the expulsion, which was designed to resolve once and for all the Jewish 'problem', had only made matters worse by swelling the numbers of *conversos* within the population. Santiago's Other had still not been annihilated, and the Inquisition's executioners would be kept busy for centuries to come.

NO WAY

It's accepted now that Columbus was not the first European to cross the Atlantic: archaeological research has proved conclusively that the Vikings beat him to it by several centuries. What's not so well known, however, was that he wasn't even the first person to make the attempt from Spain. The Arab historian Al-Masudi relates how a captain from Caliphal Cordoba named Khashkhash sailed on a voyage across the 'Circumambient Sea' as early as the ninth century. 'He was absent for a time, then returned with rich booty and his exploit is well known among the Spaniards.' Frustratingly, Al-Masudi doesn't provide further details, although a second historian relates how Khashkhash later died in 859 fighting the Vikings, no less.

Under the Almoravids, a second expeditionary voyage left Spanish shores some time during the first half of the twelfth century under a captain Raqsh al-A'azz, who died. But then a third attempt left Moorish Lisbon to cross the 'Sea of Darkness' to find out 'what it contained and where it ended'. Eight cousins described as 'adventurers' set sail, first travelling west for eleven days, then south for a further twelve, at which point they arrived at an 'island of goats'. The twelfth-century Ceutan geographer Al-Idrisi takes up the story:

> *After sailing for twelve more days they saw an island*
> *which seemed to be inhabited and there were cultivated*
> *fields. They sailed that way to see what it contained.*
> *Soon boats encircled them and made them prisoners*
> *and transported them to a poor village situated on the*
> *coast. There they landed. The sailors found there*
> *people with red skin with little hair on their bodies,*
> *and with very straight hair on their heads. They were*
> *all very tall and their women were extraordinarily*
> *beautiful. The sailors were taken to another island,*
> *where they were imprisoned for three days. On the*
> *fourth day someone came to them who spoke Arabic,*
> *interpreting for the chief of that place . . . Then the*
> *natives prepared a boat, blindfolded the sailors and*
> *sailed with them for three days till they left them on*
> *the coast.*

The Moorish adventurers finally made their way back across the Atlantic, and the city of Lisbon named a street in their honour – *Darb al-Mugharririn*, the 'Street of the Adventurers'. 'Red-skinned' people with very straight hair sound a lot like native Americans, but some historians have concluded that the Portuguese cousins only got as far as the Canaries. What's curious is that they should have found an Arabic speaker on their distant shore. But then Columbus himself took an Arabic interpreter on his first voyage, expecting him to converse with the natives on the other side. The

Moors, in his mind, weren't only to be found on his doorstep in southern Spain and the Mediterranean, but on the far side of the globe as well.

Columbus's voyage of discovery is born out of a Christian victory over Muslims: the fall of Granada meant Ferdinand and Isabella could turn their minds to other matters, while a long and costly war meant they were in desperate need of new potential sources of wealth. Military success over Spanish Muslims also emboldened the Catholic Monarchs to attempt a much greater conquest: Columbus expected to find the eastern shores of Asia – the 'Indies' – on the other side of the Atlantic, and Arabic-speaking Christian communities who would ally themselves with Spain in a pincer campaign against the Islamic heartlands, attacking from both east and west in order to conquer Jerusalem. It is interesting to note, however, that his discovery, which would lead to Western Christian culture dominating much of the world, was built on anything but Christian foundations: the technology he used – astrolabes, caravel ships and maps – were of Moorish origin, while the money for the trip (1,140,000 maravedíes) came from the Jewish moneylender Luis de Santángel, a Valencian. In a fascinating development, 'the three Spains' – Christian, Islamic and Jewish – combined, despite being ostensibly opposed, to make the Columbus voyage possible.

The result was the emergence from the Spanish crucible of a new creative burst which sprang from the darkness, much in the way of the Toledo School of Translators or the court of Abd al-Rahman III centuries before. And like its predecessors, the Columbus voyage would leave an indelible imprint on the world, marking a very clear 'before' and 'after'. Our world today is unthinkable without the *Pinta*, the *Niña* and the *Santa María* arriving back from the Caribbean with news of their famous discovery.

Yet with the white comes the black, Spain's checkerboard history in evidence once more in the Columbus story. The conquering spirit which brought about the end of Moorish Spain – thereby creating the possibility for Columbus's voyage – was now translated to the New World. It is estimated that in 1491 around 145 million indigenous people lived in the Americas; two hundred years later that number had fallen by some 130 million, or by around 90 to 95 per cent. Massacres, forced labour and new diseases meant that Columbus's arrival and the wave of discovery which followed was anything but a moment of enlightenment for many. Spanish culture, with its ages-long Manichaean struggles between good and evil, arrived in the New World with explosive force. It changed the world, but only at very high human cost.

NO MISTAKE

The marriage of Ferdinand and Isabella, and the subsequent events of 1492, did not create Spain, but they made Spain a possibility. Castile and Aragon did not become a single nation or kingdom at this time. In fact they would continue to have different laws, customs and even currencies for centuries to come. But following the Catholic Monarchs' deaths and the accession of their offspring, the crowns of the two kingdoms would henceforth be held by the same person, who, despite not being officially the 'King of Spain', would now begin, in part, to be considered as such. 'Spain' itself, however, was still a difficult thing to define, and over the next few hundred years monarchs would commonly be referred to as the king of *las Españas*, 'the Spains', plural: Spain as a single coherent political entity was still a very distant proposition (and, arguably, has yet to be fully realised to this day).

Marriage, however, was one thing. Kingdoms had been joined in the past through the same practice only to break apart again – indeed, this had happened in the case of Castile and León several times. What helped to seal the possibility of unity that 1492 represented was the emphasis on the one thing around which Spaniards could theoretically be joined: the Catholic faith. The conquest of Granada and the expulsion of the Jews need to be seen in this context: Catholicism would provide the common culture which could unite Castilians and Aragonese (and others). In a land of many different languages and traditions, a single faith would be the unifying factor. Which is why Ferdinand and Isabella became known jointly as *los Reyes Católicos* – the Catholic Monarchs. There was still no 'Spain' in a political sense, but through unity of belief such a state might be brought about. Hence the need to bring an end both to the last Muslim kingdom as well as the large, and powerful, Jewish community. From now on, to be 'Spanish' would be synonymous with being 'Catholic' (the remaining Muslims, the Moriscos, would have to wait until 1609 for their own expulsion, but as mere artisans and farmers they were, for the time being, seen as less important).

A single faith, then, provided the ideological basis needed for the creation of 'Spain', and this was reinforced by Ferdinand and Isabella working closely together in matters of state. Spanish schoolchildren are taught that the phrase which encapsulated this collaboration was *'Tanto monta, monta tanto'*, meaning that the one and the other acted in unison. And although this is true to an extent, the motto was in fact Ferdinand's, a reference to the Gordian Knot and to Alexander the Great, whom Ferdinand liked to emulate. The phrase was first suggested to the Aragonese king by a scholar, Antonio of Lebrija, who has an interesting postscript to the story of 1492, for it was in that same year that the Andalusian presented Queen Isabella with a curious new kind of book he had written, *La gramatica de la lengua castellana*.

Grammars of Latin existed aplenty, but not of any 'vulgar' tongue. When handed it, Isabella looked at the book and, perplexed, asked Antonio what it was for. In attendance was the Bishop of Avila, Hernando de Talavera, a relatively open-minded churchman ensuring, temporarily, that the Moors of conquered Granada were being treated fairly under the terms of their capitulation. A policy soon to be changed by the arrival in Granada of Cardinal Cisneros, who favoured forced conversions and the burning of thousands of Arabic books. He stepped in and answered on Antonio's behalf:

> Now that Your Highness has made subject barbarous peoples and nations of many tongues, with conquest comes the need for the conquered to accept the laws of the conquerors, among them our own language. With this book they will be able to learn it, just as we learn Latin through works of Latin grammar.

The queen was impressed by his answer, and gave her royal approval. She was the ruler of something new: the first Western European empire, a precursor to the French and British, and other European empires which would follow centuries later in Spain's wake. Such tools would come in useful. Not only faith, but eventually a common tongue, would help to unite the many peoples now living under the joint rule of the Catholic Monarchs.

Did Isabella read Antonio's preface to his historic tome? We don't know. But as the Spanish Empire burst violently into life, with many more bloody battles ahead of it, she might well have been surprised to come across the author's words:

*The old wars have been won, the old religions put
aside, and the old languages translated. The only thing
left to cultivate is peace.*

Castile and Aragon were joined, but very separate. It would take
centuries for the two kingdoms to be administratively combined.
With so much emphasis on religious unity, however, there was one
state organisation which bucked the trend and acted in both
nations as one body: the Inquisition.

INTERLUDE

SCENE ONE

THE INQUISITION

The Spanish Inquisition operated as a state-run thought police, persecutor of minorities and censor throughout the Peninsula from the late 1400s until 1834. During this time it prosecuted as many as one hundred and fifty thousand people, sentencing anywhere between two thousand and five thousand of them to death. The initial targets of the inquisitors were Jewish converts to Christianity who secretly remained true to their original faith. But with time this remit was extended. 'Crimes' investigated by the Inquisition included all forms of heresy, as well as blasphemy, homosexuality, witchcraft and Freemasonry. During interrogation, a prisoner was kept in the dark about what they were accused of, and who their accuser was. Torture was sometimes used to extract a confession. Sentencing was carried out in highly popular and well-attended public ceremonies – *autos da fé* – in which victims were humiliated by being paraded in special robes and tall, conical hats. Those who were sentenced to death were handed over to the civil authorities, who carried out executions usually on the outskirts of the town or city later the same day. The preferred execution method in the earlier years was burning victims alive. Later, if prisoners 'confessed' at the last minute, the executioner would strangle them to death to spare them the agonies of the flames. Other execution methods included the garrotte and hanging, which became more common in later years. All the assets of a condemned person passed automatically to the Inquisition itself.

These are the recognised facts about the Spanish Inquisition. Intense debate continues to this day, however, about the finer details, and about the 'uniqueness' or otherwise of the organisation in its historical context. The Spanish Inquisition has got a lot of bad press over the centuries – justifiably so, for it was a wicked institution which had an enormously negative effect on Spanish life and culture. But was it any worse than other similar 'inquisitions' in existence at the same time? Is it fair that Spain's image abroad should have been so badly degraded because of its own inquisition's activities? The answer to these questions is, no.

Historians trying to place the Spanish Inquisition in context emphasise other persecuting movements in the rest of Europe of the same period, principally the witch-burning craze which saw tens of thousands of innocent people executed across much of the Continent over the sixteenth and seventeenth centuries, numbers which far exceed the Inquisition's death toll in Spain. Less mention is given, however, to the long tradition of persecuting unorthodox and minority beliefs within the Peninsula itself. The Spanish fourth-century bishop Priscillian, as already mentioned, was the first person ever to be executed by the Church for heresy, while anti-Semitic persecution, in particular, was anything but new: the Visigoths had introduced anti-Jewish laws in the sixth century, almost a thousand years before the establishment of the Spanish Inquisition. The creation of a Muslim state in the Peninsula brought a pause in anti-Semitic violence, but with time it resurfaced. In 1066 Jews were massacred in Muslim Granada as the more tolerant atmosphere of the Umayyad era gave way to more hard-line tendencies. A less open-minded attitude then became more entrenched over the eleventh and twelfth centuries, first under the Almoravids, and later the Almohads, who introduced specific anti-Jewish measures, such as closing down synagogues and forcing Jews to wear distinctive clothes or badges. It was as a direct result of this persecution that Maimonides, the most celebrated Jewish philosopher of the Middle Ages, author of *The Guide for the Perplexed* and native of Cordoba, fled Spain, eventually settling in Cairo. Ironically, it was his teaching that it was acceptable for Jews merely to pretend to convert while secretly remaining faithful to their religion which caused many Jews still living in Spain grave problems over the centuries to come.

With Al-Andalus on the back foot, it didn't take long for a persecuting mindset to re-infect Christian Spain. Fernando III, the conqueror of Cordoba and Seville, imposed harsh penalties on heretics, having them branded with hot irons or even, according to some sources, boiled alive. Then came the pogroms of the 1300s. These in turn served to strengthen anti-Semitism on the Peninsula so that, by the late 1400s, with Granada conquered and the possibility in sight of a purely Catholic realm, it was almost inevitable that an organisation such as the Inquisition, focused on rooting out anything but State-sanctioned belief, should come into being. As a tool of persecution, the Papacy had already used it to great effect against the Cathars in France during the twelfth and thirteenth centuries.

And in some ways the Inquisition continued the tradition established over centuries of 'Reconquest', in which Christian

Spain saw itself embodied in Santiago Matamoros, the Slayer. Notwithstanding his nickname's emphasis on 'Moors', the point was to eradicate nonconformists of any description. The inquisitors became, in effect, the frontline troops of what might be seen as Spain's *Terreur*, 'Purges' or 'Cultural Revolution': the initial war had been won, but the process it had been built on – the Christianisation of the Peninsula – was viewed as far from complete. The battles no longer took place out on the field, but in people's homes, and in their minds. Anything from what you ate to the clothes you wore became the focus of State attention, as these were often clear and powerful signifiers of belonging to one or other group. A very easy way to tell if a seeming convert was secretly following Jewish or Muslim rites was to check whether in the larder there was any pork, forbidden to both religions. Consequently, the public consumption of pork and the annual slaughter of a pig by each family (traditionally on the Feast of St Martin, 11 November), became well rooted in Spanish culture, and is still very much in evidence today, as anyone who has spent time in the country can testify.[1]

The Inquisition was not only about rooting out heretical belief, however. It was also about power. Mob suspicion of Jews, Muslims and 'crypto-Catholics' was rife, and by creating an organisation specifically to persecute such people, the State was winning itself much public support. And herein lies the fundamental difference between the Spanish Inquisition and other similar bodies which had existed before: rather than being controlled by the Papacy, it was directly under the control of the monarchy, in other words, the

---

1 The small Portuguese hill town of Belmonte was the only place on the Peninsula where Jews managed to survive the Inquisition. When, finally, they were discovered in the early twentieth century, it was revealed that one of their survival techniques had been to make fake pork sausages using chicken. Interestingly, the Belmonte Jews thought for a long time that they were the last Jews in the world, having been completely cut off from any other Jewish communities for centuries.

State. All Spanish Inquisition documents begin with the same formula: *Su Majestad manda* . . . – 'His Majesty commands . . .' The Inquisition as an organisation was active in both Castile and Aragon (and, later, Navarre, following its conquest in 1512), had a single director in the shape of the Inquisitor General, and was effectively a State ministry answerable to the monarch alone. Which in turn gave the monarch much greater power over his dominions.

And a large part of its popular appeal was drawn from the fact that many Jews and *conversos* held positions of political power and influence. A culture which valued education and which taught its children diligently to read and write was always going to have an advantage, no matter how small, over the illiterate majority among whom it lived. Ordinary Christians of low social standing had formed the foot soldiers of the 'Reconquest', but they saw 'heretics' enjoying the fruits of victory, through intermarriage with aristocrats, and by exercising influence through their wealth and moneylending. Sheer envy drove much of the early persecuting zeal, and the monarchy, forever keen to curb the power of its aristocratic rivals and enrich itself in the process, happily provided the process by which this emotion could be channelled.

And the lower classes could be satisfied with themselves. They were largely 'clean'; they weren't 'stained' with Jewish blood. So began an obsession which would dominate much of Spanish public and private life for well over a century, that of *pureza de sangre*, 'purity of blood'. Under the influence of the Inquisition, anyone wishing to obtain a position within the State or Church administrations had to provide a document proving that they had no Jewish or Morisco family. The measure had an element of class war about it, as it was generally easier for the lower classes to satisfy the authorities on this point than it was for those higher up.

But by the mid-1500s the Spanish Inquisition was morphing into something else. Within fifty years it had managed to eradicate most false Jewish converts, either by exposing and executing them, or by forcing them into exile through a climate of fear. New targets were required to justify the organisation's continued existence, and so other heretics such as Protestants or Illuminado mystics came under suspicion. And as the Inquisition was mostly self-funded, the emphasis on execution began to wane in favour of fines and other measures which helped fill the organisation's coffers.

How true are the stories about the horrors of Spain's Inquisition? It's clear now that they have been exaggerated: close analysis of Inquisition records shows that, for example, torture was used quite sparingly, and that the numbers of those executed were far lower than has been stated in the past. Inquisition jails, in fact, were considered to be superior to those housing ordinary criminals, who, on occasion, would deliberately blaspheme in order to be moved to the slightly more salubrious accommodation provided by the Holy Office. But while it's important to get a more exact idea of what the Inquisition did, its effect on Spanish culture and society was immense. In the end it wasn't so much about the precise number of people burnt at the stake as the climate of terror and suspicion which it promoted and extended for some three hundred and fifty years. And with time this got worse: Spain during the late 1400s and early 1500s had a vibrant intellectual culture, but by the reign of Philip II, when the Inquisition began widening its gaze beyond mere Jewish *conversos*, this had all but ended. Protestantism was now viewed as a major political threat in Europe, and so the Dutch Revolt against Spanish rule, with tensions over the new religious ideas at its heart, naturally placed Spain at the vanguard of the pan-European faith-driven wars of the period. And yet at the same time, Spain in the latter half of the sixteenth century became, in the words of the twentieth-century writer Ortega y Gasset, the 'Tibet of Europe', isolated and paranoid. Philip drew the Inquisition closer to the crown, relying on it to strengthen his own power,[2] and as a result all forms of intellectual endeavour came under threat: Spanish students were forbidden from travelling abroad (although some still managed to do so) and the import of foreign books was banned.

Previously, in the Middle Ages, intellectually curious Europeans had flocked to Spain. Now they avoided a country in which religious fanaticism and obsession with racial purity became State policy.

But the overriding pattern of Spanish history once more comes into play: the black and the white coexisting in explosive and often creative tension. At this time of great darkness appear new powerful and influential lights, seen clearly in literature and painting produced during this period, some of the finest ever made anywhere in the world. Yet even still the sombre backdrop to this cultural flourishing can be gleaned from the masterpiece of the period, *Don Quixote*, for example in the famous book-burning scene. Or in this line by the Morisco, Ricote, reporting on his observations of life outside Spain:

> *I arrived in Germany, and there it seemed I might live*
> *in greater freedom because its inhabitants do not*
> *trouble themselves with the details of others' lives: each*
> *one lives as he chooses because, in the most part, they*
> *have freedom of conscience.*

---

2 The clearest example of how deep his paranoia ran comes with the arrest in 1559 of the very head of the Spanish Church, Cardinal Carranza. Despite being a former persecutor of heretics himself, Carranza was locked up for seventeen years on charges of . . . heresy. He later died in Rome after lengthy trials ended in his absolution.

The contrast with his native Spain could not have been greater. More damning insight into a growing suspicion of 'thought' and culture at the time comes in a passage Cervantes wrote in one of his *Entremeses*, in which he asks a villager if he can read. To which the man replies:

> 'No, of course not. Nor will it be shown that anyone in
> my lineage would be so stupid as to learn these
> chimeras, which lead men to be burnt and women to
> houses of ill repute.'

Thinking, ideas, the world of books and learning, far from advancing human culture had become dangerous. The examples of Cordoba, Toledo and elsewhere centuries before, movements which had changed the world, were all but wiped from memory. Three hundred years after Cervantes wrote those words, much of Spain would have looked very familiar to him, with rural areas in the early 1900s reporting illiteracy levels of close to 100 per cent. The darkness which the Inquisition ushered in remained in place for a very long time indeed.

With time, the Inquisition became more and more degenerate, while continuing to enjoy popular support. With fewer and fewer heretics to persecute, it busied itself with other matters, such as sexual habits or superstitious beliefs. In contrast to much of the rest of Europe, witchcraft on the whole was ignored, although one famous case, that of Zugarramurdi in 1610, in which six women were condemned to death, stands out. By the eighteenth century the number of executions had diminished; the organisation, now corrupt and decadent, dedicated its energies to persecuting new 'liberal' political ideas or policing the import of indecent illustrations and books from abroad. Even wax busts in the windows of hairdressers were targeted, their necklines and cleavages deemed too revealing.

But Spain was changing. Despite its greatest efforts, the Inquisition couldn't stem the flow entirely of new, Enlightened ideas arriving from across the Pyrenees. The organisation's last victim was a schoolteacher in Valencia who refused to teach the Catechism. Cayetano Ripoll was executed by hanging in August 1826. In June 1834, the Holy Office was finally abolished.

Yet the Inquisition had left an indelible mark on the country. It was later revived in all but name during the Spanish Civil War, and continued almost to the present day: even as General Franco was dying in late 1975, left-wing nonconformists were being executed on his orders using one of the favoured methods of the Inquisitors, the garrotte.

SCENE TWO

A MIXED PALATE

Spanish cuisine reflects much of the country's character: its division into multiple parts, its tendency to 'forget' its history, its blending of many influences from abroad, and its simultaneous experimentalism and conservatism. As with many cultures, understanding Spanish food goes a long way towards understanding the place itself.

Olives and grapes, staples of a more sophisticated Mediterranean diet, first arrived in the Peninsula from the East with the Phoenicians around three thousand years ago, but cultivation and development were slow and only began to gain importance once the Roman conquest was under way. Spain became, in time, an exporter of *garum* – a fish sauce much used in the Roman diet – to the rest of the empire, and the remains of an ancient *garum* factory, where fish entrails were fermented, can still be visited near the southern town of Tarifa. Rome also laid the groundwork for irrigation systems within Hispania, but the real revolution in cuisine and agriculture came with the Moorish invasion of the eighth century.

Hailing from drier climes, the Arabs were nothing if not respectful of water, a fact shown in their frequent use of it in decorative pools and fountains for their gardens. Once established in the Peninsula, they introduced more sophisticated irrigation techniques, as well as new crops which could benefit from the more efficiently tended soil. In the south, water from the Guadalquivir was extended across the flat valley plain, while around Valencia in the east a vast market-gardening area was created around the city which was still providing Spain's biggest foreign exports earner as late as the twentieth century. Apricots, artichokes, carob, rice, saffron, sugar cane, aubergines, parsnips, lemons, oranges, grapefruit, carrots and spinach were all introduced and cultivated on a mass scale during this period, as their names – almost all of Arabic or Eastern origin in Spanish and English – testify.[1] This 'green revolution' not only made Spanish food more interesting, but led to something of a population explosion as people began eating far more healthily: the foundations for one of the world's healthiest diets – the Mediterranean – and the reason why Spain today enjoys some of the highest longevity rates anywhere, can be found in the Moorish period. Indeed, the irrigation network around Valencia has barely changed in a thousand years and is still very much worked by hand, with mounds of earth running in lines in the fields to form mini-barriers which control and divert the course of the water as it enters from the channel running along one side. The legal authority in charge of any disputes – *El Tribunal de las Aguas* – was set up during the reign of Abd al-Rahman III in the tenth century and still meets every Thursday (the last day of the Islamic

---

1 'Apricot' is curious in that the Arabic name 'al-barquq' comes from the Latin 'praecox', because the tree blossoms early in the year. 'Praecox' went on to give us 'precocious', while 'al-barquq' passed through Spain to become 'albaricoque' and in time the English 'apricot'.

213

working week) at midday outside the cathedral (formerly the site of the city's main mosque). It is one of the oldest functioning legal institutions in the world and continues an old Berber practice of indicating whose turn it is to speak by pointing with feet rather than fingers. In the *Huerta*, as the fertile lands are collectively known, you can still hear the elderly using occasional Arabic words, for example *ma* meaning 'water' directly from the Arabic, as opposed to the Castilian *agua* or Valencian *aigua* from the Latin *aqua*.

The rice that was introduced to the Valencia area and grown to the south of the city in the Albufera wetlands, went on to become the most important ingredient, along with saffron, in what is arguably Spain's national dish: paella. But paella is problematic, for despite having spread across most of Spain to become a staple dish, and even beyond Spanish borders to become a culinary symbol of Spain, argument rages about its accepted ingredients. In typical Spanish style, disagreements on the subject can, at times, become quite vocal and even heated.

On the one side are the purists, defenders of *la paella valenciana*, the original incarnation of the dish. (At this point I have to put up my hand and admit that my sympathies lie with this particular faction, although I have softened somewhat in my previously paella-fascist stance . . .) Even here there are discrepancies and disputes, but *essentially* it is made with chicken, rabbit, *bachoqueta* green beans and *garrofón* butter beans, along with paprika, tomato, rosemary and *Valencian* rice. Ordinary household *Bahía* or the newer *Albufera* varieties are fine. Food snobs who bang on about more expensive *Bomba* rice being the best are merely following the example of restaurants, who only use it because it is harder to overcook and therefore more useful in a busy restaurant environment. Hardly anyone uses saffron any more because it is expensive and most of the stuff on sale is fake (marigolds and all kinds of rubbish are packaged up as 'saffron' these days). Ordinary Valencian folk use an orange food colourant instead, which is almost 100 per cent tartrazine, and therefore less than ideal from a health perspective. A handful of Valencians are starting to use small amounts of turmeric as a substitute. What almost everyone agrees on, however, is that hard, chalky Valencian water is needed to make real paella. Nothing else will do. A friend who drives every summer from Valencia to Italy to visit his extended family there actually fills the back of his car with containers of tap water just so he can make 'real paella' for them once he gets over the border.

Much more could be written about authentic Valencian paella, about how it should be cooked over a fire made using the wood from pine and orange trees, about the finer points of the gooey *socarraet* at the bottom of the pan where the rice begins to stick, about the permitted use of certain other ingredients depending on the time of year or village in which it is being prepared, such as snails, or cow's liver . . . But I shall restrain myself.

The argument over authentic paella ingredients is echoed in the debate over its origins. The word 'paella', according to the orthodox view, comes from the Latin *patella*, which was a kind of flat pan. And although this has a ring of truth about it, it fails to embrace the Eastern origins of the dish's two most important ingredients: rice and saffron. An alternative etymology derives from the Arabic for 'leftovers', *al-baqiyya*, sometimes pronounced *al-ba'iyya*. It has to be pointed out that neither of the two cookbooks which survive from Moorish times talks about anything like a paella dish existing from that era, and yet anyone who has eaten Persian stuffed-rice dishes will perceive a direct link, not least between the *socarraet* of paella and the crispy *tahdiq* of the Eastern equivalent.

Given all these arguments and disagreements, it is perhaps not surprising, then, that paella has become Spain's *de facto* national dish. Could we imagine anything else from a nation so divided by internal conflict and warfare?

The veil drawn over any connection between paella and Eastern rice dishes marks a trend, however, and part of one of the major patterns which governs Spanish history – that of periodically 'forgetting'. As we've seen earlier, food was an important signifier of faith in the past, so much so that an emphasis on pork-eating became inevitable as a way of showing oneself not to be either Jewish or Muslim in the paranoid years of the Inquisition. Yet it went further than this. As noted before, olives had been a Spanish crop since Phoenician times, and yet the Inquisition tried – and thankfully failed – to eradicate them from the local diet, considering them Moorish. 'True' Christians came from the north of the Peninsula, where they cooked with lard and butter, which were therefore viewed more favourably. Part of the problem possibly lay in the fact that despite having Latin-based words for 'olive' and 'oil', Spanish had adopted Arabic-based words for them instead: *aceituna* from *al-zeitun*, and *aceite* from *al-zeit*. Moorish doctors and writers had also extolled their virtues, including the great Averroes, who wrote:

> When oil comes from ripe, healthy olives and its
> properties have not been tampered with artificially,
> it can be assimilated perfectly by the human body.
> The quality of fried eggs [and other foods] improves
> greatly if fresh olive oil of little acidity is used.
> Generally speaking, all olive oil is excellent for people.

Other ingredients, however, do appear to have vanished from the Spanish kitchen in the wake of the Inquisition's cultural purges. Unleavened bread was a staple, but was stamped out. Moorish recipes commonly use coriander, yet when I first lived in Spain in the early 1990s, the herb was unknown. It later made a reappearance with the influx of immigrants from Latin America in the 2000s, who unwittingly brought back with them flavours which had originally been Spanish and had travelled with the Conquistadors across the Atlantic in the first place. Another example is couscous, which was very common in Moorish Spain, so much so that it gave birth to the Spanish word *alcuzcúz*. Yet having been wiped from collective memory by the spirit of the Inquisition, when it made a reappearance in the late twentieth and early twenty-first century in Moroccan bars and restaurants, Spaniards referred to it as *el cuscús*, unaware that their own dictionaries already had a word for this 'new' exotic dish from across the Strait.

There is even a suspiciously Moorish angle to Spain's obsession with eating pork. Yes, it is permitted by Christianity and forbidden by Islam and Judaism, but in many ways Moorish traditions surrounding lamb appear to have been grafted wholesale on to the unsuspecting pig. As the Spanish today use every conceivable part of the animal in their cooking, even the ears, so Moorish cookbooks recommended the same for lamb, and recipes for it far outweigh those for chicken and beef. And as Muslims ritually slaughter a lamb once a year on the Eid al-Adha festival, so it was common until relatively recently in Spain for every family to kill a pig on the feast of St Martin. Likewise, a dish my wife often makes, *arroz con espinacas*, could easily come from the Middle East: simply substitute the pork with lamb and add coriander and other spices which disappeared in the past, and you have something recognisable as far away as India. The meat in question has changed, but structurally there are many similarities.[2]

A similar case of a food falling foul of the political correctness of its times is the humble *ensaladilla rusa* – 'Russian salad' – found in bars practically everywhere across Spain. Made with a variety of ingredients including peas, potato, olives and peppers mixed together with mayonnaise, during the Spanish Civil War it had to be re-baptised in Francoist areas as *ensaladilla nacional*, as anything 'Russian' was considered communist and therefore offensive. Likewise a coffee made with meringue milk known as a *ruso* had to be called a *nacional*.

Modern Spain has moved in new culinary directions, most notably with a healthy number of Michelin-starred restaurants and chefs such as Ferrán Adriá who have become international cooking stars. Innovation has been the watchword, and for a while it seemed that all foods, including Spanish standards such as gazpacho and tortilla de patata, were to be converted into concentrated and very small portions of flavoured foam as part of the new culinary wave. Yet despite cities like San Sebastián and Barcelona becoming foodie-meccas, not everywhere has enjoyed the advances in cooking styles and techniques. Andalusian food is generally still very oily, and it is hard to find a non-Andalusian ready to extol the virtues of the cuisine of this southern part of the country. Elsewhere in Spain, for example in the high plains, 'food' is almost synonymous with 'stews' of varying description, some better than others – hearty meals designed for life at high altitude. Travel across the country,

---

2 In a similar fashion, a Moorish influence helps to explain the common use of 'Jesús' as a first name in Spanish- and Portuguese-speaking cultures, a practice almost unheard of elsewhere. When you take into account the many centuries Christian Spaniards spent living side by side with people who frequently named their sons after *their* prophet, Muhammad, it makes more sense.

and barring a few notable exceptions, you'd be hard-pressed to identify a single Spanish cuisine at all. Or even a drinking culture: try asking for a *fino* – a 'sherry' – in many areas, particularly in the north, and you will frequently be met by blank stares.

Despite its high-speed trains, its motorways, modern communications and even the Internet, food still divides the Spanish subcontinent as much as it always has.

PART FOUR

AUSTRIAN SPAIN

THE OUTSIDER

Joined by the marriage of Ferdinand and Isabella, Castile and Aragon were meant to be ruled under a single Spanish-born monarch following their deaths, thereby cementing the union of the crowns. But these carefully laid-down plans were shaken by the joint forces of mental instability and lust: there would eventually be a single king once the Catholic Majesties were gone, though he was anything but Spanish.

The original heir to the throne was the couple's second-born son, Prince Juan. Juan, however, married Margaret of Austria who, in the space of a few months, had despatched the unfortunate nineteen-year-old to the next world through an excess of marital congress.

'We should give him a rest,' alarmed court medics had warned Isabella. 'Such frequent copulation is harming the prince's health.'

But his mother wouldn't hear a word of it.

'Men cannot separate those whom God has joined in conjugal union.'

And so the shagged-out crown prince breathed his last.[1]

Juan had a sister, named after their mother, but she died shortly afterwards as well. Which left the young Princess Juana. Some at the time thought her quite capable of taking the reins of power. But they were wrong: Juana was, in fact, a basket case, remembered by history as *la Loca* – 'the Mad'. As a girl she had displayed excessive mood swings and extreme hypochondria. She married Philip 'the Handsome', son of the Holy Roman Emperor, and bore six children, but with each birth her mental health deteriorated, worsened by a growing obsession over Philip's infidelities. When her husband died suddenly at the age of twenty-eight (some say poisoned by his father-in-law, Ferdinand) Juana became so unstable that she was removed from power. For the rest of her life she was effectively imprisoned at Tordesillas, dying at the age of seventy-five in 1555, having barely reigned a day.

Some have questioned Juana's madness, suggesting that her father made out that she was mentally unstable to further his own political ends. But her mother's will, written as she was dying of uterine cancer in 1504, suggests that there were doubts about Juana from the start: Isabella passed the crown of Castile to her daughter, but added the proviso that should she be incapacitated, her father should act as regent until Juana's son, Carlos, came of age.

Ferdinand certainly had an eye on the Castilian crown, now further enriched by the treasures beginning to arrive from the New World. But such were the rivalries and historic tensions between Aragon and Castile that he was unable to take on the role of regent

---

1 Margaret, his wife, went on to give birth to a stillborn daughter. She later married Philibert II of Savoy, who also died after three years of marriage, at which point Margaret tried and failed to commit suicide by throwing herself out of a window. Other possible husbands were suggested, including the widowed Henry VII of England, but Margaret refused ever to marry again. She later became regent of the Netherlands, in which position she is generally regarded to have excelled.

he desired. So divided was 'Spain' even at this point after decades of joint rule by the Catholic Monarchs that the idea of an Aragonese king ruling over Castilians was unthinkable. And so Cardinal Cisneros took the position instead. Still, however, Ferdinand thought he might secure the joint throne for his own Spanish offspring, and married a Frenchwoman, Germana de Foix, in an attempt to produce a new heir. But his efforts not only proved fruitless, they killed him. Already in his sixties, Ferdinand relied too much on the Viagra of the moment for his project, potions made from the emerald-green beetle *Lytta vesicatoria*, known as Spanish Fly. A highly toxic substance, the 'aphrodisiac' causes severe gastrointestinal bleeding, renal failure and eventual death.

And so Castile and Aragon got their new joint king, but not one envisaged in the original plan. Carlos, son of Juana the Mad and Philip the Handsome, was a Habsburg, born in Flanders, educated at the Flemish court, and could barely speak a word of any of the Hispanic languages. It wouldn't take long for the Spanish to express their disquiet.

Carlos was sixteen when finally he arrived in Spain as king. One of the first things he did was become enamoured of Ferdinand's widow, and his own step-grandmother, Germana, who soon fell pregnant by the lusty young Habsburg. Carlos also brought most of his Flemish courtiers with him to the Peninsula, who proceeded to treat the new kingdom as a cash cow and did everything they could to steal as much as possible. As they felt little or no attachment to the lands of Castile and Aragon, such behaviour is perhaps not surprising. Carlos was the most powerful person on earth: Holy Roman Emperor, heir to the Habsburg territories scattered over Europe, lord of most of the Iberian Peninsula and now master of new and exciting lands being explored and claimed by Spanish

Conquistadors on the other side of the Atlantic. But local Spanish issues quickly brought him back down to the ground.

Ordinary Spaniards quickly grew unhappy with the rapacious new court, and two simultaneous but unconnected rebellions rose up: movements known as the Comuneros in Castile, and the Germanías in Valencia. Of the two the Comuneros were the more threatening, garnering a large amount of support in the largest and richest of the Spanish kingdoms. And by declaring the imprisoned Juana as their rightful monarch, the Comuneros could claim a certain legitimacy for their cause. Several aristocratic families whose noses had been put out of joint by the arrival of Carlos and his foreign retinue sided with the rebels, and the conflict turned into another civil war to join the long list of Spanish civil wars.

But both the Comuneros and Germanías revolts failed by demanding too much. They became social movements, dominated by leaders from lower classes demanding more rights for their own kind. As a result, support for either cause began to dwindle: not enough people at the time were in favour of social revolution. And Carlos, realising that Spanish pride had been hurt by his foreign airs and ways, took the necessary measures to make sure he was better loved: Flemish courtiers were sent back home, the king made efforts to learn Castilian, and he generally went 'native', developing an apparently genuine love for the Peninsula which was underlined by his eventual decision to retire to the Extremaduran countryside at Yuste when, worn out from ruling half the planet, he abdicated in favour of his son Philip II.

But Carlos (I of Spain, but V of the Holy Roman Empire) never ceased to be a foreign king, linked through his lineage to the traditional Habsburg territories and the geographical centre of Europe. And it was here, with the rise of Protestantism, that the running sore which would define so much of Spain's 'Golden Age' would open. Catholicism, as mentioned before, was the one unifying and identifying factor within the Peninsula, the belief system which made a political, as opposed to a purely geographical, Spain a possibility. Carlos was not the 'King of Spain', because no such kingdom existed, but he was the inheritor of a specifically Catholic realm which was already far into the process of 'purifying' itself and ridding the Peninsula of Jews, and, eventually, Muslims. So, given that Carlos was also leader of nations experimenting with new versions of Christianity, it was inevitable that Spain should be dragged into the religious wars which now ignited in the Old World. Some historians lament the arrival of Carlos and the Habsburgs, suggesting that without them Spain might have remained apart from the religious conflicts of the sixteenth and seventeenth centuries, and have enjoyed the wealth from the Americas for herself rather than seeing it wasted on long-running and highly costly military campaigns. But given her already intense obsession with the imposition of Catholic orthodoxy, it is hard to imagine the Spanish kingdoms remaining on the sidelines while Lutheranism and Protestantism took root in other parts of Europe. Christian Spain had long considered itself at the heart of the military wing of the Catholic faith, a role constructed over many centuries of 'Reconquest' and battling against the Moors. It was a part symbolised succinctly in the manifestation of the country's patron saint, Santiago, as a warrior. Battle-hardened and devout, Spanish soldiers would inevitably have been key players in the European religious wars which dominated the sixteenth century. Fighting in the name of Rome was all they knew; the battlefield simply shifted now from their own southern borders to northern Europe, and the other side of the world.

Nevertheless, the subsequent conflicts in the Netherlands, in Germany, in France and across the Mediterranean against the Turks, put Spain under enormous pressure. To be the guardian of Catholic orthodoxy was expensive, bloody and exhausting. No sooner had treasure ships arrived at Seville from the Americas than their booty was absorbed to pay the debts brought on by multiple wars. Spain herself saw relatively little of the famed gold and silver from across the Atlantic. She was open to the world, as Carlos's new motto for the country showed: the *Nec plus ultra* of antiquity which had insisted there was 'nothing beyond' the Strait of Gibraltar, was changed to the defiant *Plus ultra* – 'Yes, there *is* something beyond.' But the price for this new world-dominating role was very high.

As the situation worsened, so the strain began to be seen particularly in Castile, which paid the largest amounts in tribute and provided the majority of fighting men required for the armed forces. From being the most populated part of the Peninsula, with its rich merino wool trade, the kingdom became increasingly depopulated over the sixteenth century, the wool markets shrinking in size and importance. Wealth may have existed in great abundance on the far side of the world, but with religious wars raging on many different fronts at the same time, a black hole had effectively been created which could never be filled.

By the mid-sixteenth century, Spain was becoming stuck in an international quagmire with no easy way out. Carlos's response was to take early retirement. Philip, his son, would have to sort out the mess.

HUMAN RIGHTS

Was a Spaniard one of the founding fathers of the international human rights movement?

In 1550, two of the different versions of Santiago – the Slayer and the Seeker – met at Valladolid to hold a debate. The first was represented by a Cordoban philosopher named Juan Ginés de Sepúlveda, the second by a Dominican from Seville, the Bishop of the Mexican diocese of Chiapas, Bartolomé de las Casas. The debate was arranged by order of Carlos V and the question on the table was, how to treat the indigenous populations of the New World.

Less than sixty years after Columbus's discovery, the Spanish territories in the Americas had grown enormously. Spain was the most powerful nation in the world, a great empire stretching over several continents; nothing quite like it had ever existed before. And the subject peoples it had conquered had suffered enormously through warfare, disease and enslavement. De las Casas had seen this first-hand and had written about it in his *A Short Account of the Destruction of the Indies*. He had been one of the early colonisers in Mexico, but then turned his back on his former life in the face of growing moral doubts over the treatment of local peoples. He had taken these doubts directly to the emperor himself, advocating much gentler treatment.

Carlos's reply was to arrange the debate.

The Amerindians, de las Casas argued, had souls. As such they should not be enslaved. Nor should they be forced to adopt Catholicism. Rather – in the way that Cardinal Talavera had argued following the conquest of Moorish Granada – they should be encouraged through argument and good works to come to the Christian fold voluntarily. Above all, their mistreatment by Spanish colonisers should stop.

The Pilgrim – gentle, seeking, finding new territories, seeing things in a new way – had made his pitch.

But the Slayer now had his say.

Sepúlveda had never been to the Americas. But like his fellow Cordoban of four hundred years before, Averroes, he was well versed in the theories of Aristotle. And the Philosopher made everything clear in Book I of his *Politics*:

> *Those whose condition is such that their function is the*
> *use of their bodies and nothing better can be expected*
> *of them, those, I say, are slaves of nature. It is better for*
> *them to be ruled thus.*

What's more, Aztec human sacrifice and cannibalism were proof that Mexicans were not as 'human' as the Spanish. Which meant that they should continue to be enslaved while useful, and killed when not.

The debate continued for several months. Both sides claimed victory. And on the ground little really changed. Spain continued its conquests, further extending its territories and bringing new populations under its rule.

But a precedent had been set: for the first time a colonial power had asked itself a moral question about the people it was subjugating. Other European empires would take centuries to do the same, some never doing so at all.

De las Casas became celebrated for raising the question in the first place. There are those who would have him made a saint. Yet he is controversial: at first, his proposed solution to the manpower shortage caused by freeing Amerindian slaves was to import new slaves from Africa instead. Later in life he changed his position, insisting that Christ's message was true to all humans. Yet some blame him for kickstarting the mass importation of Sub-Saharans to the New World. Others say the African slave trade was already under way and that de las Casas's early arguments made no difference.

So is he Santiago the Seeker? Or actually another Slayer?

The two manifestations of the saint wrap around each other so tightly it is not always easy to untangle the one from the other. As if they were one and the same thing.

Which, of course, they are.

THE INSIDER

Carlos was a man of the flesh, a lusty, gluttonous warrior who found relief from his arduous imperial duties in delighting in sensual pleasures. His heir, Philip II, could hardly have been more different, a cripplingly shy and punctilious control freak who hid himself behind the mountains of paperwork now being produced by his increasingly bureaucratic domains. Philip had inherited the larger share of the Habsburg territories from his father – Spain and its American conquests, as well as southern Italy and Sicily, Milan and the Netherlands. He was master of a vast empire, yet by nature he was a micro-manager, indecisive, stubborn and superstitious. He marked the turning point in the country's international fortunes: from the world's most powerful nation (even while it had yet to become a 'nation' itself), Spain embarked on a slow, staggered decline during Philip II's reign.

Unlike Carlos, Philip was Spanish-born and Spanish-speaking, and his successes as monarch were mostly limited to domestic, Iberian, affairs. Under him, Spain – still more a geographical than a political reality – took further, if hesitant, steps towards becoming a united country. He established Madrid as a de facto capital, breaking with the tradition of moving the administrative centre around the various regions in order to keep everyone happy. He subdued a rebellion by Moriscos in the Alpujarra area south of Granada, a final whip in the tail of the centuries-long Reconquista wars and the last battle between Moors and Christians. Likewise, a revolt by the Aragonese was successfully put down. And in a *coup de main* Philip managed to claim the crown of Portugal for himself in 1580 when his nephew, King Sebastian, died without an heir. For the first time since the Visigoths, the whole Peninsula was united under one Catholic monarch.

Philip made history, yet his success was an illusion. His Iberian realms were still separate kingdoms with independent administrations. The revolts he quashed were reminders that holding the many different parts of Spain together was still the near-impossible juggling act that it had always been, no matter who was in charge or what religion they professed. Where one challenge to central authority was put down, another would soon take its place, and within sixty years Portugal would break away again, while Catalonia would simultaneously attempt to do the same. At this moment of its greatest 'unity', Spain remained an ever fragile concept.

If Philip's record domestically was mixed, on the international level it was disastrous. Victory over the Turks at the great sea battle of Lepanto in 1572 (in which Cervantes was wounded) was celebrated at the time as having checked Ottoman expansion westwards, yet it ultimately failed to give Spain control over the Mediterranean. Ships from Muslim ports – 'pirate' vessels in Spanish eyes – continued to harry Christian merchantmen for centuries to come. Meanwhile, in northern Europe, Philip engaged in further wars which brought few, if any, results, and deepened the bottomless financial pit which no amount of treasure arriving from the Americas could ever fill.

Philip's problem was that when it came to matters of religion, he was intransigent. His contemporary, Henri of Navarre, was pragmatic enough to swap his Protestantism for Catholicism in order to take the French capital and thereby end his country's religious civil war. 'Paris,' in Henri's words, 'was worth a mass.' And so he became Henri IV of France and founder of the Bourbon dynasty.

For Philip, such an attitude was anathema. 'I would rather lose my states than rule over heretics,' he declared. God had shown his pleasure with Spanish militant Catholicism by granting victory over the Moors. Defeating the new face of heresy, Protestantism, was merely a continuation of a divinely given role. And as head of state, Philip had a specific part to play.

The result was that Spain became entangled in long-running conflicts with northern European Protestant states that drained its resources. England had briefly been an ally when Philip had married his first cousin once removed, Queen Mary. But Mary died childless, and when her half-sister Elizabeth acceded to the throne and made England Protestant again, the two countries were set on a collision course. The Spanish Armada of 1588, with its one hundred and thirty ships intent on invading England and conquering it for the Catholic faith, turned into a well-known disaster, and a huge shock for Spain.[1] Philip's response was to send two more armadas over the coming years, convinced that England would eventually fall. But made up largely of lighter ships suited to

---

1 An interesting side effect of Spanish ships smashing against Atlantic rocks during the ill-fated Armada voyage was that, according to legend, the Irish were introduced for the first time to a New World food found on board – potatoes.

the calmer waters of the Mediterranean, they fell foul of more virulent Atlantic conditions.

The defeat of the Armada and the actions against Spanish ports and ships by *el pirata Drake*, as Sir Francis is known to this day in Spain, still rankle, centuries on. But the really damaging war during Philip's reign was the conflict against the Dutch Protestants, heretics within his own territories who threatened the Catholic hegemony of his kingdoms. The Dutch Revolt would become 'Spain's Vietnam', a long, costly and eventually unsuccessful war against a native population intent on expelling a foreign superpower. For decades Spanish *tercios* – among the most feared troops in Europe at the time – would make their way from the Peninsula across Philip's lands in Italy northwards to combat the rebels. The result was a bloody quagmire, a conflict Spain could never win yet from which it could not extricate itself; the more men, money and national pride it poured in, the deeper it got stuck. The Dutch wars emptied Spain of its wealth, contributing to three bankruptcies during Philip's reign. And it also drained her of a vital energy which only recently had made her the most powerful country on earth. The result was defeat: Holland and her Protestant allies eventually gained their independence, but at the expense of a running sore which continued to bleed through the seventeenth century, long after Philip had gone.

In 1598, when Philip died, Spain still had an empire, it had taken tentative steps towards becoming a politically unified nation, and it was still a player in Europe, albeit a diminished one. Yet beaten in its struggles against the Dutch and the English, still threatened by the Turks, and increasingly isolationist as the Inquisition and Counter-Reformation stifled intellectual curiosity, it was listing, a country already in decline. The seventeenth century would tell the tale of its final collapse, while simultaneously sowing the seed of its eventual unification as a country.

CAPITAL CAUSE

It's freezing in winter and suffocatingly hot in summer. The river which passes close by (and which doesn't even run through the centre) is unnavigable and barely warrants the name, being little more than a muddy stream. It has no great cathedral – even the locals are underwhelmed by the one they have – nor an abundance of monumental architecture to boast of. And sitting at some 650 metres (c. 2,100 feet) above sea level, it is, by most measurements, at mountain height. Yet Madrid is Spain's capital, and is at once a symbol of the unity and division within the country.

The truth is that Spain doesn't have a natural capital because as a nation it is an amalgamation of 'countries'. Toledo served as the seat of government for the Visigothic kings, but the fact that it did not regain this status under Ferdinand and Isabella is testament to how different were the many 'bits' that made up Spain. Toledo in the fifteenth and sixteenth centuries could serve as a capital of Castile at best, but held no resonance for the Crown of Aragon.

The solution for many years was not to have a capital at all, and simply move the court around, spending a year or two here, then there, in a complicated and expensive way of trying to please everyone. Then one day in 1561, Philip II took his royal train to Madrid, a middling-sized town in Castile with around thirty thousand inhabitants, and never moved on. And although he later continued to travel around his domains, the offices of state would henceforth (excepting a brief interlude in Valladolid in the seventeenth century, and another during the Spanish Civil War) remain where they were. Madrid became the Spanish capital more by accident than by design.

There are several reasons given as to why Madrid had this role thrust upon it. All of them are legitimate and none definitive because Philip almost certainly never consciously made such a decision. In fact, it was only as recently as 2006 that the city's role as capital was sanctioned by a specific law.

The most commonly cited reason is because Madrid is *mathematically* at the heart of Spain. Supposedly, if you measure all the land in the country and then work out its exact centre, you end up in Madrid, specifically its central square, La Puerta del Sol. Originally set on the outskirts of the medieval town, the square owes its name to an image of the sun that used to be found on the east-facing gate. It marks *kilometro cero*, – 'kilometre zero' – the starting point of all the major roads in Spain, which radiate out from the city like the hands of a clock.

That was a later development, however, in the eighteenth century. In 1561, Madrid was not quite a backwater, having hosted the royal court several times already over previous decades, but neither was it a cultural or economic hub. It did, however, have several features which pleased the king. First, it was good for hunting, and the Casa del Campo, the large parkland area to the west of today's city centre, commonly hosted Philip and his successors in the preferred aristocratic pastime of the age. Second, there was no bishopric of Madrid at the time, so clerics posed little threat to royal authority, unlike in Toledo, seat of the Primate of the Spanish Church. Third, the town had a large castle dating from Moorish times, the Alcázar, which was strong enough to serve as the prison for King Francis I of France after his capture at the Battle of Pavia in 1525. And fourth, lying south of the high Sierra de Guadarrama, there was ample good-quality water (despite the Manzanares being such a sorry excuse for a river).

In addition, Philip's third and favourite wife, Isabel de Valois, liked Madrid, claiming the climate suited her health. Sadly, it didn't prevent her from dying shortly after childbirth in 1568, but by this point Philip had yet another reason for staying in Madrid – the construction only a few miles north of his architectural magnum opus, the Escorial.

Meaning 'the slag heap', El Escorial overcame the unpromising connotations of its name to become one of the most imposing buildings in the whole of Spain. Philip started it in 1563, practically coinciding with his arrival in Madrid, and paid for its construction using New World treasure not absorbed by the costs of his multiple wars abroad. It was intended to be the last resting place of his father, Carlos V, and then of Philip himself and all future kings of Spain. Carlos himself had died only five years before in 1558. With failing health, he had told his son to bury him wherever he saw fit. And so Philip had come across a slag heap near an old mine nestling in the southern foothills of the Sierra de Guadarrama, and decided this should be the spot.

It took twenty-one years to build. The vast rectangular structure was constructed on a grid pattern, and as St Laurence was said to have been burnt alive by the Romans on a gridiron of similar shape, it was named after him: El Monasterio de San Lorenzo de El Escorial. Built out of pale limestone and with almost no decoration on the outside (by Spanish standards), it echoes much of the man behind it, with his austere, Counter-Reformation aesthetic and need to build high walls around himself: although punctuated by neat small windows and an occasional column or two, there is no mistaking that the monastery owes much of its outer appearance to the concept of a castle, a place designed to keep people out, much like Philip's Spain itself. El Escorial was designed to be a symbol of the power and resilience of the Catholic faith.

Today it is still the final resting place of kings and queens of Spain, their bodies installed in *el Pudridero*, the 'rotting room', for the first twenty-five years before passing through to the Pantheon, where their desiccated and shrivelled remains are placed in special, one-metre-long coffins.

Yet if its function and outer appearance are offputting for the visitor, the inside of El Escorial is a gem. Frescoed walls and ceilings are home to one of the most important libraries in the country, while the chapel could serve as a cathedral given its size. The monastery itself became Philip's favoured living quarters, making it not only a place for religious devotion but also a royal palace.

El Escorial is as much a reason for Madrid becoming Spain's capital as any. Yet if placing the seat of government at the geographical heart of the country made sense on one level, it made none at all pragmatically. No boats could make it up the Manzanares, so from its establishment as the capital, for the following three hundred years Madrid had to be supplied by pack animal. Only with the coming of the railways in the late 1800s and the construction of modern roads in the early 1900s did it find itself properly connected to the rest of the country. That it survived so long as the seat of government in such circumstances – and given Spain's tendency to break apart at the slightest opportunity – is little less than a miracle. But the fact remains that until just over a hundred years ago Madrid was more capital in name than anything else, effectively cut off not only from the rest of the country, but from the vast empire of which it was also, in principle, the heart.

And yet, despite all its problems, Madrid has *something*. It's not always easy to define, but there's a quality to the spirit of the place and its people which is special, a combination of pride, stubbornness, liveliness, friendliness and earthiness which is unique. This is the city which, despite throwing everything he had at it and with huge numbers of supporters on the inside, Franco could not conquer through military force. It is also home to many thousands of bars which have become almost synonymous with the city and Spain as a whole. It was here, in its frenetic and energised atmosphere, that the greatest cultural movement to emerge after Franco's dictatorship – La Movida and the films of Almodóvar – was forged. And while there is beauty in abundance to enjoy in El Prado and other art museums, Madrid is less a city to look at than to *feel*.

WORLDS BEYOND
WORLDS

One of Spain's greatest gifts to the world has been its mystical traditions. Any vision of Spain which does not include this current is incomplete, for it is the power behind so much Spanish artistic and creative expression: Man's eternal search, and his struggle with life and destiny born out of separation from the divine. This is the Spain of Santiago the Pilgrim, ever wandering, ever seeking answers, the Spain that wishes to explore and innovate, to find new ways, new thoughts, and break with orthodoxy.

Who were the Spanish mystics of prehistory? We can't give them names, but the powerful ancient cave paintings at Altamira give a hint to their existence, extraordinary images which show a sense of awareness of realms beyond ordinary experience.

Historically documented mysticism in Spain begins with Priscillian, the gnostic. But while the militantly orthodox Santiago managed to slay this particular pilgrim brother, his influence continued for many years after his death (and, as mentioned earlier, may even be preserved in disguised form in the Camino de Santiago itself). 'Mystic idealism', according to the early twentieth-century Spanish scholar Miguel Asín de Palacios, is, in fact, embedded within the Spanish 'race' and cannot be subdued. And, following Priscillian's example, it subsequently emerged in the ninth century in the shape of a man named Ibn Masarra.

Of local Hispanic origins, Ibn Masarra was born in Cordoba within a family that had previously converted to Islam. His father's skin was said to be so pale that when travelling in the Islamic heartlands he was often mistaken for a northern European and had to take care not to be sold into slavery. Ibn Masarra is the first notable mystic of Al-Andalus, and as a Muslim and Arabic speaker his thinking is bracketed within the Sufi tradition, the mystical current associated with Islam. But mysticism by its very nature draws lifeblood from sources existing outside ordinarily understood confines of time and space. As Asín Palacios says, despite the oriental origins of his ideas, 'the analogies which Ibn Masarra's Sufism present with the Manichaean Gnosticism of Priscillian are so remarkable that one could take Masarrism as a continuation of Priscillianism'. Points of similarity include the existence of a 'universal prime material' from which everything is made, a divine origin for the soul, and its redemption via the teachings of prophets sent by God.

For Asín, Ibn Masarra not only takes up the torch of mysticism left by Priscillian, but firmly re-establishes it in Spain, providing the basis for many of the esoteric traditions which flourish in the country over the following centuries and which have a powerful influence on thinkers in the rest of Europe.

Followers of Ibn Masarra were concentrated in the southern city of Almería and at one point established a kind of Sufi republic there, where mystical ideas about the unity of the human soul with the divine were openly preached in the street. Spanish Sufis could be people of action as well as of otherworldly thought: one of their number even ruled a *taifa* kingdom in the Algarve until his assassination.

Following Ibn Masarra, however, the next major mystical expression came from Ibn Tufayl and his novel *Hayy bin Yaqzan*, mentioned earlier. Ibn Tufayl was the teacher of the philosopher Averroes, who lived long enough to meet the man considered the greatest mystic Spain has ever produced: Ibn Arabi. Born in Murcia in 1164, Ibn Arabi went on to be hailed as the *Sheikh al-Akbar*, the 'Greatest Master', a title which was translated by medieval Europeans as 'Dr Maximus'. Like Priscillian before him, Ibn Arabi walked a dangerous tightrope between free-thinking mysticism and the orthodoxy of his period. He professed acceptance of the strict doctrines of his age, dominated by the Berber Almohad movement which had taken over Al-Andalus in the twelfth century, but simultaneously spent time with Sufis, eventually composing some of the most celebrated mystical verse ever written. His *Interpreter of Desires* is on the one level a collection of romantic and erotic poetry directed towards a beautiful young woman called Nizam. When he was attacked for producing this apparently impious work, Ibn Arabi then wrote his own commentary on it, showing his detractors how, in fact, it fitted their interpretation of Islamic law.

It was not enough, however, to protect him. Travelling from Spain across North Africa to the central Islamic countries, Ibn Arabi 'the Andalusi' was often violently attacked, only narrowly escaping death at the hands of a fanatic in Cairo. He finally died in his seventies in Damascus in 1240, but his influence continued to echo for centuries: Asín claimed that the writings of the Spaniard inspired Dante's vision of Paradise, while a whole future school of Spanish mystics wrote in such a way that strongly suggests a link or connection with the Murcian.

Mystical writing and thought in medieval Spain was not the preserve of Muslims; the Jewish community also developed its own mystical school at the same time, and it was in Spain that the Kabbala, as it's called, took greatest root, producing some of the most important figures to emerge from the Jewish mystical tradition. Among them was the philosopher Ben Gabirol, who drew on Ibn Masarra's work as later Sufis did, developing ideas of the intelligent 'prime material' forming the building blocks of the universe. But perhaps the most important figure for the Kabbala is Moses of León (d. 1305), widely thought to be the author of the *Zohar*, the 'Radiance'. This is the foundational book of Kabbala, published by Moses in Spain in the thirteenth century. Moses claimed it was actually the work of a second-century rabbi who had escaped Roman persecution by living in a cave, where he studied the Torah and was inspired by the Prophet Elija. It is believed that the book is, in fact, the concealed or esoteric part of the Oral Torah. The Kabbala movement went on to form an important element within the Spanish Jewish community and beyond. One of its centres was established in the Catalan city of Girona.

As well as producing one of the key figures in Sufism (Ibn Arabi) and Kabbala (Moses of León), Spain was also the birthplace of two of the most important mystics of the Christian tradition: the sixteenth-century saints, Teresa of Avila and John of the Cross. Many links have been drawn between the writings and beliefs of these two 'Doctors of the Church' and Sufi ideas, not least St Teresa's concept of the seven castles surrounding the human soul.

But if all true mystics are inspired by the same non-worldly source, then such historical connections are only, at best, of academic interest. What is remarkable about these two figures is not only how they continue a long Spanish pedigree of producing giant figures within mysticism itself, but, as with Priscillian, Ibn Arabi, Ramón Llull, Ansemlo de Turmeda and others, they successfully did so in the face of violent and potentially stifling orthodoxy.

The Spain of these two 'pilgrims' is the paranoid and increasingly insular country of Philip II and the Counter-Reformation. They themselves were persecuted by it: St John was imprisoned and tortured in Toledo by his enemies for several years before managing to escape. Yet against this unpromising backdrop both saints managed to shine a powerful light, not only reforming the decadent Carmelite order, but also producing some of the most sublime verse ever written in the Castilian language. St Teresa's writings are still, today, among the best-selling books in the Spanish-speaking world. At a time when thinking and speaking beyond the tight strictures of a narrowly defined orthodoxy could bring great physical pain and death, these two mystics were able to write openly and elegantly about the direct relationship of the human soul with the divine – a dangerous idea which, paradoxically, threatened the role of a Church meant to act as an intermediary in such matters and whose entire power derived from the general acceptance of this 'truth'.

Santiago the Slayer may have murdered Santiago the Seeker, in the shape of Priscillian and others, but at the height of his powers, with the Inquisition ruling almost supreme, his Pilgrim brother produced not one but two shining lights, the culmination of mystical thought in Christian Spain, and an inspiration for religious expression and belief at a time of persecution and State-sponsored paranoia.

In the seventeenth century mystical thought took on a less religious tone, becoming, in a way, more secular. The 'unreality of reality', the transient nature of the ordinary physical world, however, still lay at its heart. The key book to deal with this was the world's first 'modern' novel, *Don Quixote*, while it also played a part in the creation of Velázquez's masterpiece, *Las Meninas*.

Cervantes plays with our sense of reality with the very first sentence of his great work: '*En un lugar de la Mancha, de cuyo nombre no quiero acordarme . . .*' – 'Somewhere in La Mancha, in a place whose name *I do not care* to remember . . . [my italics]'. Whether Cervantes has a specific town in mind or not is unimportant; we are already in a vague terrain, undefined, dream-like – as in a fairy tale – where strange and curious things can happen. Geographically, La Mancha is the closest thing in Spain to a blank canvas, huge, empty, dry and mostly flat, well inland and with few features beyond its featurelessness. It is a perfect setting for the novel, a world where it's hard to know what's what, in the company of a protagonist with a singularly loose grip on 'reality'. Impoverished and proud, he dreams for himself a different life, in which his chamber pot becomes a helmet and he himself an upstanding knight from Spain's Heroic Age. His ordinary surname, Quijano, takes on the more romantic associations of Sir Lancelot ('Lanzarote' in Spanish) by changing to 'Quijote'. The ordinary serving girl in the next town becomes his beloved, the village idiot his 'page', and, of course, mere windmills on the horizon are in fact giant, terrorising monsters for him to slay.

Cervantes is writing at a time of rigorous censorship. And yet he manages to slip dangerous concepts through to his readers nonetheless. Early on he explains that the book is not, in fact, his work at all. He is, rather, merely copying down a translation from the Arabic of a much older, *Moorish* text, penned by one Sidi Hamete Benengeli. 'Sidi' is an honorific a bit like the Spanish 'Don' which we have already come across in the form of 'El Cid'. 'Hamete' could pass as a garbled version of 'Muhammad', while 'Benengeli' suggests *ben* – 'son of' – *engeli*, very similar to the Spanish *ángeles* – 'angels'. At the very height of the Counter-Reformation, then, with persecution of religious minorities at its most intense, Cervantes managed to produce a bestseller purportedly written by a Spanish Muslim (a Moor) who is, in fact, a 'son of angels' – an echo of the very direct relationship between man and God which St Teresa and St John had been championing only a few years before.

But there's more. Why windmills? Why, of all things, in his most celebrated scene, should Don Quijote tilt at these structures? A clue may lie in the supposed Moorish origins of the book. As mentioned before, the Spanish Inquisition was not the first organisation to impose strict religious orthodoxy on the Peninsula through violence. Similar movements had existed within Al-Andalus, particularly under the Almohads, who persecuted Jews in particular and forced many Christians to flee to the northern kingdoms. The Almohad leader was known in Arabic as the *Emir al-Mu'minin*, a figure of terror on the Christian side. Memories of this 'bogeyman' remained in folk culture, but his name was garbled, becoming *Miramamolín* in Spanish. Which is where an enticing play on words emerges related to *Don Quixote*, for *molino* means 'mill' or 'windmill', while *mira* means 'Look!' So by having his hero tilt at windmills, Cervantes is saying, 'Look at the windmill,' which in turn evokes memories of the Almohads and their policy of religious persecution. So who is Don Quijote really charging at? On one level, yes, mere windmills which in his mind are evil monsters. Yet this is a world where things are not what they seem, and those windmills, in fact, are symbols of violently imposed religious orthodoxy, or in other words, of the inquisitorial society in which the author himself lived. In an upside-down world, one must be upside down in relation to it oneself in order to see things as they really are. As Cervantes said: 'Too much sanity may be madness. And maddest of all to see life as it is and not as it should be.' Cervantes is holding up a mirror, showing Spain to herself.

And he is not alone. The theme of things not being what they seem becomes common in Spanish artistic expression during the seventeenth century, and is, perhaps, its most lasting legacy. Playwright Calderón de la Barca explored it in his *Life is a Dream*, whose most famous lines read:

> *What is life? It is an illusion,*
> *A shadow, a fiction,*
> *Whose greatest value is only small:*
> *All of life is a dream.*
> *And dreams are only dreams.*

Priscillian, Ibn Arabi and St Teresa would all have agreed. Those words could almost read as an interpretation of *Don Quixote* itself, and also of the greatest painting to emerge from seventeenth-century Spain, Velázquez's *Las Meninas*, painted in 1656.

Few other paintings in Western art have been the subject of so much analysis. Myriad interpretations abound, even some which insist astrological constellations are hidden within the image. But that the painting is saying *something* is clear as, just with Cervantes, it states quite boldly that appearances are other than they seem. Is it a group portrait of the five-year-old Infanta Margarita and her ladies-in-waiting? Is it a self-portrait by Velázquez? Is it actually a scene showing Velázquez painting a portrait of King Philip IV and his queen, whose reflections are visible in a mirror? And the shadowy figure at the back, holding a curtain as though to beckon us through to another realm – what's his significance?

With such a complex painting there is a sense that it expresses the difficult nature of reality itself, a place where solid definitions dissolve. Such a realm is in keeping with the tone set by Cervantes and others: it is Spain itself, the accidental world empire already crumbling, held together more by faith and self-belief than real power. And it is also a representation of our world, the everyday world, a thing which has less solidity than we believe, which is, in fact, an illusion. We must see it as such, become aware of its fragility and inherent madness so that, perhaps, like the mystics of the previous century, we may break through and perceive something other, something beyond.

Decadent Spain, crumbling Spain, the Spain that is losing her empire and her position of power and authority to the new vigorous power that is France in the seventeenth century, is no longer dazzled by the gold and silver from the New World because this is running out. And so, ever more cut off from the rest of the world, fearful and paranoid, it must look deeper within itself. And there, in the darkness, it finds light – the light of *Don Quixote* and of *Las Meninas*, two of the greatest works of art in the world.

What these works are hinting at is the existence of another perspective: the mirror to see ourselves, an open doorway to pass through. For centuries Spain has been locked in its dualistic struggle, between two faces of its patron, Santiago, between the Slayer and the Seeker, the Inquisitor and the Converso, the Moor and the Christian, the black and the white. Yet there is a third face to Santiago, his original one, one which many have lost sight of: Santiago the Apostle, the disciple of Christ, the figure who has been as close as is possible to the Divine. Cervantes and Velázquez remind their compatriots that there is another dimension to their national story, that while the Manichaean fight continues and will continue, one can step out of it and see the whole, a whole made up of these two battling parts, neither of them right or wrong, but caught in eternal struggle, each trying to annihilate the other while not understanding that to do so would be to annihilate themselves. This is the mirror with the two royal faces in *Las Meninas*, king and queen as physical embodiment of their realm. And through self-awareness, by recognising this dual nature, a way out opens up, the queen's chamberlain holding open the curtain at the back for the couple to step through the scene in front of them and out into a lighter world. That is the eternal challenge that Spain must face, a truth reflected in her greatest painting.

It is said that after Velázquez died, Philip IV himself painted the red cross of the Order of Santiago which adorns the chest of Velázquez's self-portrait, for the painter had still not been awarded this highest of honours when the painting itself was executed. It is an interesting theory, and places the figure of Santiago, the three-faced saint, at the very heart of the image. Did the king himself realise the symbolism of his action?

MOORS OUT

Al-Andalus came to an end with the fall of Granada in 1492, but Moorish Spain itself continued to exist for almost another century in the form of Muslims who remained in the Peninsula, people referred to as 'Moriscos'. Like the *conversos*, they had been forced to convert to Catholicism. But as with many Jews, they continued to practise their religion in secret. Yet with the desire to create Spain in one singular Catholic image, it was only a matter of time before this remnant of a more plural past would be eradicated.

By the sixteenth century the Morisco community was made up mostly of farmers and artisans, people of low social class, but vital for the economy. With the loss of political power, most of the wealthier and more learned Muslims had gone into exile, including jurists and Islamic scholars. The rump of Moorish Spain they left behind was culturally a far cry from its illustrious predecessors, but was proudly aware of its heritage and resentful of Christian authorities who had broken the generous terms given at the fall of Granada and instead imposed harsh restrictions on their Muslim subjects. Forced conversions were combined with a banning of the use of Arabic and the wearing of Moorish-style clothes: not only the Moriscos' religion, but their entire culture, was under attack.

Although scattered widely across Spain, the bulk of Moriscos lived in Valencia and Aragon, and in and around their former stronghold, Granada. Here, settled in remote villages of the Sierra Nevada, they tried to continue their lives as before. Yet a bloody revolt in the early 1500s, in which both sides carried out acts of unprecedented brutality against each other, set the tone for what was to come: Christian authority was re-established, but Morisco resentment continued to seethe.

Things came to a head in the late 1560s. By now Spain had changed, becoming ever less tolerant of religious minorities. Previously, Church and State authorities had been more concerned with Jewish *conversos*. Morisco farmers and craftsmen had been of little concern. But now they, too, became a cause for alarm, not least because they were being perceived as a potential 'fifth column'[1] for the Ottoman Turks, an ever-threatening Muslim presence in the Mediterranean. New rules in 1568 reinforcing previous but only partially imposed measures against Morisco traditions provoked a second rebellion.

This new civil war was a bloody and drawn-out affair. Don Juan of Austria, Philip II's half-brother, led the Christian troops at one stage, sacrificing many of his own men in the conquest of Morisco villages and towns high in the Alpujarra mountains south of Granada. Women and children not sold into slavery were frequently slaughtered, while any male over the age of twelve was killed without mercy. Meanwhile, the Moriscos themselves carried out their own acts of brutality: during the siege of Galera, they captured

---

1 The term was coined during the early months of the Spanish Civil War by a Francoist general referring to secret supporters inside besieged, Republican-held Madrid.

a knight from the Order of Santiago; seeing the distinctive cross on his garments, they tore him apart limb from limb.

Despite holding out for over two years and making good use of the mountainous terrain, the Moriscos were eventually defeated, their cause undermined by divisions on their own side. The Christian authorities, for their part, were determined not to allow a similar revolt to take place again, and expelled all survivors to other parts of Spain, leaving the Alpujarra empty while they searched for Christian families to repopulate it from the north.

The end of the second rebellion, and the defeat of the Turkish navy by the Spanish at the Battle of Lepanto in 1572, only brought temporary respite, however. The Moriscos may have been removed from their southern mountain stronghold, but still numbered in their hundreds of thousands and were particularly concentrated now close to the eastern coast, within easy reach of Muslim naval forces, either Barbary pirates or Ottoman ships. And what had become increasingly clear to the Inquisition authorities was that the Moriscos were particularly stubborn in clinging to Islam. Bereft of their religious leaders, and now barely capable of speaking Arabic, they had developed their own patois and a written 'language', Aljamiado – Castilian Spanish written with Arabic letters.

Nonetheless, a last-ditch attempt at reconciliation came from within the Morisco community itself when two men from Granada carried out one of the most daring religious forgeries in history with the 'Sacromonte texts'. 'Miraculously' discovered between 1595 and 1599 in the Sacromonte area of the city, they purported to be ancient writings from the time of Nero comprising a 'Fifth Gospel' revealed to Mary *in Arabic* to be divulged specifically to the Spanish people. The city authorities were unable to decipher the texts, which were discovered next to the burnt remains of what was assumed to be the body of a first-century Granadan Christian martyr. So they gave them to a couple of Moriscos to translate. These men, Miguel de Luna and Alonso de Castillo, had been instrumental in the discovery of the writings to begin with, and unbeknownst to the authorities, were their actual authors. The two then 'interpreted' the ancient message from Mary. It was an attempt to syncretise Christianity and Islam, and to engineer a more tolerant climate for the Morisco community. According to the 'gospel', Arabic was the ancient language of Spain, and of the first peoples in Granada, who had been Christians. The cult of the Virgin and worship of relics was praised, but aspects of Christianity unacceptable to Muslims, such as the Trinity and Jesus as the son of God, were rejected.

Many in Spain were excited by the discoveries, including Philip II himself, but from the very start there were doubters. It took the Vatican until 1682 to declare them forgeries, but by then they had become an irrelevance, for in 1609 the inevitable decision was taken: the Moriscos would be expelled from Spain en masse.

In France, Cardinal Richelieu commented that the expulsion of the Moriscos constituted 'the most barbarous act in the annals of mankind'. Yet he might well have celebrated it as it served seriously to weaken the economic power of his southern neighbour and rival. A Peninsula denuded of its Morisco population constituted a far less vibrant country (which, in time, would be conquered by French troops). That Spain carried out such an act of self-harm, however, fits with the pattern of self-inflicted damage brought on as one 'Spain' tries to dominate and eradicate the other. A precedent had been set in 1492 with the expulsion of the Jews. Then, just as in the early 1600s, there were warnings of serious consequences – including economic ones – for the country as a whole by the forceful removal of an entire (and in the case of the Jews, very wealthy) section of society. But then the Americas had been discovered and the gold and silver had begun to flow. This hadn't prevented multiple bankruptcies, but the arrival of wealth from the New World had an intoxicating effect: if Spain could do it once, she could do it again.

And so the decision was made: after a hundred years of rebellions, unrest and unsuccessful conversion campaigns, the Moriscos were forced to flee. In 1609 there were some five hundred thousand of them in Spain, around 5 per cent of the population, with around half of their number concentrated around Valencia. Here they formed up to a third of the population, generally settled in the countryside, where they farmed one of the most fertile areas in the country, *la huerta*, using irrigation systems established centuries before during the Umayyad caliphate. When news of the expulsion was announced, it began in Valencia on 22 September, and by 30 September the first ships were taking Moriscos to North Africa, a final insult being that these Muslim Spaniards had to pay for their own fare to leave their home country. Within mountainous areas a rebellion began, but was eventually crushed, and by the end of the year over one hundred thousand people had been forced into exile, only allowed to take with them what they could carry. Dwellings passed to the crown and anyone caught burning them down was executed.

It took three years for the expulsion to be effected throughout Spain, and the result for the State was the loss of up to half the country's revenues in taxes. But by 1614, nine hundred years after the Moorish invasion of 711, the last remnants of Moorish Spain had gone.

Or had they? Recent historical research suggests that not a few Moriscos managed to avoid the expulsion, while many who did sail away eventually found their way back and reassimilated. Spanish-speaking and Spanish-born, they had little in common with the North African communities among whom they were supposed to start a new life. And after a nine-hundred-year presence in Spain, they were ethnically closer to their Christian persecutors than their co-religionists on the other side of the Mediterranean. Just as with the expulsion of the Jews, the language used to describe events hides an important fact. These were not acts of Spaniards expelling non-Spaniards or foreigners who they happened to find in their midst: these were mass expulsions by Spaniards of other Spaniards. By 1609 there was barely even a linguistic barrier between Moriscos and Christians. This makes the argument that many secretly returned more compelling: as Spaniards it would have been easy for them to pass unnoticed back into the land which had rejected them.

Whatever the truth about the numbers who returned, however – and this is still debated – the fact remains that the Valencian economy in particular collapsed with the removal of the Moriscos, the very men and women who farmed the land and kept the local economy afloat. And the move came as the flow of precious metals from the Americas was diminishing. Spain could ill afford such a blow, and the consequences were to be felt over the coming years and centuries as the country slid into decadence and decline. The Moors had brought greatness to Spain. Now, with their final removal, came disaster.

GOLDEN YEARS

The seventeenth century is known in Spain as the *Siglo de Oro*, the 'Golden Century', not for the gold from the Americas, which had run out years before, nor for any major success internationally, but for the writings and paintings produced in the country at the time. This is the period of Cervantes and Velázquez, of Calderón de la Barca and Lope de Vega, architects of modern Spanish culture. Yet, in a trend which appears to be repeated time and again in world history, this artistic rise runs in parallel with political decline. Spain at the start of the 1600s is damaged yet still powerful. By the end of the century, however, her collapse is complete.

Yet things might have gone differently. Decline was not inevitable, and Spain came close to taking an alternative path, but old patterns of behaviour came into play, reinforcing the country's downward spiral.

Much of the reign of Philip III (1598–1621) coincided with a period of peace with France, England and the Dutch. Problems with the Turks rumbled on in the Mediterranean, but the absence of wars on multiple fronts couldn't have come at a better time for

Spain, whose wealth had evaporated over much of the previous half-century. Rather than serving as a period of healing and new growth, however, the early seventeenth century witnessed further decline. The disastrous decision to expel the Moriscos was the brainchild of Philip III's chief minister, the Duke of Lerma. Yet if Lerma's wisdom at expelling a highly productive section of the population was questionable, he inflicted further damage through his own corrupt practices. Unlike his father, Philip III was happy to take a back seat when it came to affairs of state, with the result that for a while Lerma tried to run the country as his personal fiefdom. In a move which today's corrupt Spanish political class could only envy and admire, he managed to move the capital from Madrid to Valladolid having previously bought up large amounts of real estate in the city for next to nothing which he then sold on at a vastly inflated price. The move lasted for six years, before the court was bribed by Madrileños to return to its former home.

Corruption at the very top of public life is a refrain running through Spanish history, and it has a long pedigree, but the Duke of Lerma set a precedent which his successors emulate to this day.

Philip III died, it is said, because a heating stove had been placed too close to him against the cold March winds, making him sweat. Strict court protocol meant that only one person could mention this to the monarch, but by the time that official was found and brought into the royal presence, Philip was already drenched in his own perspiration. That night he caught a fever and died.

The tale might easily act as a metaphor for Spain at the period, so rigid in its own grandeur that it marches relentlessly towards doom.

But another Philip – IV – brought in changes and placed a man in charge who came close to reversing the country's slide. This was the Count–Duke of Olivares. Olivares had a vision for Spain to become a truly unified country, rather than the collection of kingdoms and principalities which it still was, albeit all under the same king. In a secret memo of 1624 called *el Gran Memorial* he wrote: 'The most important business facing the monarchy is to reduce the kingdoms which make up Spain to the laws and ways of Castile, without any difference among them. If your majesty achieves this, he will be the most powerful prince in the world.'

A hundred and forty years after Ferdinand and Isabella united the crowns of Castile and Aragon, someone was seriously working out a way for 'Spain' to become more than a mere concept. Yet the solution – to Castilianise the Peninsula – held the seed of its own failure. Common Spanish values would not form the basis of a united state, but the imposition of one element – admittedly the largest – on the rest.

It would work for later generations – at least in part. But Olivares was a man ahead of his time. What's more, he made the mistake of reigniting the war against the Dutch Protestants, reopening a wound which merely brought the same results as before: financial exhaustion and ultimate defeat. With inflation rising and the government running out of money, the currency was devalued. Another bankruptcy ensued. Olivares declared war on France, as though that would help matters. But they only worsened.

The spark for full-scale rebellion came when troops fighting the French were stationed in Catalonia, the Catalans being made to pay for their upkeep from their own pockets. Tensions soon boiled over and in 1640 Catalonia broke out in revolt. The movement sprang up among rural farm labourers – *segadors* – who gave their name to what turned into a twelve-year struggle with Madrid and the temporary breakaway of Catalonia from the rest of Spain. In

Barcelona, a republic was very briefly declared, only for allegiance to be sworn to the French crown in opposition to the Spanish. Yet the Catalans quickly learned that the French were no easier masters than the Castilians. Their own concerns were merely a detail within the greater struggle between Paris and Madrid. Eventually the French retreated, leaving the Catalans to their own devices. In 1652, after a lengthy and bloody siege, Barcelona was recaptured and the rebellion quashed.

Yet on the other side of the Peninsula, the Portuguese – few of whom had ever been in favour of a Spanish king – seized their moment and placed their own man, the Duke of Braganza, on the throne. Caught up with the Catalan rebellion, the Spanish could do little to respond, not least because in Andalusia a similar independence movement decided that it would also make a break for it at the same time. The Iberian Peninsula, united only sixty years before under Philip II, was once again splintering into its constituent parts.

Through use of force, Catalonia and Andalusia were checked and brought back into the Spanish fold. But Portugal had gone, never to return. With it went Olivares as well, fallen from grace amid the general collapse. Philip IV carried on, and for a while tried to follow his grandfather's example by taking on the reins of government himself. But he lacked the right temperament, preferring the cultural and sexual delights offered by monarchy over the hard graft of ruling.[1] Humiliation came for Spain with the Treaty of the Pyrenees of 1659, and the loss of Roussillon to France. Henceforth the slide became unstoppable. Philip IV was sixty when he died in 1665, but looked eighty. The doctors had him sleep in the same bed as the mummified remains of the sixth-century St

---

1 Philip IV fathered as many as forty-six children, thirteen of whom were legitimate.

Isidro, yet to their surprise no miracle was forthcoming and the king breathed his last.

Philip's greatest failing, however, was to pass the crown to his son, Carlos II. Generations of inbreeding amongst the Habsburgs created an individual utterly incapable of ruling himself, let alone an empire still stretching over half the globe. An epileptic and paranoid schizophrenic, when he was born Carlos looked so strange that protocol was broken and he wasn't presented before the court. As a boy he failed to develop any teeth until he was two, continued to suckle from his fourteen wet nurses until he was four, learned to walk when he was six, and was an adolescent before he could – barely – read and write. He had sticking-out eyes, a nose which drooped over his top lip and a vastly oversized jaw. People said he was so ugly 'it was frightening'. Of him, the Papal Nuncio wrote:

> *His body is as weak as his mind. On occasion he shows*
> *signs of intelligence, of memory and a certain*
> *liveliness, but not now; he generally has a slow and*
> *indifferent appearance, is awkward and indolent and*
> *comes across as rather stupid. One can do with him*
> *what one desires as he lacks any self-will.*

The poor man should have been in special care. Instead he was on the Spanish throne and expected to produce an heir, a matter further complicated by his possession of only one testicle. He became known as 'Carlos the Bewitched'. The whole of Europe waited in anticipation: without any offspring, Spain's line of Habsburgs would die out, and the throne would be up for grabs.

Meanwhile the country as a whole was suffering from over a century of mismanagement and wars. Famine, disease, foreign adventures and a large section of the population taking religious orders meant that over the 1600s the country's population plummeted from nine to seven million. The ailing king in Madrid personified a nation sick to the heart, the former master of the Continent and of much of the wider world now brought very low.

Finally, in November 1700, Carlos died at the age of only thirty-eight. An autopsy revealed 'a heart the size of a peppercorn', corroded lungs, gangrenous intestines and 'a head full of water'. The king had produced no heir. The Habsburg line was finished and the country was in ruins, yet still it possessed an empire, and represented a potentially rich prize. From being the Continent's strongman, however, it was now a mere pawn in the European game. Ordinary Spaniards could only watch as, in future years, the country's fortunes were decided not by themselves, but by powers abroad.

FRENCH SPAIN

SPANISH SUCCESSION

The eighteenth century was one of the more peaceful periods in Spanish history, but not to be outdone, it had – like every century in the story of Spain – its own civil war.

The loss of Portugal in 1640 signalled the beginning of a serious decline in the fortunes of Castile. The Catalan revolt which began in the same year only enjoyed limited success, but did give the region the taste of twelve years' separation from Madrid, and a sense that at some point in the future greater independence might be achieved. It also marked the start of an economic and demographic shift away from the centre: where Castile had once been the powerhouse, the strength of areas on the Peninsula's periphery, such as Catalonia, Valencia and the Basque Country, now began to grow.

The death of Carlos II brought an end to the Spanish Habsburg line, to Austrian Spain. For the country as a whole it was a low point. And yet it brought with it the chance of rebirth, and in the Spain that emerged from the ruins lay the possibility that the country might finally become a politically united nation.

But first there had to be another civil war.

Childless, Carlos II had named a successor to his throne on his deathbed: Philip, Duke of Anjou – a Bourbon from France and grandson of Louis XIV. Despite not being the best of friends, and having fought several wars against each other, the Habsburgs and Bourbons had intermarried in the past, meaning that Carlos was Philip's great-uncle.

The news of Philip's accession came as a shock. A Bourbon on the throne of both France and Spain raised the spectre of the two countries uniting, which would create an over-powerful European super-state. Protestant England and Holland in particular were disturbed at the prospect.

And so a second claimant to Carlos's crown was found in the shape of the Habsburg Archduke Charles of Austria (there were up to three at one point, but the third, Prince Joseph Ferdinand of Bavaria, died). Bourbon and Habsburg were pitted against each other again, this time for control of Spain. The result was the War of Spanish Succession. Spain itself was now a mere battlefield for much larger Continental struggles.

But this is to see the war from only an exterior perspective. In a similar way to the Spanish Civil War – in which Hitler and Mussolini supported one side, and Stalin the other – the War of Spanish Succession was not only a conflict between outside powers, but was also concerned with local Spanish issues. And the most important of these was the ever-present struggle over the power balance within the Peninsula.

The Bourbons were known centralists, following the example of Louis XIV in creating a nation centred around his very royal self ('L'etât, c'est moi'), so they were natural bedfellows for Castilians wishing to bolster their traditional yet weakening domination of the Peninsula. Meanwhile, the Habsburg pretender cleverly promised autonomy and respect for regional rights and privileges. This went down particularly well in the lands of the Crown of Aragon, who swiftly declared for him.

War ensued. Concerned at the rise of Bourbon power, England and Holland duly joined the Habsburg forces of the Holy Roman Empire's candidate. For a while Spain was split along old lines: the Bourbons held Castile, and the Habsburgs Catalonia, Valencia and Aragon. The union forged by the marriage of Ferdinand and Isabella, and the very building block of 'Spain', was under threat.

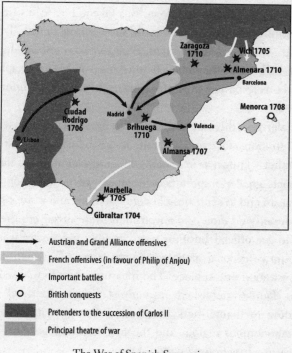

	Austrian and Grand Alliance offensives
	French offensives (in favour of Philip of Anjou)
★	Important battles
○	British conquests
	Pretenders to the succession of Carlos II
	Principal theatre of war

The War of Spanish Succession

It was a close thing. The Valencians were roundly defeated in 1707, but the Habsburg alliance made a comeback, even briefly occupying Madrid. Archduke Charles installed himself in the royal palace expecting to rule. But events outside Spain changed his fortunes. Back in Austria, his brother, Joseph I, died, meaning Charles was now the heir to the Holy Roman Empire. If the concept of a Bourbon super-state worried England and Holland, the threat of a Habsburg one, with echoes of Charles V, concerned them just as much. Almost overnight, Charles lost his international supporters. As a consequence, his lines were successfully pushed back by the Bourbons, and on 11 September 1714 the last major Habsburg stronghold, Barcelona, was taken. The War of Spanish Succession came to an end with the signing of the Treaty of Utrecht. The Bourbon claimant, Philip V, was confirmed as king, but at high cost: the Spanish territories of Milan, Naples and Sardinia were passed to Austria, while Britain took Minorca and Gibraltar.

Catalans to this day remember their defeat in the war, and demonstrations to commemorate it are held every year on 11 September – known as *la Diada* – in a movement which has taken on much greater importance in recent years. Bourbon victory brought an end to centuries-old regional rights and institutions: the city council and *diputació* government were dissolved, the use of Catalan for official business was banned, and power was taken away from the local aristocracy, with a new, Castilian-speaking administration put in place. The measures were formalised in the *Nueva Planta*, published in early 1716, a document which, according to many, marks the end of Spain as a collection of semi-autonomous regions and the final creation on paper of the country as a functioning nation state.

This is true to an extent, but the view has to be modified. First, the reforms imposed on Catalonia and Valencia were largely punitive in nature: Navarre and the Basque Country had supported the Bourbons, with the result that their regional rights were, paradoxically, respected by the 'centralising' new dynasty. A precedent had been set in which Castile acted as an authoritarian husband, whipping its wayward partners into line, punishing them for misdemeanours and rewarding them for their loyalty. The pattern would be repeated many times in the future.

Secondly, and ironically, by taking power away from the old Catalan aristocracy, the Catalan middle classes were given a boost, principally merchants who were strengthened in their position as the backbone of the local economy. This further cemented the growing economic power of the region, and with it the Catalans' reputation as serious and hard-working (less generously, some non-Catalans would say 'obsessed by money and tight-fisted . . .').

The result was that Castile could no longer dominate the Peninsula through its sheer size. From now on, Madrid would have to hold 'Spain' together by resorting more and more to the threat or use of violence. A country born out of war would only survive intact through many more wars to come.

BORING DOWN

More civil wars in Spain, however, would have to wait. At least for the time being.

For much of the eighteenth century, the country enjoyed a period of relative stability – as did the rest of Europe in the quiet hiatus between the religious struggles of the sixteenth and seventeenth centuries, and the revolutionary ones just around the corner. This was a time of 'enlightened absolutism', of monarchs beginning actually to care for their subjects (to some degree) and their welfare. And in the Spanish experience, the man who best exemplified this was Carlos III.

Carlos III was a dullard. Nonetheless, apart from giving his name to one of the better mid-range Spanish brandies, he is remembered as the king who did much to unify the country. It was Carlos III who gave Spain its national flag, adopting the pennant of his navy to become the *Rojigualda*, as it is called.[1] It was Carlos who built canals and roads to improve communications around the country and properly connect high, remote Madrid to the regions.

---

1 The flag had to wait until 1843 to be officially recognised as the State symbol.

The mirror: Velázquez's *Las Meninas*. *(© Prado, Madrid, Spain/Bridgeman Images)*

The end of Moorish Spain: the Moriscos set sail from the port of Valencia. *(Wikipedia)*

The struggle against the French begins: Goya's *Dos de mayo*. *(© Prado Museum/Josse/Bridgeman Images)*

Blood begins to flow the next day: Goya's *Tres de mayo*. *(© Prado, Madrid, Spain/Bridgeman Images)*

(*above*) Peninsular War violence was as much between Spaniards as against the French: from Goya's *Los desastres de la guerra*. (© *Private Collection/Index Fototeca/ Bridgeman Images*)

(*left*) The worst king: Goya's portrait of Fernando VII. (© *Prado, Madrid, Spain/ Bridgeman Images*)

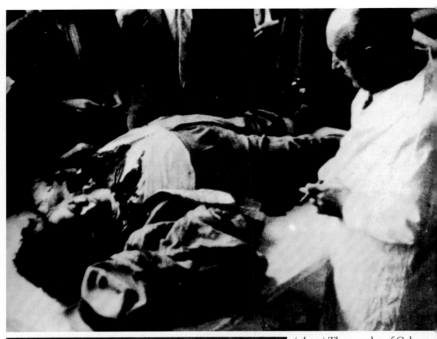

(above) The murder of Calvo Sotelo lit the blue touch paper for the military coup attempt of 1936 which led to the Spanish Civil War. *(© Photo 12/Universal Images Group via Getty Images)*

(left) A meeting of minds. *(© Keystone/Getty Images)*

The Basque terror group ETA won friends in the early 1970s by assassinating Franco's chosen successor, Admiral Carrero Blanco.
(© Bettmann/Getty Images)

King Juan Carlos was groomed for his future role by the dictator.
(© Bettmann/Getty Images)

Tejero's coup attempt of 1981: how many were actually in on it?
(© Bettmann/Getty Images)

(*above*) Francoist memorials still remind contemporary Spaniards of those who died fighting the Republic during the Civil War. Only in recent years have memorials to the Republican dead been erected. (*Jason Webster*)

(*left*) The town of Belchite was destroyed during the Civil War and never rebuilt. Today it is an open museum. (*Jason Webster*)

Spot the difference.
(AP/Shutterstock)

Graffiti appeared in
Barcelona streets at
the time of the 2018
Catalan referendum
on independence: a
diabolical Franco asserts,
'I'm back!' *(Jason Webster)*

Franco's mountain mausoleum had been slowly fading from memory, but recent calls for his body to be disinterred have awakened sleeping giants. *(Jason Webster)*

Tourists now visit the site in Barcelona where dozens of children were killed by a Francoist bomb in 1938. *(Jason Webster)*

As a delicate marriage of multiple ingredients, paella is an ideal symbol of the country for which it has become the national dish. *(Jason Webster)*

It was Carlos who set up the national lottery, established early chambers of commerce, and gave Spain its national anthem.[2] He was responsible for some of the most emblematic buildings in Madrid, including the Prado Museum, the Puerta de Alcalá Arch, and the Casa de Correos in the Puerta de Sol. He divided the country into administrative districts which are followed almost exactly to this day in the shape of the current *comunidades autónomas* and *provincias*. And although Spain never recovered Gibraltar, his reign marked something of a second summer for the Spanish Empire, with new territories from Florida to California added following the American War of Independence.

Despite being a devout Catholic, Carlos also did his best to curb the power of the Church, expelling the Jesuit order in 1767 and clipping the wings of the Inquisition (although stopping short of abolishing it).

Not everything went smoothly in his reign: riots broke out in 1766 when Carlos and his chief minister tried to impose French ways – including French styles of clothes – on the population. And the Gypsy community do not remember him fondly as he forced them away from their life of 'idleness' and into royal factories and businesses.[3] Violence in the form of civil wars was less evident during this time but in many ways was becoming codified in the art form of bullfighting. *La tauromaquia* had existed in some description in Spain since ancient times but it was in the eighteenth century that the first specially made bullrings were built, and the pageantry associated with the modern spectacle was established.

---

2 To this day the anthem has no lyrics, as, in an eternally divided nation, no one can agree what they should be. In addition, there are those who claim, with some justification, that the tune derives from an ancient Moorish song.

3 This is why, some hundred years later, Mérimée's Carmen – the inspiration for Bizet's opera – is working in the tobacco factory in Seville: as a Gypsy, she has little choice.

Bloodletting through internecine conflict had temporarily abated, but was still present in ritualised form.

On the whole, Carlos III's reign is viewed as a success, almost as a Silver Age. In the words of two Spanish historians:

> *The final years in Carlos III's reign are of maximum vitality for 18th-century Spain. There is something of a feeling of promising new times, as if the national symbols adopted then . . . acted as identifying signs of resurgence, as though a new period of plenty had begun.*

The sentiment was reflected in inscriptions on triumphal arches:

> *Happy Spain, because you are ruled over by Carlos III, a great, compassionate and august king . . .*

In some ways, Carlos III fits the pattern identified earlier of the 'Man from the East', bringing new ways and civilisation to Spain. Although born in Madrid (to a French father and Italian mother), before becoming king of Spain he ruled in Naples for twenty years, which is where he tried out his 'enlightened' policies before taking them to the Peninsula. He arrived, then, in a similar vein to Hercules, Santiago, Abd al-Rahman and others, to bring a new era in Spanish history, a relatively enlightened moment which has left its indelible imprint on the country: much of what we think of when we think of 'Spain' is thanks to him and his reign.

Historically speaking, though, Carlos III was also lucky: he had the good fortune to die in 1788, one year before the beginning of the French Revolution, and events and developments which would see the overthrow of his Bourbon cousins across the Pyrenees, and change the course of European history.

But the challenges that the new order would bring he happily and ignorantly left to his descendants.

A NEW *FITNA*

Spanish history from 1808 to 1874 is a big bloody mess – in every sense of the term. Civil wars, coups, invasions and massacres now shift from being merely frequent to becoming almost everyday occurrences. If it weren't so tragic it would be farcical, with cartoon-like characters appearing briefly on stage for short cameo roles before – usually – being despatched in violent fashion to make way for the next clown. There are so many *pronunciamientos* – coups or coup attempts – during this period that history books refuse to count them all (in 1843 alone there were over a hundred), while at times up to three different civil wars took place *simultaneously*.

Amazingly, at the end of this period, 'Spain' still exists, but has undergone enormous change: an absolutist monarchy has given way to a constitutional one (via a very brief foray into republicanism); its empire has been all but lost, the final remnants disappearing in 1898; and a partial move towards industrialisation has begun. Much, however, remains the same. Church power has been curtailed in part through the final suppression of the Inquisition in 1834 and the selling off of Church lands, but on a social level still has considerable authority. Regional separatism is in abeyance but only temporarily, as regional differences have been a major factor in the longest-running civil war of the century; divisions between rich and poor are still huge and, if anything, now worse as the selling off of Church and municipal lands has only concentrated land ownership in the hands of a few. And the use and threat of violence in State affairs is now deeply entrenched following decades of internal warfare and military interference in government. All these elements would go on to culminate in the massive violent conflagration of the twentieth century which we today call the 'Spanish Civil War'.

And while the details change, the story of Spain in the nineteenth century continues as always, that of a country wrestling with different identities, each one trying to impose itself over the others. The masks change – no longer 'Moors' versus 'Christians', or 'Castilians' versus 'Aragonese', but 'liberals' versus 'conservatives' or 'guerrillas' versus *'afrancesados'*. Behind the masks, however, the players are the same, the opposing manifestations of Santiago slugging it out for domination. While from the side the third Santiago, the Apostle, watches events, increasingly moved and saddened by the horror he is forced to witness, and finding new expression for his visions.

VIOLENT CONSTITUTION

Thanks to the Bourbons, in the eighteenth century the French brought to Spain the beginnings of a centralised state. In the early nineteenth century France further aided the construction of a shared Spanish identity by providing Spaniards with a common enemy.

What in English is known as the Peninsular War in Spain is called the War of Independence. The term is misleading as it suggests a country united to defend itself with single purpose against a foreign invader. And in part this is true, but an important minority within Spain supported the French occupation of their country – and the 'Enlightened' thinking it brought – with the result that the struggle to eject the foreigners took on the characteristics of a civil war. It turned out to be merely the first of many which would blight the country over the next seventy years.

With the same dynasty on the throne in both Paris and Madrid, it was inevitable that the French Revolution would have significant ramifications within Spain. And so it proved to be. The fall of Louis XVI in 1789 and his eventual execution in 1793, combined with the American Revolution and War of Independence, changed the world and heralded over a century of social convulsion. Spain was affected as much as any country – in some ways even more so.

At the time the country was ruled by Carlos III's son Carlos IV, a man generally derided as indecisive and weak-willed (and even cuckolded by his first minister). The initial Spanish reaction to events north of the Pyrenees was to join other European powers in trying to bring down the French revolutionaries, launching its own invasion from the south in alliance with Britain and Austria. With the resultant Revolutionary victory, however, the Spanish were pushed back, and French troops even crossed into the Peninsula. Peace was eventually restored, and with time geopolitical priorities prevailed: Spain renewed its old alliance with France in the face of what it saw as the greater threat of British influence in the Atlantic. The man behind this policy was Manuel Godoy, a soldier from an impoverished noble family of Extremadura who went on to become the most powerful man in Spain and even the queen's lover (and, it is rumoured, the real father of her offspring, the future Fernando VII). Godoy's decision backfired, however, when, at the Battle of Trafalgar, Nelson destroyed not only the French but also the Spanish navy. An alliance with France was starting to appear less attractive. Things, however, were about to get even worse.

Portugal was Britain's ally. And as Britain was France's great enemy, so Portugal became a target for Napoleon. But in order to invade and subdue it, French troops would first have to cross Spain. Spain was still France's ally at this point, and so she opened her doors. Soon as many as one hundred thousand French soldiers were stationed around the country, preparing for the invasion of Portugal.

But Napoleon had his eye on Spain itself, and believed that in Godoy he had a pliable ally in Madrid. In exchange for promised titles, the Corsican planned to extend the French border as far as the Ebro – in effect absorbing Catalonia – while palming Godoy and Spain off with bits of Portugal.

But with more and more French troops on Spanish soil, fears among ordinary Spaniards began to grow. Godoy himself could see which way things were going. In March 1808 he gathered the royal family at the palace of Aranjuez with the intention of evacuating them to safety on the other side of the Atlantic. But he was stopped in his tracks. Godoy's many rivals, including heir-to-the-throne Prince Fernando, organised a mob to storm the palace. In the chaos, Godoy hid in an attic behind a carpet, fearing for his life. Carlos IV, relieved of his chief decision-maker, abdicated in favour of Fernando in an attempt to calm the situation. The plan worked, but only for a while. Carlos then went back on his word, insisting that he was still king.

In the confusion, Napoleon stepped in, offering to resolve the issue. Carlos and Fernando both agreed to travel to Bayonne for an audience with the emperor. Once they crossed the border and were in French hands, however, Boney played his hand. Neither man, he simply informed them, would henceforth be king of Spain; he was handing the crown to his elder brother Joseph.

With one deft move the Bourbons were simply removed from the picture – for the moment. Neither Carlos nor Fernando could refuse. Fernando, in fact, revelled in his forced exile and quickly settled into a life of French luxury, playing billiards with his friends, being pleasured by the string of 'actresses' which his host sent his way, and writing sycophantic letters to Napoleon asking if he could become his adopted son (the emperor never agreed).

Meanwhile, back in Spain, a lot of people were less happy about the situation.

Large numbers of Napoleon's troops had walked into Spain without a shot being fired. Many Spaniards, intellectuals for the most part, actively supported their presence as an important step away from the corrupt absolutism of the Bourbons. But they were outnumbered. The majority hated the idea of foreigners in control, and wanted no change at all. These Spaniards were about to disrupt Napoleon's plans for a takeover of their country, no matter how 'Enlightened' it might be.

It's possible that if the French hadn't imported the idea of a centralised state to Spain in the first place, the reaction in 1808 and the subsequent war would have taken on a quite different flavour, one in which – like the War of Spanish Succession a hundred years before – regional identities and separatist tendencies could have been exploited. But 'Spain' was becoming a singular kingdom rather than the collection of loosely connected countries it had been under the Habsburgs. It had the symbols of political unity: its own flag and national anthem. And now, in addition, it had a singular common enemy. As embodied in the shape of Santiago Matamoros, Spanish identity is forged around a negative, around what the Spanish are *not*. But by the early 1800s the traditional 'Others' had gone: Jewish and Moorish cultures had both been eradicated. Now, however, into the gap stepped a new 'them': the French. And the Spanish War of Independence – the Peninsular War – began.

The war originated in a mass, spontaneous, unorganised reaction against the French takeover. The conflict sparked into life on 2 May 1808. The true extent of what the French were doing was still unclear at that point, but Carlos and Fernando were absent and French troops were now stationed in Madrid. Two young Bourbon princes were still in the capital and Napoleon wanted to get them out before announcing his coup. But when word leaked that the boys were being smuggled away, the people of Madrid rose up, no longer in any doubt about French intentions. The rebellion was violently suppressed: the French cavalry, including Mamluke mercenaries from Egypt, charged at the mob. Summary executions followed through the night and into the following morning. For a moment it seemed as if Napoleon might prevail.

Yet brief and unsuccessful as it was, news of the Madrid uprising sparked similar movements around the rest of the country. The French were unable to extinguish them: the war itself had now begun.

The Peninsular War gave the world two new words: 'guerrilla' and 'liberal'. And, arguably, saw the establishment of the first concentration camp: the Balearic islet of Cabrera became a makeshift prison for captured French soldiers. Of the 9,000 men sent there, only 3,600 survived. Cabrera preceded the British concentration camps of the Boer War by almost a hundred years. 'Guerrilla' comes from the Spanish meaning 'little war', describing the nature of much of the conflict: this was unorthodox fighting which, despite a number of set-piece battles, involved much skirmishing and ambushes by Spanish irregulars against the occupation force. As with the Americans in Vietnam one hundred and fifty years later, the French were never in total control of the country: any territory not directly in their hands was effectively held by the *guerrilleros* – guerrilla fighters who in some cases were little more than small bandit gangs. These were, however, very effective, and sometimes managed to create standing armies by absorbing soldiers from the Spanish army who deserted to fight the invaders.

The result was the Battle of Bailén, the first time Napoleon's forces were defeated in open field in a major engagement. Victory gave an enormous morale boost for the anti-French cause, but also came close to destroying it: on hearing the news, Napoleon decided to strengthen his forces on the Peninsula, despatching his Armée d'Espagne of nearly three hundred thousand men to 'pacify' the rebellious Spaniards. It was a disaster for Spain: Napoleon's men ransacked the country as levels of violence were stepped up. To this day the scars of the conflict can be seen, with cannonball craters in old city walls, and many national monuments razed to the ground. Napoleonic troops were responsible for the destruction of Sahagún, once the most powerful monastery in Spain and headquarters of the Cluniac order (whose mother monastery in France had also been destroyed during the Revolution). And as is inevitable in a guerrilla war, atrocities became common, with civilians drawn into – and often participating in – the escalating violence. But it wasn't a simple question of 'Spaniards' against 'French': *los afrancesados*, Spanish supporters of Napoleonic rule, were often targeted by the rebels, identified by their French styles of dress or mannerisms.

Some of the most graphic depictions of the violence appear in the work of the most important artist to emerge from the time, Francisco Goya. The events which sparked the war led to two of his masterpieces, the *Dos de mayo* and the *Tres de mayo*. But perhaps more interesting from a historical point of view are his series of prints *Los desastres de la guerra – The Disasters of War*, a work which acts as a mirror by reflecting back at his fellow Spaniards the ambiguity of a civil war that was never declared as such, and the deeply uncivil nature of the conflict. Like Cervantes and Velazquez before him, in Goya we can feel the presence of the third face of Santiago, the Spain which watches from a distance the incessant struggles between his two other manifestations, between the Pilgrim and the Slayer. But now the humour of *Don Quixote* and the clear reflection of *Las Meninas* have gone, replaced by something darker. The Spain Goya is reflecting back through his art is one of pain and despair, of grotesque violence, perpetrated not only by the invading French soldiers, but by his own countrymen against each other. A sense of hope present in the work of Cervantes and Velazquez is beginning to wane. The mirror has become tarnished.

Today, Goya is regarded as the first 'modern' painter. He is one of Spain's artistic greats, a cultural giant produced by the same country that gave the world Averroes, Alfonso X, St Teresa and so many others. And the torch that he ignites later inspires not only painters throughout the Western world, but that other towering Spanish artist, Picasso, whose masterpiece *Guernica*, which owes so much to Goya, would later act as a prescient mirror reflection from Spain's twentieth-century conflagration of the horrors about to occur all over the globe in a Second World War.

In the end, Napoleon was defeated by a combination of guerrilla warfare and the intervention of the British under Sir Arthur Wellesley, later Lord Wellington. Irregular action wore the French down, but their army still needed to be defeated in traditional fashion on the battlefield, and this combination of tactics eventually drove the invader out in 1813. Joseph Bonaparte – known as José I in Spanish history – fled Madrid, in many ways a victim of the rapacious French troops he had been powerless to control. With him went as many as twelve thousand Spanish families into exile, supporters of his moderate reform programme, and fearful of retributions which would inevitably come with the establishment of the new regime. This was headed by the wretched Fernando VII, who now returned to Spain like a Messiah.

With Napoleon's defeat in the Peninsula, Spain once again showed itself to be ahead of the curve: the Battle of Bailén broke Napoleon's air of invincibility, and the Corsican himself later blamed his Spanish venture for his eventual fall.

> *The unfortunate war in Spain ruined me* [he wrote on St Helena]. *All my reverses originated there.* [It] *destroyed my reputation throughout Europe* . . .

The Spanish reaction against the French hadn't only expressed itself in the form of irregular warfare, however. In a hugely significant move, middle-class intellectuals and free-thinking clerics had mobilised during the conflict to set out their own ideas for how 'Spain' – still a nascent political entity – should be shaped once the invader had been removed. The result was the Constitution of Cádiz of 1812, the brainchild of a group of some three hundred 'liberals, centrists, army officers and ecclesiastics' who managed to congregate from most areas of the country in the one place which resisted the French assault, the ancient Herculean city of Cádiz.

It was entirely appropriate that the Constitution of 1812 should be drafted in the three-thousand-year-old city given Heracles's role as the mythological founder of Spanish civilisation.[1] The document became the cornerstone of the modern Spanish state, the text against which all other Spanish constitutions (and there have been a few) are measured. Apart from three very brief periods, however,

---

1 The document still referred to Spain in the plural, with Ferdinand as '*rey de las Españas*'. The first mention of 'the Spanish nation' was not until the Constitution of 1869, while a subsequent Constitution of 1876 referred to King Alfonso XII as, for the first time, 'king of Spain', singular.

the 1812 Constitution, known affectionately in Spain as *La Pepa*,[2] was not implemented. But following the example already set in the US, it was an attempt to create a country around a set of ideas, to find common cause based on 'reason' around which Spain could unite. And those ideas were 'liberal' in the sense of the times in that they espoused a constitutional monarchy, free enterprise, freedom of the press, votes for men of means over the age of twenty-five, and the right to own property. Freedom of worship, however, was not allowed, nor were rights for women addressed. Nonetheless, it was a radical step, the first written constitution in European history, which went on to inspire similar documents in Norway, Portugal and Mexico over the next few years, as well as the Italian liberal movement. In fact, the word 'liberal' arrives in other European languages in its political sense from the Cádiz conclave.

One of the things which makes the 1812 Constitution special in Spanish history is that it was written by men from almost all parts of the country. In response to the French invasion, clandestine local parliaments – *juntas* – had been set up in opposition to the new regime. At most other times in the country's past, the breakdown of central authority has a centrifugal, fracturing effect. During the Peninsular War, however, given the common enemy, the mood was uniquely different. The authors of the Constitution were deputies from the various regional bodies who managed to smuggle themselves through occupied territory to reach Cádiz and take part in the *Cortes Generales*. That they risked their lives to get there is a sign of how significant the occasion was, for there was an overwhelming desire to lay the foundations for a united Spain in which the Spanish people themselves – not their kings – held the country together:

---

2 It was signed on the Feast of San José – St Joseph – *Pepa* being the shortened feminine version of José.

sovereignty, under the terms of the document, lay in the 'nation', not in the monarchy. If the supporters of José I sought reform under the French model, then the Cádiz deputies were inspired more by ideas emanating at the time from Britain and the English-speaking world.

La Pepa is another example of illuminated Spanish ideas in the midst of darkness. As Averroes established Western rational thought in the face of Almohad religious fundamentalism, and St Teresa and St John of the Cross wrote of their heavenly visions against the paranoid depths of the Inquisition, so out of the destruction and violence of the Peninsular War emerges the 1812 Constitution, another Spanish vision which would go on to have great impact around the world. In the decade that followed – the 1820s – almost all Spain's foreign possessions broke away; *La Pepa* ignited the spark which led to their eventual independence with the simple and powerful idea that people, not monarchs, were the basis of nations.

But just as Averroes's rationalism went on to have greater influence outside his own culture than within, so the ideas of Cádiz had only a limited impact within Spain itself. One version of Santiago had shown his face, with new ideas and an open mind. But he had the other Santiago to contend with. This time the Slayer appeared in the shape of the very man in whose name the new Constitution had been written: Fernando VII.

A FERNANDO TO END
ALL FERNANDOS

Spanish history has produced its fair share of ogres, but Fernando VII is among the worst. And like the monsters in fairy tales, he didn't just have an evil character, but was physically repulsive as well. His prominent forehead, huge nose, depressed upper lip and exaggerated chin made even the later Habsburgs appear handsome, and have led some to conclude that he suffered from a genetic disorder known as Crouzon syndrome. He was also obese, had terrible halitosis brought on by constant cigar smoking, went prematurely bald, had small, devious eyes and was afflicted with gout from eating too much red meat. That's not all: Fernando also had a complaint which led to hypertrophy of the genitals, making intercourse generally difficult and painful for his partners; it took him over a year to consummate his first marriage. In fact his bride, María Antonia of Naples, almost fainted the first time she clapped eyes on the 'monstrous' royal member.

None of this might have mattered or even have been remembered were it not for the fact that Fernando was also a vile human being, at once vengeful, petty, treacherous, cowardly, deceitful, ungrateful and self-obsessed. A later Spanish historian described him as 'utterly lacking any aptitude to be king'.

Despite this, at the beginning of his reign most Spanish people loved him. Fernando was, in their eyes, *el Deseado*, the one they had longed for during the cruel years of the Peninsular War, their exiled king in whose name they had fought and died in their many thousands against the French. Unknown to the Spanish, however, during his 'exile' Fernando had been trying to ingratiate himself with Napoleon the entire time, and had even written letters to the emperor congratulating him when French troops defeated the Spanish in battle. His subjects could not have read their 'saviour' any more wrongly.

Further examples of his duplicity were not long in coming once he returned triumphantly to Spain in the wake of the French defeat. The liberals who had drawn up the 1812 Constitution insisted that he could only be king if he accepted their document. Of course, said Fernando, anything you say. But before he had even reached Madrid he turned on the very people who gave him his crown, rejected *La Pepa*, and had as many of its authors rounded up as possible. Spain might have changed dramatically during his absence, but Fernando would do his best to pretend that nothing had happened and revert to the *ancien regime* ways of before.

His task was made easier by displays of mass support for an absolutist monarchy: as his train passed through Valencia, bystanders surged forwards to unhitch his horses and pull the royal carriage themselves. *¡Vivan las cadenas!* went the cry – 'Long live our chains!'[1] Ordinary people were, on the face of it, happy and willing

---

[1] It's uncertain in which Spanish city the event actually took place, but its symbolic importance remains nonetheless.

to be subjugated. And so Fernando destroyed the infant liberal state and ushered in a new period of paranoia and repression in Spanish history. With echoes of Philip II's reign, censorship was imposed and the universities were closed. Thinking was once again deemed dangerous in the police state which was effectively ushered in. The 'other' Spain had to be annihilated, a task Fernando saw to himself on many occasions by arresting suspects in person.[2]

And in the most visible statement that the old order was back, he reinstated the Inquisition, briefly suppressed during his absence. It comes as a shock to many to learn that the Spanish Inquisition was still persecuting people over their beliefs as late as the 1830s. What's even more striking, perhaps, is that in general the Spanish people at the time applauded the 'Holy Inquisition', seeing in it a symbol of national identity and difference: one of the other cries to greet Fernando's return to Spain was 'Long live the king! Long live the Inquisition!'

Fernando's reign was an unmitigated disaster. The country had suffered badly during the war. Agriculture and infrastructure were damaged and the economy was in a mess: prices dropped by 50 per cent in only six years as a deflationary cycle started. What made things worse was that the Latin American colonies now started to break away and became independent, cutting Spain off from its sources of wealth across the Atlantic. A token force was all that Madrid could afford to try to halt the independence movements, and it proved ineffective. By the end of the 1820s all that was left of Spain's mighty empire was Cuba, Puerto Rico and the Philippines, with former colonies from Mexico to Argentina having separated from the mother country. As other European empires were still

---

2 Just over a hundred years later Franco insisted on ratifying in person all death penalties against his enemies.

expanding, Spain, as so often, preceded its neighbours by already entering a 'post-colonial' phase, well over a hundred years before them.

And as if further confirmation was needed that Spain was no longer a major player in Europe, the French invaded again in 1823. Liberals within the army had rebelled and forced Fernando to swear loyalty to the 1812 Constitution. Fernando, conniving as ever, played along, and for three years Spain moved to become the liberal country that the authors of *La Pepa* had dreamt of. But the liberals themselves were divided, while royalists (secretly supported by Fernando) formed guerrilla forces and fought back. The conflict turned into another civil war largely between the progressive urban middle class and rural artisans and farm labourers of more conservative views. The clash only came to an end with the arrival of the French – the 'Hundred Thousand Sons of St Louis' – troops sent from Louis XVIII's now conservative France, who marched in and restored 'order' once more. This time the crowds cheered the foreigners where only a decade before they had fought them to the death. 'Long live the absolutist king!' came the cry again. 'Long live religion and the Inquisition!'

As if economic disaster, loss of empire and inviting the French in again wasn't enough, Fernando's greatest disaster lay in his failures in the bedroom. Without an heir, his crown would pass to his younger brother Carlos, who, amazingly, was even more conservative and absolutist than Fernando, and was already stirring up trouble. Desperate to avoid such an eventuality, and beginning to feel his age, Fernando married for the fourth time in the hope of producing offspring. The lucky bride, María Josefa Amalia of Saxony, promptly produced a child – a daughter, Isabella. Earlier in Spanish history this wouldn't have been a problem, as the accession of Isabella the

Catholic to the crown of Castile shows. But the Bourbons had imported the Salic Law from France, as well as absolutism, which meant that only a male could succeed to the throne.

Fernando's solution was to promulgate a law overriding the Salic one, making Isabella next in line to the throne. It could have worked, but brother Carlos was already preparing himself to lead the country. In 1833 Fernando died aged only forty-eight. Little Isabella was a month shy of turning three. Spain stood on the brink.

The response was a new civil war.

CARLIST WARS

The conflict which spilled out over the liberal 'triennial' from 1820 to 1823 was repeated on a grander scale on Fernando VII's death in 1833. This new war of Spanish succession was to dog the country over much of the rest of the century, breaking out on three different occasions. The battle lines were complex, but centred on the identity of the country: was 'Spain' to be built around tradition, or new ideas?

The division between the two sides was not always clear-cut, or static, but roughly speaking an urban and progressive minority went head to head with a majority living in the countryside which was unenthusiastic about change. The liberals became synonymous with the cause of the infant Queen Isabella, whose regent, the Queen Mother María Cristina, needed their support (despite not being particularly liberal herself). They were largely supported by the nobility – who were appeased by liberal ideas about property rights – by the urban Church hierarchy, who also supported Isabella's cause, and by most of the army. On the opposite side, artisans, farm workers and the rural clergy rallied to

Carlos's side. As in all Spanish civil wars, regional identities played a significant role, becoming one of the most decisive factors in the conflict: the centre was once again at war with the periphery.

If in the War of Spanish Succession of the early 1700s the Basque Country and Navarre had largely remained on the sidelines by backing the Bourbon winners (while Catalans and Valencians supported the Habsburg 'regionalist' cause), now this northern corner of the country became the epicentre of the new hostilities. Unlike the territories of the old Crown of Aragon, the Basques and Navarrese had not had their local rights and traditions (*fueros*) taken from them . . . that is until the rise of the liberals with the 1812 Constitution, which sought to forge a united Spanish nation and ruled out any autonomy for the regions. Now these regions had much to lose. And in opposition to the liberal cause

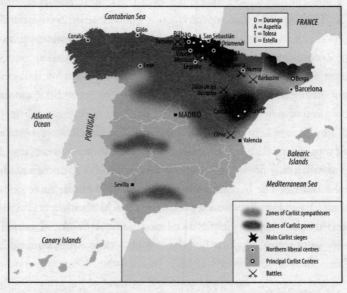

The centre against the periphery once more: the First Carlist War

stood Don Carlos, the absolutist younger brother of Fernando, pretender to the throne who believed in the divine right of kings and in keeping everything as it was. For the Basques and Navarrese he was their man. And so they proclaimed for him. The First Carlist War had begun.

There is a sad irony in the fact that, as an absolutist, Carlos's first act had he won the war would have been to tramp over the regional rights and privileges that many of his supporters were fighting to defend. Unluckily for him, however, he never got to exercise royal power. But he came very close: in 1837 his army reached the outskirts of Madrid, and he might have taken the capital, but at the last minute lost his nerve. It was a turning point: from then on Carlism was on the retreat, finally being defeated in 1840 by the better organised and better equipped liberals, who this time received support from both the French and the British.[1] Focal points of Carlist support, however, continued to survive for decades, not least in the eastern Maestrazgo mountains, which had fallen to the Carlist leader Ramón Cabrera, nicknamed *el Tigre* for his cruelty. Cabrera's merciless treatment of prisoners only worsened when the liberals captured and executed his mother. His exploits highlight the very bloody and vengeful nature of the conflict: as many as three hundred thousand Spaniards lost their lives over the course of the Carlist Wars, a figure comparable to the number killed during the Spanish Civil War. Summary executions and reprisals became the norm, one notorious incident being the shooting of one hundred and eighteen Isabeline prisoners by Carlists at the Basque town of Heredia. An agreement to limit the atrocities was brokered by the British diplomat Lord

---

1 The Spanish derogatory word for northern European, *guiri*, dates from this time: the foreigners fought for the cause of Isabella's mother, María Cristina, Cristina being pronounced in Basque 'Guiristina', hence *guiri*.

Eliot in 1835, and for a time enjoyed some success, but violence behind the lines soon resumed. One member of the British Legion wrote that prisoners were 'mercilessly put to death, sometimes by means of tortures worthy of the North American Indians'.

El Tigre later died peacefully in exile near London, having married an English girl and moved into the country estate which in time would become Wentworth Golf Course. But the scars left by the First Carlist War were slow to heal: the war reignited twice more over the coming decades, in 1848 and then again in 1872, with the Carlist cause continuing to exist well into the twentieth century.[2] The conflicts set a dangerous precedent which would be followed time and again of putting military generals at the heart of political developments. And although the Carlist wars eventually drew to a close, the basis of what they were fought over – tradition versus change, orthodoxy versus free-thinking – not only echoed the civil wars of the past, but also, in many ways, gave birth to their descendant: the Spanish Civil War itself.

---

2 And even to today: the current Carlist pretender to the Spanish crown is Carlos Javier de Borbón-Parma, born in 1970.

A SECOND (CLASS) ISABELLA

Fernando VII baptised his daughter and heir Isabella in the hope that his subjects would accept a sovereign queen named after the great Isabella of Castile of blessed memory. His plan was only a partial success, however, as testified by three Carlist civil wars over the following decades aimed at overthrowing the girl-queen in favour of her uncle. In addition, Isabella II's personal failings further scuppered her father's designs, eventually leading to the (albeit temporary) fall of the Bourbon regime and Spain's first dalliance with republicanism.

If having a psychopath as a father wasn't bad enough, Isabella was less than fortunate in having a corrupt and rapacious mother who quickly remarried following Fernando's death and dedicated herself to bringing up her new, rapidly expanding family and lining her own pockets. All of which wouldn't have been so bad except that at the same time Maria Cristina was supposed to be acting as regent for her infant daughter, as well as providing a decent education for the future monarch. So neglected was the young queen that at the age of ten she could still barely read, write or do basic sums, could only express affections towards her cuddly toys and dogs, and had non-existent table manners. Perhaps not surprisingly, given the absence of any real parenting, courtiers and others around her took advantage and initiated the queen in the only activities for which she is really remembered, namely her colourful sex life. It is said that she was deflowered by her own chief minister, Salustiano Olózaga, although various tutors were not far behind. One of them, José Vicente Ventosa, was later expelled from the palace for 'serious' misdemeanours. Isabella became notorious for having a string of lovers, many of whom were politicians or high-ranking military officers (she also had a penchant for opera singers), such as General O'Donnell, or Lieutenant Enrique Puigmoltó, who is generally regarded as being the father of Isabella's son and heir, the future Alfonso XII. Rumours of her many affairs provided material for popular songs of the age, as did the sexual inclinations of her husband and consort, Francisco, who was nick-named 'Doña Paquita' for his supposed lack of interest in women. A series of over one hundred caricatures were drawn at the time, not unlike those depicting the antics of Britain's Prince Regent, in which Isabella's erotic encounters were illustrated in full porno-graphic glory, including acts of group sex and bestiality (although not at the same time).

Her adulterous tendencies were so widely known of that when Pope Pius IX agreed to baptise the infant Alfonso XII voices were raised in the Vatican that the Spanish queen was a *puttana*.

'A whore, yes,' the pontiff replied, 'but a pious one.'

And the child was embraced to the bosom of the Church.

While bed-hopping was the norm within the palace, outside in the rest of the country a curious parallel existed on the political scene, with the years of Isabella's reign marked by a truly dizzying number of coups, revolts and changes of government. Most of them failed, but some succeeded. Changes in government, in fact, only ever came about during this period through violence, always instigated or supported by various military factions, a precedent which would have lasting repercussions for Spanish history and which can still be felt to this day. This is the period of Spanish history which gives us the word *pronunciamiento*, the act by which some high-ranking officer would declare umbrage with the government, and perhaps shoot a few people just to show he was serious, only to be shot down himself as his call to arms generally failed to muster the support he needed. With hindsight they can appear almost comical, but at the time they kept the country in an almost permanent state of emergency. Occasional moments of stability came, but were brief. O'Donnell was in charge of the longest of these, five years which, miraculously, managed to buck the general trend of the period.

And behind the rebelliousness lay serious questions: Spain now finally existed, but there was no consensus about the kind of country she wanted to be. So-called 'liberals' were often at the forefront of the political debate, but their liberalism amounted to little more than oligarchy. In addition, they themselves were deeply divided between 'moderates' and 'progressives', rivalry between the two factions very often resulting in bloodshed. With time these groups would become political formations, forerunners of the parties which have governed Spain since 1978. Meanwhile, regional identities continued to add further dimensions, and among the multiple coups and revolutions were uprisings in formerly independent states, including an insurrection in Barcelona in 1842 which only ended after the army used heavy artillery to bombard the city into submission. Regionalist sentiments, in fact, never went away, exploding brightly – if briefly – in 1873 and then feeding a new Catalan independence movement which would develop towards the end of the century.

Meanwhile, Spain was changing radically. The first railway lines were built at this time, a transformative leap in communications within a country in which numerous mountain ranges traditionally highlighted a lack of cultural cohesion. And with trains came the beginnings of industrialisation – principally in Catalonia, where textiles took off, and the Basque Country, which developed a steel industry. That the new forms of wealth would be concentrated in these fringe areas with strong cultural and historical identities would have – and still has – significant consequences.

Socially these developments had a huge impact, but more importantly on a national scale was the effect of the forced sale of Church and municipal lands at this time. The Church owned a third of the Spanish land mass, and wresting it from ecclesiastic hands had long been an ambition of liberal governments, not least to weaken Church power. But while the idea was that rural communities would be strengthened by the move, the result in many ways was the reverse. Most of the land sold passed into the hands of already-wealthy landowners whose power simply increased further. Free Church-based education began to disappear as priests founded private schools in order to make up for lost revenues. The new landowners in many cases tore up the contracts of their farm workers and forced them to become *jornaleros* – men who were only ever employed for a day at a time, with no guarantee of future work beyond the goodwill of the manager. A similar development meant that many former skilled artisans became mere labourers.

This shift turned the political sentiments of Spain's lower classes on their head. If in the 1830s they had supported the conservatism of Church and absolutist monarchy as the guardian of their traditions and way of life (*¡Vivan las cadenas!*), by the 1860s they had become highly radicalised and very open to the new anarchist and socialist ideas developing in the rest of Europe. Thirty years of Spanish history, of generals interfering in politics, of a corrupt ruling elite seemingly incapable of steering the ship of state, of violence taking centre stage in the national identity drama, of a State taking on the power of the Church, of disastrous rural reforms which ruined the lives of those they were designed to help, of one Spain and another fighting it out. This was Isabella II's reign.

CHAOS

To say that the six-year period from 1868 to 1874 was an almighty mess is an understatement, even by the standards of a country no stranger to political turmoil. In an almost farcical string of developments, during that very short time Spain managed to squeeze in: a revolution; a civil war; the overthrow of the reigning monarch; the setting up of a provisional regime; a new constitution; a regency; a constitutional monarchy with an invited, foreign king; the assassination of a king-maker; an abdication; the establishment of a unitary republic (the country's first); then a federal republic (regarded as a continuation of the first); the break-up of the country into autonomous inter-warring 'cantons'; three *simultaneous* civil wars; a *coup d'état*; another regency (or dictatorship); and finally the restoration of the Bourbon monarchy whose overthrow had initiated the chaos (albeit in the form of a new king, Alfonso XII). Astonishingly, the period turned out to be the last hurrah of the roller-coaster ride of the nineteenth century as it was followed by twenty-five years of peace and stability, ushered in not least by collective exhaustion after so much infighting and disorder.

The revolution of 1868 which sparked the turbulence could well have gone the way of the many hundreds of *pronunciamientos* which preceded it. But the shift in Spanish society played a decisive factor: ordinary people, who only recently had put a brake on reformist-driven military coup attempts, now became more radicalised, angered by the drop in their own standards of living, fed up with a corrupt ruling class, and buoyed by the new political ideas arriving from the rest of Europe. To the cries of *Abajo la Isabelona, fondona y golfona* ('Down with big-arsed, sex-mad Isabella the Fat'), they rallied to the cause of the rebellious generals. A brief civil war ensued in which Isabella's loyal troops received a bloody nose outside Cordoba at the hands of one of her majesty's former lovers, General Serrano. The queen herself, spending the summer months in San Sebastián on her doctor's orders, realised the game was up and slipped across the nearby border into French exile (she died in Paris in 1904). The Bourbon dynasty, brought in amid the violence of the War of Spanish Succession in the early eighteenth century, appeared to have ended.

Spain, however, had a problem: after so many, mostly failed, attempts over previous decades, a *pronunciamiento* had now finally brought about a quite spectacular result. Which meant that those who had been calling for change and reform now found themselves in the position of having to follow their words with deeds. Unfortunately for Spain, they were not up to the job. The country needed urgent answers to the questions that had dogged it for so many centuries: what was it? What kind of a country did it want to be? There were a multitude of possibilities, none of them with a clear majority of support. Over the next few years a number of them would be tried out on a suck-it-and-see basis. All of them failed. And in the meantime the country resorted to its default setting when the political centre crumbled – of breaking up into its multiple parts.

In the absence of any better ideas, the first step was the creation of a provisional government by supporters of a constitutional monarchy. They drew up a new magna carta in 1869 introducing reforms such as universal suffrage for men, and freedom of press and worship. They also made first mention in an official state document of the 'Spanish nation' but, curiously, declared that the country was a hereditary monarchy. Given that they had just kicked out the ruling, hereditary dynasty, this gave them a problem. The proposed solution was to shop around for a new king. And so began an absurd, Pirandello-style drama of subjects in search of a sovereign. The spectacle was made all the more poignant by the fact that no European prince wanted to touch Spain with a barge-pole, not surprisingly given its recent history. Eventually the prime mover behind the idea, General Prim, found a willing victim in the shape of Prince Amadeo, Duke of Aosta, who agreed to take the crown. It appeared the charade could come to a close. But on the very day that the hapless duke arrived to be declared King Amadeo I of Spain, Prim, his one and only supporter, was assassinated. The rest of the political class made no bones about the fact that they didn't welcome the newcomer, who was immediately isolated. The poor man struggled on for a couple of years, surviving assassination attempts on his own person all the while, only finally to abdicate in 1872, unable to make headway or any sense of the chaos which he had inherited. 'I don't understand anything,' he declared. 'This is a madhouse.'

In his farewell speech he went further: 'Spain lives in constant infighting . . . Those who perpetuate and worsen the ills of the nation with the sword, the pen or with words are all Spanish.'

He left for Lisbon, eventually returning to his home town of Turin, where he died in 1890 aged forty-four.[1]

With no king, the logical step was for Spain to declare itself a republic, which it duly did in February 1873. It was a farce from the beginning, as no one could agree what kind of a republic it should be, not least because most of the deputies in parliament who voted it in were actually monarchists . . . The eleven months of its existence saw the coming and going of four presidents, none of whom could bring order to the further chaos into which the country was descending. Things got worse when one of them, Francesc Pi y Margall, who managed to hang on to power for a staggering thirty-seven days, suggested that Spain should be a federal republic, with power flowing from the bottom upwards. According to his political model, families joined to form communities, communities to form 'cantons', cantons to form provinces, provinces regions, and regions combined to form a nation. Federalism, in his view, would serve to unite the country. Curiously, Pi y Margall was a historian, which makes you wonder how he thought the plan could possibly work, given Spain's track record. Not surprisingly, the federal model only pushed an already crumbling state into anarchy, with the establishment of thirty-two cantons around the country centred on major towns and cities, all of them autonomous and beyond central control. The *taifas* of the Moorish period were back. And just as in the past, they immediately started fighting amongst themselves: Jaén declared war on neighbouring Granada; Utrera went to war with Seville; Coria was at war with Cáceres; and the most belligerent and successful of all

---

1 Brief, ill-fated reigns became something of a family speciality when Amadeo's grandson held the throne of Croatia for, again, just two years from 1941 to 1943 as Tomislav II, a puppet monarch of a kingdom invented by Hitler and Mussolini.

the cantons, Cartagena (which had its own flag and currency), went to war with none other than Madrid itself in a five-month-long struggle which even saw a battle at sea! If that wasn't bad enough, the third and final Carlist War was simultaneously under way in the north of Spain, while civil war had broken out in the country's last important colony, Cuba.

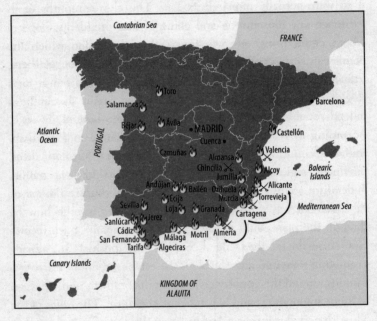

The chaos of the Cantons

Things were at their lowest ebb, but the chaos still had some life in it yet. In January 1874 General Pavía rode on horseback into the parliament building and staged a coup. Not wanting power himself, he handed it over to General Serrano (Queen Isabella's former lover who defeated the royalist forces in 1868). Serrano ruled as dictator until Christmas that year when he was himself overthrown by another general, Martínez Campos, who brought an end to the years of political experimentation by restoring the Bourbon monarchy. Isabella II's son, Alfonso XII, was asked to take command. He did so, and the whole of Spain gave out a long sigh of relief. Peace and stability were restored. The generals put away their swords. Party politics took centre stage, alternating power between reformists and moderates like clockwork for the next few decades.

Exhausted, Spain as a whole basked in its new-found serenity. Perhaps it could exist, in fact, as a peaceful, harmonious country, free from bloodshed and civil conflict. And for a while it seemed that it might. The new constitutional monarchy appeared to function, and in time the country began to prosper.

But before too long, events were to occur which would shake the new regime, events which would bring an end, as in the past, to the brief pause in internal fighting. Soon Spain would be pitted once more against Spain. The greatest civil war of them all was just over the horizon.

PART FIVE

BEFORE

THE ROAD TO A
SECOND REPUBLIC

The Bourbon monarchy was restored, republicanism was buried, regionalist dreams were in abeyance . . . For a full
quarter-century from 1874, Spain knew only peace and prosperity
and political stability. As if by magic, all the convulsions of the past
vanished in a puff of smoke. Yet it was a charade, a game most
agreed to play through sheer exhaustion after the high drama of
the previous six years. The architect of this oasis of calm was a man
called Cánovas de Castillo, commonly regarded as the ablest politician Spain has ever produced. Cánovas was the driving force
behind the new constitutional monarchy and installed a bi-party
system along the British model; he led the conservatives himself,
and found an obliging opponent to head the liberals in the shape of
a politician of almost equal skill named Sagasta. These two men
effectively shared power until the end of the century, their parties
alternating in office in mechanical fashion, and always mutually
respectful of each other's decisions and achievements. And,

amazingly, the system worked. But it could not last indefinitely for the simple reason that it was a sham. The 'elections' in which one or the other party 'won' the popular vote were rigged, specifically designed to ensure that the swing should continue to operate. The idea that the government in any way enjoyed democratic support was a joke, not least because, in addition, any parties that didn't support the system were automatically banned from taking part. Worker groups such as the union movement and the anarchists, or regional parties such as the ones developing in Catalonia, the Basque Country and elsewhere, had no voice. Which meant their activism was consequently clandestine and increasingly radicalised.

Nonetheless, things continued at their gentler pace, with the young Alfonso XII as titular head of state. Even the shock of the king's death at the age of twenty-eight in 1885 (from tuberculosis) was skilfully sailed through, and his widow, María Cristina – a Habsburg, no less, and daughter of the Archduke of Austria – took over as regent. She was pregnant at the time, and to the delight of all, later gave birth to a son, a boy who, from the very first breath he took, was king of Spain, Alfonso XIII. María Cristina continued at the helm while her offspring grew up, strictly following the last piece of advice given by her dying husband: 'Cristinita, you know what to do: Cánovas to Sagasta, and Sagasta to Cánovas. And don't shag about!' (¡Guarda el coño!) For her scrupulous morals she became known as Doña Virtudes ('Mrs Virtue'), and proved a steady hand on the tiller for the next twenty years.

And then everything began to fall apart.

The first blow came in 1898 in an event which became known simply as The Disaster. For a while the US had been arming and supporting rebels in the Spanish colony of Cuba. When the USS *Maine* blew up in Havana harbour, killing over two hundred men on board, passions were already running so high that war between the two countries became inevitable.[1]

The resulting conflict was a huge embarrassment for the Spanish in which their naval and land-based forces were rapidly outclassed and outmanoeuvred by a virile new country testing its strength on the international stage. The Spanish military suffered combined losses over the period of some sixty thousand men, and in the peace agreement that followed, in December 1898, the once great empire on which 'the sun never set' (the British later copied the phrase) was reduced to nothing: Spain's last overseas territories were lost, with the Philippines, Puerto Rico and the jewel in the crown, Cuba, all passing into American hands. (A band of Spanish soldiers held out in a besieged church in the Philippines until June 1899, waiting for a relief that never came; when they finally surrendered they were hailed by their opponents for their bravery and tenacity.)

There is, of course, an irony in the fact that an empire which was built on the discovery of America should be dealt its death blow by a son of the new continent, Spain's Uranus defeated by the USA's Zeus. And a poetic justice in an accidental empire (no one was expecting to find a whole new world across the Atlantic) brought low by another accident, in the shape of the *Maine*'s sinking. But the reaction within Spain to the news was anything but sanguine. Final loss of empire came as a huge blow and led to several years' 'post-colonial' soul-searching and introspection to try to explain how such a terrible state of affairs could have come about. It in turn gave birth to a generation of writers and intellectuals

---

1 Recent historical research suggests the Spanish had nothing to do with the sinking of the ship, which went down because of an accident on board: at the time, most of the ship's officers were busy enjoying the fleshpots and other delights of the Cuban capital while their vessel was heading to the deep.

known as the *Generación del '98*, people who sought to identify the source of the country's woes in everything from rampant corruption to social inequality, or historical anomalies (from a Euro-centric perspective) such as the Moorish period of the country's past.

El Desastre also woke other forces into action, however, and eventually brought the stable, alternating bi-party system to an end: the Cánovas–Sagasta duopoly was mortally wounded, not least because – in an event which curiously augured what was about to happen to the country as a whole – Cánovas had been assassinated the year before by an anarchist. The cry went up for a real democracy, with new republicans and revolutionary worker movements demanding a role. In addition, Basque and Catalan industrialists, who had had important interests in the now lost colonies (Bacardi rum was a Catalan concern) turned away from a central state which, in their eyes, was incapable of defending their markets, and started to move towards the respective burgeoning independence groups in their regions.

And into the middle of all this, in 1902, stepped Alfonso XIII, declared by the government to have come of age and now able to reign as king. He was sixteen.

Alfonso was a spoilt brat, mollycoddled by a mother and aunt who constantly reminded him that he was king and hence above the law and able to satisfy his every whim and desire.[2] The new king was also physically weak and emotionally dependent on his mother. In fact his eventual downfall and capitulation in 1931 might be explained in part by his mother's death two years earlier, leaving Alfonso alone and depressed, unable to cope with affairs of state. Like his grandmother Isabella II, he liked sleeping around,

---

2 Spain's equivalent of the tooth fairy, *el Ratoncito Pérez*, was first dreamt up by a palace priest to explain how milk teeth could possibly fall out of the royal head.

having dozens of mistresses and even a private collection of porn films made specially for him by the Count of Ramanones (a prime minister on several occasions). In 1905 he married Queen Victoria's favourite granddaughter, Victoria Eugenie, who duly converted to Catholicism and brought with her the same family-bred haemophilia of the Battenbergs which so blighted the son of Tsar Nicolas II. Two of Victoria Eugenie's sons would inherit the disease.

Just as the arrival of Alfonso XII in 1874 had ushered in a new era for Spain, so did his son's. But not in a good way. Despite being head of state of a constitutional monarchy, Alfonso XIII arrived at the first meeting of his council of ministers only to put his feet on the table and start ordering everyone about like a tinpot dictator. That someone so lacking in political skills should take command at such a moment could hardly have been worse timed, for in the wake of the loss of empire, Spain was facing many more problems.

Now that the gloves were off politically, infighting and backstabbing became the norm, and instead of regularly alternating governments, the country reverted to short-lived and often ineffectual administrations coming and going in chaotic fashion, not least because rather than remaining aloof, the king got involved in the fight. In the first four years of his reign, eleven different governments were sworn in.

Meanwhile, in order to soothe her wounded imperial pride, Spain took control of northern Morocco as a kind of mini-empire meant to boost its role on the world stage. The problem was that the locals, Riffian mountain people, were anything but docile, taking umbrage at the idea that *anyone*, let alone the Spanish, should order them about. Using guerrilla tactics which the Spanish themselves had so successfully employed against Napoleon a hundred years before, they engaged the invaders in painful attritional warfare which turned into a long-running and very bloody sore. The violence escalated on several occasions and in time Spain's African territory would have a game-changing role in the Spanish Civil War. But the first serious sign that the country's Moroccan entanglement wasn't quite the adventure originally envisaged came in 1909 with what became known as the 'Tragic Week'. After suffering heavy defeat at the hands of the Moroccan 'irregulars', the Spanish government called up forty thousand young men to fill the army's numbers. They were nothing more than cannon fodder, sons of poorer families who couldn't pay the several thousand pesetas that the wealthier handed over to remove their own children from the draft. In Barcelona a crowd bidding farewell to a troopship grew restless and events quickly turned into a full-scale insurrection. Several churches were burnt down in the resulting clashes, with priests seen as defenders of the ruling classes. The police and military responded aggressively, arresting over a thousand people and condemning seventeen to death. Of these, five were eventually executed, including the anarchist thinker and activist Francisco Ferrer. Such was the national and international outcry over the move, however, that Alfonso panicked and sacked his prime minister, installing yet another new government.

'Tragic Week' was over, but was a signal of more to come, both in Morocco and at home, particularly in Barcelona. Spain remained neutral throughout the First World War, and her industries – Catalan textiles, Basque iron and Asturian coal – thrived as they happily did business with both the Allies and Central Powers. But the consequent boom brought higher prices and more demands from worker groups for improved labour rights and higher pay. The year 1917, so crucial in Russia, came close to bringing about a similar outcome in Spain when street violence broke out and a 'revolutionary strike' was called in which up to two hundred people were killed. In the crackdown many leaders were arrested and sentenced to death, although this time their penalties were commuted. Among them was union leader Francisco Largo Caballero, later a Socialist prime minister during the Civil War.

More violence followed, however, with Barcelona at the epicentre. For two or three years gunmen (*pistoleros*) engaged in shootouts between worker groups and big business in which up to one hundred and fifty people were killed. More strikes were called; further assassinations took place: prime minister Eduardo Dato was gunned down by anarchists in Madrid in 1921. Later that year came another 'Disaster', the massacre of thirteen thousand Spanish soldiers by Moroccans at Annual. It was another huge blow for Spanish morale, and added to the sense of a country on the brink.

The mood was summed up by playwright and leading member of the *Generación del '98* Ramón María del Valle-Inclán in his play *Bohemian Lights*, published around the same time. As Cervantes, Velazquez and Goya had done before, Valle-Inclán placed a mirror before his audience, this time in his depiction of the last night on earth of an ailing poet called Max Estrella. Slowly going blind from syphilis, and in despair at the decline of his country, Estrella eventually commits suicide after witnessing the shooting by police of a Catalan revolutionary. Yet Valle-Inclán's mirror is not the simple glass of his predecessors: in Goya's vision it was already becoming stained; now in the twentieth century the faithfulness of the mirror itself came into question. In central Madrid was a bar which had placed convex and concave mirrors in its windows to attract visitors, who would then stand in the street and stare at the deformed images of themselves. This warped looking glass formed the basis of Valle-Inclán's new perspective, in it finding a reflection of Spain as nothing more than 'a deformation of European civilisation'. There was, in fact, no hope for the country. Estrella – Valle-Inclán's incarnation of Santiago the Apostle, the third face of the country's patron saint – looked into the future and saw only darkness. And his response was to take his own life.

And then, on cue, the old patterns reasserted themselves. In September 1923 there was a military coup, the constitution was suspended, and a dictatorship set up. The new strongman was a general by the name of Miguel Primo de Rivera.

A LITTLE DICTATORSHIP

I t's often forgotten that Spain in the twentieth century saw two dictatorships, not one. The first, that of Primo de Rivera, was short, lasting just six years, but it re-established a pattern which would have huge repercussions for the years to follow: the military were back in politics.

The coup was planned by a group of army officers involved in Morocco, soldiers who were known as *Africanistas* for their time spent on the other side of the Strait. This was now Spain's only overseas territory, and the sole arena in which ambitious men could see frontline service and accelerate their rise through the ranks. *Africanistas* would henceforth play a large role in Spanish political life.

Primo de Rivera's coup was welcomed by many as a necessary step to save the country from collapse. Industrialists, landowners, the Church, the middle classes, and the rest of the armed forces saw in the new dictatorship a way of halting a proletarian revolution, casting the anarchists as the principal villain of the piece. The Socialists of the PSOE party and UGT trade union remained neutral, fearing the anarchists almost as much as everyone else (the Spanish Communist Party at this point was minuscule). But importantly, Alfonso XIII hailed Primo de Rivera as 'my Mussolini', *il Duce* having risen to power in Rome less than a year before.

Miguel Primo de Rivera, however, was no firebrand or dramatic orator in the style of the Italian, nor did he appear to have any clear political ideas. Born into an aristocratic, landowning family from Jerez, he was by now in his fifties and generally regarded as a *vividor*, someone who enjoys carnal and worldly pleasures to the full. His time in power would alternate between his working long hours for stretches of time, only to disappear for some R&R in the bars and brothels of the capital, often seen wandering the streets in the early hours in an opera cape, heading back to his office where he would issue drunken communiqués which had to be rescinded the following morning.

Primo de Rivera is generally viewed unfavourably by history, not least for his uncanny ability to lose all his friends. Gradually, as his mandate extended beyond the initial ninety days that it was meant to last, his supporters abandoned his cause, for example wealthier Spaniards enraged by his new taxes on them to fund a public works programme. When that finance scheme proved unworkable, the dictator turned to raising money through public loans, which caused high inflation and led to a devaluation of the peseta.

Yet Primo de Rivera needs to be given some credit, if only for bringing to an end the long-running bloody rebellion in Morocco. He relieved inept commanders of their positions and struck a deal with the French to launch a joint campaign against Abd el-Krim and his Riffian fighters. The result was the amphibious landing at Alhucemas in 1925, regarded as the first assault in military history in which naval and air forces were combined. Armoured cars were landed on the beach in another military first, while thirteen thousand Spanish soldiers pushed into enemy territory, eventually defeating the rebels and bringing the long-standing war to an end. Almost twenty years later, Allied commanders preparing for the Normandy campaign of 1944 studied the Moroccan landings as part of their preparations.

Alhucemas was also where a new body within the Spanish military, the Legión, cut its teeth. Modelled on the French Foreign Legion and inspired by slightly dubious concepts about Japanese Bushido and the 'Samurai code', it was led by a one-eyed maniac called General Millán Astray, who told his men that he expected them to die in battle, and coined the curiously paradoxical (and somehow quintessentially Spanish) phrase 'Long live death!' (*¡Viva la muerte!*) His second in command was a young major rising very quickly through the ranks, a Galician called Francisco Franco.

From a centralist and law-and-order point of view, Primo de Rivera also put a lid on the street violence which was blighting Barcelona, as well as on Catalan independence moves. Singing of the Catalan 'anthem', *Els segadors* (a homage to the Catalan independence group of the seventeenth century) was banned, as was the raising of the Catalan flag. And by declaring a state of war, military rule was imposed and street fighting curtailed. When it surfaced again, for example with the murder of Barcelona's official executioner, two hundred people were arrested, the anarchist newspaper *Solidaridad Obrera* was closed down and all anarchist union offices forcibly shut.

In addition, Primo de Rivera established state-controlled companies such as Telefónica (still in existence), the oil and petrol concern Campsa, and the Tabacalera. Yet these achievements were not enough to make him loved by any group within society, and slowly his power waned. Rising inflation and the growing effects of the Wall Street Crash on the economy didn't help. Nor did his insistence on politicising the military, which alienated many of his fellow officers. In 1926 disgruntled generals, including the captain-general of the army and leading politicians, organised a coup attempt, La Sanjuanada, which was only foiled because Alfonso XIII learned about it and opted for the time being to stick with the dictator he already knew. Yet by 1930 Primo de Rivera saw clearly that he had the support neither of the rest of the army nor of the king. Not waiting to be overthrown, he resigned at the end of January that year and removed himself to a Paris hotel where, less than two months later, he died from diabetes.

Alfonso's response was to name a new dictator, General Berenguer, who brought in what was viewed as a 'softer' dictatorship (a *dictablanda*, in the Spanish pun, as opposed to a *dictadura*, *dura* meaning 'hard', and *blanda*, 'soft'). But too much damage had already been done. The monarchy was severely damaged by Alfonso's association with Primo de Rivera. Perhaps if the king had supported the 1926 coup he might have saved himself, but by now many in the country, most importantly in the cities and large towns, were tired with Alfonso just as their predecessors had been with his grandmother Isabella in the 1860s. A group of politicians from both Left and Right signed an agreement to overthrow the monarchy and try for a republic again. Their leader, Niceto Alcalá-Zamora, was charged with making contact with like-minded military officers to stage another coup.

In the end, however, and unusually for Spain, on this occasion violence wasn't needed to bring about change. When municipal elections of the spring of 1931 showed a clear victory for anti-monarchy parties in the cities (votes from the rural areas took longer to count) spontaneous declarations of a new Spanish republic began to sweep across the country. Seeing how things were moving, Alfonso decided to follow Primo de Rivera's example and scuttled off before anyone could overthrow him. Leaving his wife and children behind to find a different route out of the country, he hurried to Cartagena, from where a boat took him to Marseille. Landing on French soil, the deposed Bourbon king's first reaction was annoyance on learning that the city's brothels had already closed for the night.

Back in Spain, the Second Republic came into being on 14 April to great popular acclaim. The hated king was gone; the oligarchs and old regime had been swept from power. It was a new beginning, full of hope.

Yet the world economy was in collapse; Stalin ruled the Soviet Union, Mussolini Italy, and in Germany the Nazi Party was on the rise. Social unrest and political extremism were rocking Europe and much of the rest of the world. It was a less-than-auspicious time to be building a new state.

WHAT'S IN A REPUBLIC?

Historically speaking, the Second Republic is the prelude to the Spanish Civil War. How a person views the period is directly related to their perspective on the war which brought it to an end. Was the Republic good, or bad? Did it achieve anything, or was it a failure? Was it, in fact, doomed from the start (as hindsight can sometimes suggest), or could it have lasted? Did it sow the seeds of its own destruction, or was it an innocent victim of the forces which brought it down? Can we, indeed, even regard the Republic as an entity in itself, or was it never more than a very loose and temporary association of multiple groups and forces, most of which were pulling in mutually exclusive directions? The answers to these questions are entirely wrapped up with a person's views on the Civil War itself.

In 1876, when asked to define what a 'Spaniard' was for the drafting of the new constitution, Cánovas had artfully answered that a Spaniard was someone 'who could not be anything else'. It was a playful piece of sophistry which nonetheless highlighted the fact that Spain is both impossible to define and yet possessed of a powerful self-identity. But 'What is Spain?' and 'Who are the Spanish?' – these fundamental questions of national identity lay at the heart of most if not all the problems which beset the country. Which face of Santiago was the true one? Yet the problem was intractable because, as throughout its history, the one could never be divorced from the other, the Seeker and the Slayer were two sides of the same coin, aspects of the same collective self, no matter how much force and violence were employed in an attempt to settle the matter once and for all. Spain was about to repeat patterns of behaviour which had dominated its national life for many centuries. And as before, with consequences which would have a large impact on the international stage.

SECOND TIME
AROUND

The authoritarian years of Primo de Rivera's dictatorship had served a dual function of both provoking and partially restraining the many tensions within Spain at the time. The fall of Alfonso combined with the proclamation of the Second Republic was subsequently both a liberation as well as the opening of a Pandora's Box. In simplistic terms, the Republic finally fell because it failed to contain or channel the demons now freed and circling about unhindered. Whether that failure was its own fault, however, is the subject of ongoing and often heated debate.

Two developments at the very moment the Republic came into being demonstrate how explosive the situation was.

Firstly, in several cities Republican supporters celebrated the arrival of the new regime by burning down a number of churches. The Church was, not without reason, seen as part of the oppressive establishment along with the monarchy, landowners and others, who had done so much to prevent or restrict social progress over many centuries. And as such it was targeted. But to the surprise of many, these acts of vandalism were tolerated by the new government, and in a phrase which grew to haunt him, the then prime minister (and later president of the Republic during the Civil War) Manuel Azaña declared that 'all the religious buildings in Spain were not worth the life of a single Republican'. Anticlerical violence, in other words, was effectively given a green light by the government. Which, regardless of one's views of the Church at the time, did not send out good signals. In opposition to the usual pattern, a new regime had come into being without resort to violence, but within moments violence had resurfaced on the national stage.

Secondly, Catalan nationalism was reinvigorated. While spontaneous proclamations of a republic had been issued in towns and cities across Spain at the news of the 1931 municipal election results, in Barcelona the regional authorities had seized their chance and declared a Catalan Republic within an Iberian federation. For centralists, this was the nightmare scenario in which Spain could break apart (once more). At the time, the Catalans were persuaded to pull back in return for the promise of a statute of autonomy, which they accepted. But a clear statement of intention had been made which only served to make many in Spain nervous, and uncertain about the Republic. Over time, those uncertainties would grow, and when the Catalan statute went to parliament, in 1932, a new military coup was staged in an attempt to halt it. General Sanjurjo's attempt on power failed – in part thanks to a prostitute who had overheard the rebels' plans and passed information on to the police – but it demonstrated that the old patterns of behaviour remained, Republic or no.

But Catalan separatists and jumped-up generals weren't the only people threatening the new regime. Rural Spain was in crisis, with a shocking contrast in living standards and way of life which was practically indistinguishable from the Middle Ages.[1] Conditions were worst in Andalusia and Extremadura. During the 'Reconquest', Christian kings had tempted their vassals to join in (and help finance) the campaigns southwards through promises of tracts of captured lands. In the Crown of Aragon new territory had been divided a little more evenly, but in Castile great swathes of the landscape had fallen into the hands of a very few. And with the forced sale of Church and municipal lands in the nineteenth century, this situation had only worsened. The result was that in a country whose main economic activity was still, by a wide margin, agriculture, the vast majority of people in rural areas were illiterate peasants with very short life expectancy (well under forty), and with no assurance of any work thanks to the *jornalero* system of employing people on a day-by-day basis. Added to this was a peculiar absence of any spirit of *noblesse oblige*, so while country folk often went hungry, the owners on whose land they lived and worked – *los señoritos* – lived it up in the cities, ignoring the plight of their tenants and actively preventing them from scratching out a subsistence on unused fields. So bad were things getting that there were even claims that in some parts of the country, peasants were reduced to eating grass simply to stay alive.

It was during these early years of the Republic that the great Spanish film director, Luis Buñuel, made his short film *Land without Bread* after a friend agreed to finance it with money won from the National Lottery (the friend was later shot by the Francoists during the Civil War). Buñuel's powerful images of the

---

1 As my own father-in-law, an orange farmer from Valencia born in 1929, has told me, horse-drawn carts were an innovation at the time; his own father's generation had had to transport everything on mules and donkeys, with very short distances in modern terms taking up a whole day's travel or more.

peasants of the Las Hurdes area drinking water from puddles and living like animals were partly staged, but he used poetic licence to describe a truth about the Spanish countryside at the time: conditions really were horrific in certain areas.

Politically, the peasants of southern and south-western Spain felt unrepresented. But into this gap stepped the anarchists, who built one of their strongest power bases in the region.

No country in Western Europe proved to be such fertile ground for anarchist ideas as Spain. By the outbreak of the Civil War in 1936, membership of the CNT anarchist trade union was one and a half million, around double the socialist UGT. The anarchists were a long way from being a coherent group and embraced many tendencies, from anarcho-syndicalism (the CNT) to espousers of violent anarchist revolution (the FAI), to more intellectual types promoting a libertarian reform programme of education, vegetarianism and even anarcho-nudism as solutions to society's ills. Anarchism chimed both with a healthy disrespect of authority in Spanish culture, and with a sense that if things were ever going to change there would have to be a complete overhaul of the system. Communism, with its Church-like emphasis on discipline and authority, never caught on – until, that is, the outbreak of the Civil War. Anarchism, with its ideas of spontaneity, equality, and heroic and violent action to bring about radical change, was far more attractive on a mass scale.

Anarchists and many left-leaning and even centralist republicans shared many ideas when it came to social reform. Problems arose from the scale and speed of those reforms, however, and by the simple fact that anarchists wanted to bring down the entire workings of the State. They had claimed the lives of more than one prime minister, and the Barcelona shoot-outs they engaged in had been a major contributing factor in Primo de Rivera's coup: the anarchists were destabilisers by definition and as much a threat to the Republic as the monarchists and other conservatives determined to smother it from the start.

So when anarchist groups in the countryside started occupying unused rural land owned by wealthy landowners, alarms went off not only among the farmers whose fields were being forcibly expropriated, but among the liberals in government, who were pursuing a slower pace of reform. The anarchists posed a double threat, both through their own actions and as a potential trigger for a conservative backlash.

Things came to a head in an incident near Jerez at a small town called Casas Viejas. After an anarchist-inspired land takeover, the police went in hard, and in a subsequent shoot-out several locals were killed. It caused a scandal and the Socialists of the PSOE, who until then had been propping up the liberal republicans in power, pulled their support, causing the government to fall. Elections soon followed and the results brought in right-wing parties with very different ideas about social change.

The Second Republic was still alive, but it was about to be very seriously tested.

ABOUT TURN

Much of the energy bound up in the creation of the Second Republic was centred on hope. After the decline of empire, and with a feeling of being left behind by its European neighbours, many wanted Spain finally to take leaps forward and become a democratic and progressive state, free of the shackles of the past. This desire for reform can be seen in the mass school-building programme begun at the time, in which around twenty thousand new schools were set up in rural areas, filling a gap left by the Church in the nineteenth century and in many cases bringing education to parts of the country for the first time. A large number of these structures can still be seen dotting the landscape today, easily recognised because they are virtually identical, although few, if any, are now used for their original purpose.

A similar sentiment led to the establishment of *La Barraca*, a travelling theatre group which crossed the countryside bringing classic Spanish plays by writers such as Calderón de la Barca and Lope de Vega to largely illiterate backwaters. Far-right groups attacked the troupe as a propaganda tool for the Republican government, and even sabotaged some of its performances, but *La Barraca* was a powerful symbol both domestically and internationally of the new Spanish government's intentions. One of the group's originators and early directors was poet and playwright Federico García Lorca.

Another reform came with advances in women's rights. Equality of the sexes was recognised in the constitution, a liberal divorce law was passed, and women over the age of twenty-three got the vote. But this last step backfired. At the time several leading female politicians argued against it, insisting that Spanish women would need to perceive the benefits of the Republic before being allowed a say on who governed. In the elections of 1933 they were proved right: nuns and other religiously minded, conservative female voters appeared to tip the balance against the parties who had emancipated them, bringing in right-wing groups who quickly put a brake on the new reforms (the anarchists' decision not to vote, as well as divisions between Socialists and Republicans, also contributed to the change in government).

The result was what became known as the 'black biennial' by the Left (or the 'rectifying biennial' by its supporters), a period of two years in which a coalition of parties that defined itself as 'anti-Marxist' formed one short-lived government after another. And the Republic came under enormous strain not least because the party with the largest number of seats was authoritarian, anti-democratic and anti-republican. The CEDA was a coalition of right-wing groups established by its leader, José María Gil-Robles, after a visit to Germany during the early months of Nazi rule there. Inspired by what he saw at a Nuremberg rally, Gil-Robles returned to Spain and decided to follow Hitler's example of using the ballot box as a Trojan Horse to bring down democracy and set up a totalitarian regime. He styled himself *el jefe* ('the boss') as a Spanish equivalent of *führer* or Mussolini's *duce*, and spoke of a 'March on Madrid' to take power. The voice of religious conservative authoritarianism – which had existed in Spain over centuries in various guises, from the Almohads to the Inquisitors – was now expressed through the CEDA.

Gil-Robles, however, never realised his ambition of becoming dictator of Spain. Despite having the largest number of seats in parliament, he fell far short of a majority and baulked at the idea of sharing power. While for the Republic, to have given control of government to a party which was overtly intent on bringing down democracy would have been an act of suicide. So right and centre-right parties cobbled together coalitions which staggered along in highly unstable fashion. It was unsustainable, and the explosion came in October 1934.

The October Revolution is one of the most divisive moments in Spanish history, second only to the Civil War itself. And just as with the Second Republic, views on it are entirely tied up with opinions on the events of subsequent years. In fact, in many ways it was a dress rehearsal for the full-scale conflict which broke out less than two years later.

On 4 October, a new government was announced which included three CEDA ministers for the first time. Giving power to a party opposed to the Republic was unacceptable to Socialists and other left-wingers, who immediately declared a 'revolutionary strike' in response. The hope was that ordinary soldiers would join their 'brother workers' in an insurrection which would overthrow the new government. But the authorities declared a state of war and in just a few days managed to crush the uprising. Leading opposition politicians (including former prime minister Azaña, who was not involved), were thrown in jail, as well as the *president* of the Catalan region, Lluis Companys who, following a predictable pattern, had taken advantage of the chaos to declare another independent Catalan republic (while simultaneously ensuring no weapons fell into the hands of the revolutionaries whose movement he was jumping on the back of).

The only part of the country where the revolution enjoyed any success was in the mining area of Asturias, the one region where the Anarchists had joined what was a largely Socialist-organised rebellion. Here the strikers held out for almost two weeks in what became a mini civil war. In Madrid, the government called in one of the army's up-and-coming stars, Franco, now a general, who ordered in his fiercest troops – Legionaries and *Regulares* from Spanish Morocco – to crush the rebels. The result was a bloodbath in which over a thousand people died and two thousand were wounded. On 18 October, the strikers surrendered and the revolution came to an end.

October 1934 marks a 'before' and 'after' in the Second Republic. Since General Sanjurjo's coup attempt in 1932 (and arguably even before), it had been evident that conservatives were prepared to use violence to defend their vision of Spain, traditional, united and dominated by the Church. But now Socialists and other left-wingers had shown their hand and declared that they, too, would use violent means. Their justification was that it was *in defence* of the Republic, but the effect was the same: the creation of an abyss of fear and mistrust within the political sphere which would only worsen. Many large and mutually antagonistic groups were now advocating the use of arms for political advantage, not only Anarchists and right-wing generals, but the Socialist movement and also the far-Right, which had a new voice, even more extreme than the CEDA, in the shape of the Falangist party, inspired by Mussolini's Fascists and led by José Antonio Primo de Rivero, son of the former dictator. At a time when European countries were struggling with radicalism on all sides, the chances of a peaceful future were waning. Each 'Spain' saw the threat of its own annihilation in the shape of the 'other Spain': Santiago the Slayer was roused once again into action.

A further step towards the darkness came with Franco's use of colonial troops against Spanish civilians. The Legionarios were members of a death cult which glorified brutality; running a close second were the Regulares, mostly Moroccan fighters who had been given their own regiment in the Spanish army. Both would become highly effective frontline troops in the Civil War, when they would again be deployed against untrained militias. But by then any taboo against their use on the Spanish mainland against ordinary people had already been broken.

The CEDA used the October Revolution to its advantage, pressing over the following months for more cabinet members, which it got. Corruption scandals weakened the centre-right coalition governments, however, and when in late 1935 Gil-Robles, now minister of war, demanded to be made prime minister, the President of the Republic refused. Gil-Robles had placed like-minded generals in the top jobs in the military, and one of them, General Fanjul, offered to stage a coup on his behalf. Gil-Robles declined, aware that there still wasn't enough support for his cause, but already the Republic was beginning to strain under pressure. For months, other far-right groups had been talking to Mussolini, who had given his support for a future insurrection.

In early 1936, the last of the *bienio negro* cabinets fell and a new general election was called. It would bring in a new left-wing coalition of Socialists and Republicans, united once more, and with the tacit support of the Anarchists in return for the release of their incarcerated comrades.

For a moment it seemed as if the Spanish Republic might survive. Behind the scenes, however, plots to bring it down went into full operation.

PRELUDE

The Spanish Civil War started when, in July 1936, a conservative, military coup against the democratically elected government failed to take control of the entire country, splitting the nation in two and provoking a bloody conflict which lasted almost three years.

Variations on this statement have become the new orthodoxy, and while essentially true, it is also only partially true in its implication that left-wing republicans were somehow innocent victims of a one-way act of aggression. The October Revolution of 1934 demonstrated that the Socialists were as prepared to use violence for their own ends as were reactionary elements in the armed forces, or the Anarchists. Huge numbers of Spaniards – probably the majority – were getting on with their lives, at one remove from the politics of black-and-white thinking taking hold around them. That the situation was more nuanced for many is hinted at by the curious friendship which developed shortly before the war between the Falangist leader José Antonio and the poet García Lorca. But equally the fact that these two men felt a need to keep their meetings secret suggests how politically sensitive even social contacts across the political divide were becoming.[1] By 1936, years of bubbling tensions and outbreaks of violence meant that one Spain could barely look the other in the eye, so deep was the mutual hatred becoming. Each saw in the other the embodiment of their darkest fear: for one side, the spectre of a fascist-style takeover and dictatorship; for the other, a Soviet-style revolution.

The elections of early 1936 saw defeat for the Right and returned the centre-left parties and Socialists who had governed during the first two years of the Republic. As the results came in on the night of the polls, elements within the outgoing conservative government considered staging a coup to hold on to power. The military chief of staff, General Franco, was consulted, but turned the opportunity down: memories of the failed military coup of 1932 were still fresh and he thought there would not be enough support across the country to ensure success.

But as the new government, labelled the Popular Front, came into office, other generals and their supporters got to work on new plans for a rebellion. By the early summer, these were coming to fruition. The preceding months had seen an escalation of violence, with José Antonio's Falangists engaged in an increasing number of gun battles with their opponents, both Anarchist and Socialist. (The Spanish Communist Party at this stage was still very small, but organised and disciplined and already preparing the ground for the huge rise in its popularity and power once the war started.) Against a backdrop of more strikes and attacks on opponents' buildings and headquarters, the street violence escalated in the

---

1 Albeit Lorca's politics were complex; he insisted he was apolitical, and had friends of many persuasions. He would be murdered by right-wing rebels in his home town of Granada during the early days of the conflict.

middle of July when right-wing gunmen murdered a Socialist policeman in the centre of Madrid. Later that night, colleagues of the dead officer murdered a leading right-wing politician, Calvo Sotelo, in reprisal. It was a Rubicon, both sides feeling that the other had crossed a line. In effect, the first shots of the Civil War had been fired.

Calvo Sotelo's murder was of crucial historical importance because it convinced Franco, living in semi-exile in the Canaries as a perceived threat to the Popular Front government, that he should join the military coup which his colleagues had been planning for several months. Until that moment he had vacillated, but the assassination convinced many on either side that war was now inevitable. On 17 July the rebellion began when army officers took control of the city of Melilla in Spanish Morocco. The next day Franco landed at Tétouan, where he took control of the Army of Africa and secured the colony for the uprising.[2] The insurgents had the best military formations under their control, the Legión and the Regulares.

And now the Spanish Civil War had begun.

---

2 Not least through an agreement with local Moroccan leaders not to interfere too much in their affairs: for years Spanish Morocco enjoyed liberties, such as relative press freedom, which were absent in Franco's Spain.

DURING

NO ONE'S SPAIN

With its twentieth-century Civil War, Spain once again plays its traditional role of harbinger of things to come elsewhere. The fighting which was to scar the country for two and a half years acted as an antechamber for the new World War which would follow within months of its ending. Blitzkrieg techniques, mass aerial bombardments of civilians (most famously at Guernica), the use of revolutionary German Stuka and Messerschmitt Bf 109 planes, of Soviet T-26 tanks, and a military clash based on political ideology, were all prefigured on Spanish soil. Not only that: Hitler's intervention in the Civil War laid bare his aggressive intentions for all to see, striking a blow to the Appeasement policy adopted by Prime Ministers Baldwin and Chamberlain, and eventually paving the way for Britain to 'stand alone' against the Third Reich by May 1940. And although the Nazis and the Soviets supported opposing sides during the Civil War, the fact that Britain and France failed to come to the Republicans' aid during the conflict eventually distanced Moscow from London and Paris (Stalin had been trying to forge an alliance with the liberal democracies), paving the way for the Nazi–Soviet Pact of August 1936, which was the immediate trigger for the German invasion of Poland.

The parallels and precedents for the Second World War are striking enough, but the Civil War even gives a taste for the Cold War that followed, being, in one sense, a proxy war manipulated by world powers unwilling to engage in a direct fight themselves. In that way Spain's conflict also prefigures the Korean and Vietnamese wars, and the myriad battles between the Soviet Union and the West which continued long after 1945.

By that time, the country was again the 'backward' place it is more commonly seen as, remote, impoverished and isolated. But for a time, the eyes of the world (when not distracted by Edward VIII's marital complications) were focused on Spain, as if for a fleeting moment it was understood that what happened there would have important ramifications for what happened in the rest of Europe in the years to come. As left-wing propaganda posters coming out of Spain declared next to photos of dead babies and toddlers, 'If you tolerate this, your children will be next.'

Initially, the situation at the start of the war was very unclear. Franco met precious little resistance in Morocco, but on the Spanish mainland the uprising was less successful. The first days of the coup were chaotic, but it eventually emerged that the rebellion had taken control of Seville and part of Andalusia, as well as a swathe of territory in the north stretching from Saragossa to Galicia. The rebellion had failed, however, in most major cities, including Madrid, Barcelona, Valencia and Bilbao, centres of the country's industry and most of its wealth. This was less to do with any organised response on the part of the government, however, but thanks largely to spontaneous action by unions and other groups who managed to arm themselves and put a halt to the rebel takeover. The result was that in many areas which hadn't fallen to the coupists, social revolution broke out in which, for a time, the authority of central government was practically annihilated and armed militias were in charge. One Spain slipped back into an authoritarian, Catholic-dominated society in which reforms such as divorce and co-education were abolished (the Church didn't wait long to give the rebellion its blessing, dubbing it nothing less than a 'Crusade'), while the other revelled in near anarchy, embracing free love, collective property ownership and the abolition of money (in some areas), and decision-making by committee. What united the two Spains, however, was the unchecked violence and bloodletting which now broke out in both areas.

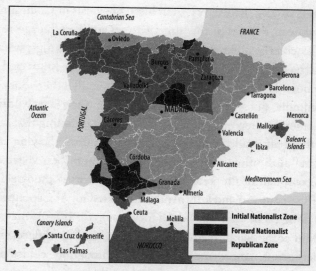

The first months of the Spanish Civil War

For the first few months of the war, thousands who found themselves on the wrong side of the new territorial divide were murdered. Within rebel-held areas, targets included unionists, known left-wingers and even schoolteachers, symbols of the educational reforms of the Second Republic. On the other side, priests and nuns in particular were singled out, but so were wealthy landowners or even men caught wearing 'bourgeois' clothes such as jackets and ties. (Such items of clothing soon disappeared from the streets, with blue workers' overalls becoming a kind of uniform and sign of solidarity with the proletariat.) In the Spain of the 'Nationalists' – as the rebels called themselves – Falangists and others would drag their ideological opponents out and shoot them, dumping their bodies in unmarked graves or by the side of the road. And in loyalist territory the story was practically the same, the men pulling the triggers calling themselves Anarchists, Socialists or Communists. Republican Madrid at this time was not unlike Chicago in the 1920s, with the different militia groups acting like gangs, roaming the streets in requisitioned cars in search of enemies and not infrequently getting into gunfights with each other. Bars and restaurants put up polite notices asking their newly armed customers to drop off their guns at the door, or failing that not to fire them off inside. Ironically, many of the films showing at the cinema at the time were gangster movies, and their vocabulary was co-opted for the new violent environment on the streets: to take someone out and kill them was referred to, Al Capone-style, as 'taking them for a ride' (*darle un paseo*).

Tens of thousands died in the bloodletting. But while the rebel leaders countenanced and encouraged it through the course of the war and beyond, within areas of Spain still nominally loyal to the

Republic politicians could only look on in horror, unable to curb or control the autonomous militia groups. It would take several months for something like central authority to be re-established, and for the violence to be curtailed.

But by then the damage internationally had already been done. It's possible that Britain and France would never have come to the aid of Spain's Popular Front government, fearful of its more left-leaning tendencies, but the violence which broke out – particularly against members of the Church – gave Baldwin's Conservative government a perfect excuse for not getting involved, still clinging to appeasement in an attempt to avoid a new European war. British embroilment in a Spanish fight between Left and Right was always going to be a very distant possibility. But denying weapons and support to 'bloodthirsty revolutionaries' was much easier than to a democratically elected government. France's own Popular Front leaders were more inclined to send materiel, but pulled back after pressure from London.

Republican Spain was on its own. The rebels, meanwhile, had enjoyed support from Mussolini even before the war began, and now Hitler, responding to a personal envoy from Franco, followed suit. Crucially, he agreed to fly Juncker transport planes to Spanish Morocco in order to airlift the Legionarios and Regulares over to Seville, from where they could be used to invade Republican territory.

Denied support from the liberal democracies, the Republic had only one European country it could turn to, the Soviet Union (Mexico supported it from the beginning, but could offer little in terms of arms). In Moscow, Stalin hesitated, but eventually decided, in exchange for 'looking after' Spain's huge gold reserves (the fourth-largest in the world at the time) to send over weaponry, including T-26 tanks and Polikarpov I-15 and I-16 planes. London and Paris may have wanted to limit the civil war to a local, purely Spanish affair, but by the end of the summer of 1936 it had escalated into a fully internationalised conflict.

Soviet aid for the Republic came not a moment too soon, arriving just as Franco's Army of Africa swept north from Seville up the western side of the country in a rapid and very bloody advance towards the capital. The Republic had no organised army to defend itself with, and militiamen armed with a few rifles were no match for professionals. In a few weeks Madrid itself was in Franco's sights. The war, it seemed, would soon be over; the Republican government fled to Valencia. But against all expectations – on either side – the capital didn't fall, saved by a combination of sheer good luck, a well-organised defence by the loyalist military commanders in charge, the lack of expertise on the part of Franco's troops in urban warfare, and the arrival in the nick of time of Soviet aid along with the International Brigades, several thousand anti-fascist volunteers from around the world.

What had looked to be a quick war would now turn into a much longer, and bloodier, affair.

EVERYONE'S SPAIN

Two factors ensured the defeat of the Republic in the Spanish Civil War: a lack of unity on its own side, and military inferiority. They were linked.

We talk about the 'Republic' during the war period as though it were a single identifiable thing, a coherent body which acted in a clearly directed fashion. Yet this is almost entirely wrong. Republican Spain was made up of a shattered spectrum of factions divided along political and regional lines whose only common feature was opposition to the military rebels trying to conquer the country. But that in itself was not enough.

It's true that leading politicians on the Republican side still held office, there was still a president and a prime minister and a cabinet. But in the revolutionary fervour of the first few weeks of the war, these figures effectively lost control to the various armed militias who now became the real authorities. From a Republican perspective, the first year of the conflict is in part the story of how centralising forces fought to wrest power back from these irregulars in an attempt to recreate a functioning state, while simultaneously defending themselves against a military insurrection. It was no easy task, not least because the biggest single group on the so-called Republican side, the Anarchists, didn't believe in the State to begin with. What's more, the various factions were frequently divided among themselves, so hard-line and moderate Socialists could hardly look each other in the eye, while the Anarchist movement turned in on itself when four leading members did the impossible and joined the government in late 1936.

The three main militia groups – Anarchists, Socialists and Communists – learned to live with each other for a while and to a degree, but generally only managed to put their differences to one side when the military rebels were on their doorstep. One example came in November 1936, when Franco's troops appeared to be on the verge of capturing Madrid. In an operation led by secret Moscow agents freshly arrived from the Soviet Union, Socialists and Communists grouped together to bus rebel prisoners away from the city centre, which was under their control, out to the surrounding countryside, dominated by the Anarchists. There, near a village called Paracuellos, the prisoners were shot dead and buried in unmarked graves in the single largest act of repression on the Republican side during the war – estimates vary, but as many as two thousand were murdered. But in a further example of how complicated political allegiances were, the massacres were only stopped when another Anarchist leader became the head of prisons and prevented any more *sacas*, as they were called, from taking place. Nominal political leaders, such as President Azaña, could only look on helplessly, meanwhile, and weep.

The political divide wasn't simply about power and fiefdoms, however. A fundamental divide lay at its heart. On the one hand, Anarchists and libertarian left-wingers embraced social revolution, the breakdown of an organised state, and rejected any form of authority. In a society in which everyone was equal, no one could tell anyone else what to do. This reached its logical conclusion even on the front lines, where a strict command structure was tossed aside in favour of soldiers holding committee meetings to decide whether or not to attack the enemy. Farcical though this may seem, it was taken very seriously by its adherents, who were sometimes more prepared to shoot those on their own 'side' who might take away their liberties than the enemy in the opposite trenches.

At the other end of the extreme were moderate Republicans who believed in basic concepts of law and order and a functioning, if liberal, state. They found new friends in the Communists.

In the 1930s, Stalin had two main obsessions, both of which would impact Spain: wiping out his perceived political opponents through 'purges'; and trying to forge alliances with the liberal democracies against Nazi Germany and Fascist Italy. To this end Communist groups outside the Soviet Union were told to lessen the revolutionary rhetoric and adopt a more 'bourgeois' appearance. Strict discipline and acceptance of authority became Communist watchwords. Far from allowing soldier committee meetings at the front, the Spanish Communists formed militia groups along traditional military lines with hierarchical command structures. Preaching a doctrine of order and unity, they quickly became attractive to many within the political class who had seen their power virtually disintegrate. What's more, their militia formations proved themselves quite capable in battle. And with the addition of Soviet, Communist, aid arriving from Moscow, the rise of the Spanish Communist Party became inevitable.

In their way, however, stood the Anarchists, staunchly opposed to any form of authoritarianism, whether from Left or Right.

Things came to a head in May 1937 in the events which George Orwell describes in *Homage to Catalonia*. Although pitched by some as an attempt to impose unity on the fractured Republic, nothing exposed its *lack* of unity more than the spectacle of 'a civil war within a civil war', with libertarians and authoritarians battling it out for control of Barcelona. In the end, the authoritarians won. The Anarchists went into serious decline, while Communist power increased.

Orwell, meanwhile, only just managed to escape Barcelona with his life. As a member of a non-Stalinist militia (the POUM), he was on the losing side. The left-wing repression he personally witnessed, however, had a powerful impact on him, providing the direct inspiration for his two most important books, *Animal Farm* and *1984*. Viewed in conjunction, the novels both explain the recent past and predict the future. Their impact and influence on Western literature and political thinking cannot be overstated. What's interesting is that, for a moment, in the shape of Orwell, Spain as Cassandra manages to escape her usual fate of having her visions of the future ignored. Orwell himself is not Spanish, he is not restricted by Cassandra's curse, and therefore he is listened to, so much so that his predictions become fully embedded in Western popular culture. It is entirely within the patterns of Spanish history, and its long-standing tendency of being ahead of its Western neighbours, that the future of a profoundly persecuting society was already developing within her borders. But the unheard prophetess had to whisper her secret warning into the ear of the foreigner, who could then smuggle her message out and repeat it in his own words, to a wider, and this time more attentive, audience.

Back in Spain, the political division described in *Homage to Catalonia* was not the only split to damage the Republican side.

True to form, the decline of central power led to a rise of regionalism. Some areas, such as the Basque Country, were barely part of the Republic even in name. The largely Catholic and socially conservative Basque people at the time had little in common with the free-love radicals charging around in Madrid and other cities. In fact, the one attractive feature of the Republic from a Basque point of view was its liberal ideas about regional autonomy, as opposed to the very strict centralism preached by the rebels. The gulf between the Basque Country and the rest of the Republic was intensified by its being cut off by a swathe of rebel-held territory, and yet it was geographically connected to Republican Santander in the west and beyond it to Asturias. These three enclaves along the Spanish northern coast, far from pulling together, however, behaved like the tiny kingdoms of the early 'Reconquest' period. Not surprisingly, the rebels found them easy pickings, conquering them one by one over the spring and summer of 1937, and in so doing capturing important steel and mining areas of the country (while their German and Italian allies experimented with mass aerial bombardment of civilian populations: the destruction of the Basque town of Guernica took place during this campaign in what was meant to be a belated birthday present for Hitler).

Other areas of Republican Spain also acted with near or sometimes total autonomy. Parts of the Aragonese countryside became totally Anarchist, with collectivised farms, the abolition of money (and the murder of local landowners) and a complete absence of State structures. In Barcelona, as Anarchist power waned, separatist politicians retook control. Eventually the Republican capital had to move there from Valencia in part as a brake on Catalan independence moves. Even when Madrid was facing its darkest hour, in November 1936, with rebel forces pushing into the southern suburbs and seemingly on the brink of victory, loyalist fighters from the rest of Spain were notable by their absence. The government ran off to Valencia, but few if any Valencians returned the favour by heading to Madrid to help in its defence. Catalan Anarchists led by the charismatic Buenaventura Durruti did put in an appearance,[1] but their presence only further highlighted the lack of formations from other parts of the country. The *taifas* were back in all but name, and each region or town was far too busy thinking about its own problems to assist anyone else.

These core divisions within the Republican side made its ability to fight back against the rebels much harder. Yet this was further exacerbated by the fact that for the first year or so of the conflict the Republic had no army to speak of. As the military rebellion spread during the first few days of the war, one of the measures taken by the crumbling government was to disband the armed forces, thereby – theoretically – making it easier for soldiers loyal to the Republic to mutiny against any officers ordering them to attack it. The plan worked to an extent, but when the coup attempt led to a full-scale civil war, it meant that the Republic couldn't send in regular formations against the highly trained troops from Morocco pushing deep into their territory. Attempts to turn the militia groups into more traditional-style military formations were seriously hampered by the libertarian approach to command structures as noted above. Attractive though the egalitarian ideals might be, in purely pragmatic terms having a committee meeting to decide on tactics is a questionable modus operandi when the enemy is about to storm your positions. And true to their beliefs, Anarchist militiamen were volunteers in the pure sense, meaning – in their eyes – that they could come and go from the front as they pleased.

---

1 Durruti himself was killed in a controversial incident near the front lines.

Which meant that the few effective military commanders present could never tell how many men they could count on from one minute to the next. The Communists were the exception to this, and their insistence on discipline and authority meant that many officers loyal to the Republic ended up joining the party. And as the Republic tried to create a proper army of its own, virtually from scratch, the Communists took a leading role.

Yet this process would take the Republic almost two years, during which time it lost huge amounts of territory and men. Soviet military aid only served to slow down eventual defeat. At times the arrival of the latest weaponry from Moscow gave the appearance of handing the Republic the advantage, for example when Polikarpov planes chased slower Italian and German aircraft from the skies above Madrid. But a telling detail shows how better hardware can only take you so far: Republican troops had Soviet T-26 tanks, superior to anything that the rebels were supplied with from their own allies, but by the end of the war there were more T-26s in rebel hands than in Republican, having been captured in battle and turned against their original users. Militarily, the rebels had the upper hand from the off, and while the imbalance was gradually reduced, it is questionable whether real parity was ever reached: when the Republic lost the Battle of the Ebro in late 1938 – the biggest battle of the war and a showcase for the Republic's 'proper' army – it had precious little left with which to continue the fight, exhausted and increasingly hungry. Final defeat was already on the horizon.

Republican disunity and military weakness could not have been in greater contrast to the other side. The rebels' control of the Army of Africa has already been mentioned, as have Hitler and Mussolini's almost immediate supplies of arms and other support. Italian forces in Spain would eventually number as many as eighty thousand, while the Condor Legion saw up to twelve thousand German military personnel operational on Spanish soil. The story of the Civil War is not one of total military dominance of one side by the other: Madrid stayed in Republican hands until the end of the conflict, while rebel offensives at Jarama and Guadalajara, for example, were stopped or defeated. But a general pattern did emerge as the war progressed of Republicans launching offensives of their own, only to be pushed back and often losing more territory in the wake of defeat. Such was the case, for example, at Teruel and the Ebro. Ever more desperate to win the support of London and Paris to its struggle, the Republic chose to

The latter period of the Spanish Civil War (Nov 1938)

fight as conventional a war as possible, spurning the guerrilla tactics which had proved so useful against Napoleon. Yet these large battles only brought defeat, collapse in morale and final exhaustion. And the Brits and the French never did come to the Republic's assistance.

Meanwhile, the rebels had a 'proper' army from the start, and one which was prepared to use terror as a weapon. Massacres in the wake of rebel victories became the norm, first by the front-line troops, who were given fifteen minutes to loot, rape and murder at free will when they took a town or city. Moroccan Regulares were particularly keen to get hold of sewing machines to send back home, while their commanders openly bragged about the brutal way they treated women. Republican depictions at the time of the *moros* as bloodthirsty barbarians may be viewed as racist today, but rebel leaders themselves, notably General Queipo de Llano, deliberately used a deep-rooted Spanish fear of the old enemy as a weapon. While the massacres, mutilations and mass rapes carried out by rebel forces spoke for themselves. The directive came from the very top: brutality was to be employed as much as traditional arms such as artillery and rifles. And in an early example of what was to come, over two thousand people in Badajoz were rounded up in September 1936 after its fall to the rebels and systematically shot.

The rebels didn't have a monopoly on the use of brutal violence against the enemy, nor in sophisticated weaponry. But what they did have, crucially, was an acceptance of the concept of a single command. Rebel – 'Nationalist' – Spain was as divided as the Republic, with factions ranging from fascists to right-wing republicans to monarchists (who themselves were divided between the supporters of Alfonso XIII and the Carlist pretender, still flying the flag for his cause over a hundred years since the First Carlist War . . .). What all these different groups could agree on, however, was the need for a *single* leader at the head of them all. At least while the war was being waged. And the man who stepped into this role as though it had been specifically made for him was Franco.

The rebels are often referred to as Francoists, yet it should be remembered that Franco wasn't behind the coup and nor was he the leader of the rebels for the first three months of the conflict. It was only as the Army of Africa, under his command, was closing in on Madrid in the autumn of 1936 that he managed to secure for himself the position of *Generalísimo*, overall commander of the rebel forces and, thanks to some sleight of hand, head of the Nationalist state. Not everyone was happy with this, and in time some of the other rebel generals realised that they had been duped. But rather than fighting among themselves – as the Republicans did – they grumbled in private while accepting Franco's fait accompli. They were, after all, right-wingers, and the idea of a strong leader historically appeals more to the Right than to the Left.

Franco was brutal, ruthless, and an average military commander. But he was lucky, and with his ability to play opponents off against one another, turned into a canny politician. Few others, perhaps, could have balanced the different factions as well as he did, eventually uniting them in a single party with a ridiculously long name which was commonly known simply as *el Movimiento*, 'the Movement'.

Rebel 'unity' was fictional yet effective, and manifested in the image of Franco himself, who drew inspiration from the great unifiers of Spanish history: Ferdinand and Isabella, and Philip II, symbols of the more glorious eras from the country's past.

Consciously or not, Franco was following a pattern from Spanish history, the predominant way in which the country has been brought together and then held united: through the efforts of Santiago the Slayer, a single, violent authority, brutally defeating anyone who would break the country apart.

For him, as for the others in the past, it worked, winning him the Civil War in 1939, and maintaining him in power until his death thirty-six years later.

AFTER

POST-WAR

Franco won the war, but peace was bloody and painful. Defeating his enemy in the field wasn't enough for the 'Caudillo', as Franco termed himself in the style of an old medieval warlord. His intention from the beginning had been to wipe out the 'anti-Spain', the other Spain. The Slayer would try to eradicate his reflection – and eternal rival – as he always does.

For decades after final victory in April 1939, Spanish executioners were kept busy cleansing the country of unwanted elements in an echo of the 'purity of blood' paranoia which had scarred the sixteenth and seventeenth centuries and furnished the Inquisition with so many of its victims. Tens of thousands of Republican prisoners were held in makeshift concentration camps dotted around the country (there were almost three hundred according to latest estimates, yet barely a trace of them remains today). 'Trials' were sometimes held, in which many were, paradoxically, accused of 'military rebellion', but these were a formality with the inevitable outcome: death, either by firing squad or garrotte. Franco insisted on personally verifying all death sentences, and the names of the soon-to-be-deceased would be read to him while he dealt with other matters of state, or even while drinking his morning cup of hot chocolate. Occasionally he might interrupt the functionary's flow, asking for details of the condemned person's political affiliation, at which point he might specify which execution method he preferred in that particular case. Garrotting, in which the prisoner is choked while a bolt is pushed into the back of the neck to break the spinal cord, was considered the harsher.

As many as twenty thousand people were killed in the post-war years, while the same number died as a result of the appalling conditions within the prisons and camps. Added to the two hundred thousand Republicans who had fallen during the actual war, and the half a million who had fled into exile following defeat, the political cleansing was extensive. All the ills of Spain as identified by the Francoists – namely, democracy, liberalism, freemasonry, Judaism and Marxism – could finally be removed and the Slayer could emerge victorious at last. The further paradox that he had used his original Other – the Moor – as his front-line assault troops in this curious engagement was forgotten. Or if questioned, dealt with by declaring the Muslim soldiers of the Regulares 'honorary Catholics'. (Albeit, questioning of the new authoritarian regime in any way at all could land you in serious trouble.)

Franco, however, was wily and never let 'facts', 'details' or even loyalties get in his way. Galicians are known in Spain as being hard to read. When you meet one on the stairs, the joke goes, you can never tell if they're going up or going down. 'Do as I do,' Franco, the dictator of all Spain, later told a journalist, 'and don't get involved in politics.' This craftiness and seeming capacity to ride currents of history which swept others away can be seen in the dictator's complex relationship with Hitler. The Führer's military support had helped Franco enormously in his rise to power, a fact which the Spaniard acknowledged in his declaration of Nazi Germany as 'the highest achievement in human civilisation', and his granting of precious iron ore to help arm the Third Reich. Five months after the Civil War ended, the Second World War began. Spain declared itself neutral at first, waiting to see how the wind blew. Then, after the fall of France and with Britain left on its own, in June 1940 Franco declared his country non-belligerent, a step just short of declaring war on the UK, whose navy could have crushed Spain easily at the time by blocking imports of desperately needed oil and wheat. When Hitler and Franco finally had their first and only face-to-face meeting, in October 1940 at a train station on the Spanish-French border, the Führer insisted that his ally take a full and active part in the war. Franco was keen to agree, but his price was high: he wanted guarantees of supplies which would inevitably be cut off by the Royal Navy, as well as control of Morocco, Algeria and huge swathes of north-west Africa in what would become a new Spanish Empire. Hitler refused, and over the coming months tensions between the two leaders intensified. Hitler even drew up plans to ignore Franco and send two German divisions through the country to conquer Gibraltar, so crucial to Britain's links with India and the rest of the British Empire.

What saved both Britain and Spain was Hitler's turn to the east and the launch of his main plan, the conquest of the Soviet Union, in June 1941. At once Spain became a sideshow. But to demonstrate his continued goodwill, Franco created the Blue Division, made up of Spanish volunteers to go and fight on the Russian front in aid of their anti-Marxist German friends. Over forty thousand Spanish soldiers passed through the division, seeing heavy fighting and casualties – as high as 50 per cent. And while most were driven by political conviction, others, such as the future film director Luis Berlanga, joined up to help members of their families jailed and awaiting death sentences for Republicanism back at home. In a kind of logic worthy of the Inquisition, youngsters fighting for Christian civilisation against the atheist hordes in the east were considered to have cleansed their blood relatives, at least in part, of their crimes.

Spain and Germany were, to all intents and purposes, close friends and allies, and the pressure for Spain to declare war on Britain remained, an outcome favoured by many within the regime, not least the Falangists, ardent supporters and admirers of the Nazis and Fascists. But behind the scenes, British intelligence officials in Madrid were busy bribing Franco's generals to stay out of the war, paying them millions of pesetas to lobby against involvement. The plan worked long enough for the Germans to be hit with their first serious defeat at Stalingrad. At which point Franco, ever the operator, saw that the wind was beginning to blow in a new direction, and gradually pulled back his support for Hitler. Falangists were removed from government and the Blue Division was disbanded.[1]

And new stories were created to explain what had happened. According to the later version, Franco's interview with Hitler wasn't, in fact, the humiliation that it really had been, but evidence of the Caudillo's cunning, cleverly keeping the impoverished and war-torn Spain out of a conflict which would have brought nothing but calamity. As further 'proof' of how he had played such a blinder, the arrival of Franco's train eight minutes late for the

---

1 Although a hard-core group of Spanish anti-Communists chose to remain in what was called the Blue Brigade; some of their number resisted to the very end, fighting around Hitler's bunker as the Red Army conquered Berlin.

interview (because of the poor state of the Spanish railways) became, in the new account, a subtle and intelligent way of showing the Führer that Spain could keep Germany waiting and was not going to be pushed around. *Con un par de cojones,* as the Spanish phrase goes. 'With a big pair of balls.' This retelling of the event is still popular today.

Spain managed to scrape through the Second World War without becoming overly involved, but this didn't mean it found new friends in return. In October 1944 Spanish Communists, thinking that the moment to overthrow Franco had come, staged an invasion of the Valley of Aran, a tiny area of the Spanish Pyrenees, hoping to drag the Allies into the fight and provoke a full-scale invasion against the dictator in Madrid. By that point, however, Britain and the US were already thinking ahead to a post-war scenario, and helping Reds in their back yard was always going to be complicated. The Communists were left to their own devices and eventually crushed by the Francoists.

But a hand of friendship towards Madrid was not forthcoming either. Spain was isolated, memories of her former ties with Hitler and Mussolini still fresh. And the people who suffered most were ordinary Spaniards, reduced to hunger and intense poverty as international political games were played around them. Many were reduced to scouring the countryside for scrap metal, selling bullet casings or pieces of shrapnel to earn enough to feed themselves and their families day by day. Even now *la posguerra* – the post-war period of the 1940s and '50s – holds a place in collective memory as a time of great suffering, a painful and drawn-out hangover after the intense agonies of the Civil War.

Thankfully, however, it was not to last. Reading the winds once more, Franco saw his opportunity in his staunch, and genuine, anti-Marxism. By the late 1940s the Cold War had begun in earnest. The US needed new allies in its struggle against the Soviet Union. And into the fight stepped Spain, with Franco as the 'Sentinel of the West' and defender of Christendom.

RECOVERY AND DECLINE

What exactly was Francoism, however, and what did Franco believe? What kind of country did he create with his dictatorial powers?

Part of the problem lies in the word 'Francoism' itself, which suggests the existence of some kind of ideology. But Franco was never a great political thinker, despite being an astute political operator. He was ambitious and had a solid belief in himself as a saviour of Spain, a man of destiny who would rescue the country at a time of great peril. In his own mind he was another Rodrigo Díaz – El Cid – a warrior knight acting on behalf of a king and yet at the same time independent, a ruler unto himself, loyal to his master's cause but also detached. A man who would carve out his own kingdom without ever becoming king.

Which is what he did. Alfonso XIII had been 'godfather' to Franco's wedding; the Caudillo had close ties to the royal family and courted their cause during the Civil War. Alfonso's third son and heir to the throne, Juan, was engaged on the Nationalist side during the conflict. Monarchists died for the sake of their king, believing that their sacrifice would help put him back on the throne. But with Franco in charge, neither Alfonso nor Juan would ever reign. The country was his and he was determined to hold on to power to the very end.

'If you give him Spain,' one rebel general commented to another back in 1936, 'he'll believe it's his and won't let anyone relieve him of his position either during the war or until after he's dead.'

Cabanellas's words were prophetic: he knew the younger general better than the others, who simply handed Franco all power. They would later regret it.

In essence, Franco was an opportunist, but it would be wrong to assume that he would have clung to the coat-tails of any ideology simply to get to the top. He was conservative, a nationalist, a devout churchgoer (he carried a relic – the withered arm of St Theresa of Avila – wherever he went), ardently anti-Marxist, and had a curious hatred towards the Freemasons.[1]

Beyond that, he rarely committed himself to any political belief system, playing the various factions around him off against one another. At the start of his rule the Falange were in the ascendant because they were closest politically to Nazism and Fascism. When the course of the Second World War changed and Spain became a pariah, 'autarchy' and isolation were touted as the new ideals, Spain proud and on her own in the face of a multitude of enemies.

Salvation for a starving nation came with the Cold War, and the US – the country which had humiliated Spain in the 'Disaster' of 1898 – now became its friend, pouring in millions of dollars to help prop up its new anti-Soviet ally. From celebrating

---

1 He was denied entry into the secretive organisation, and later amassed a large private collection of Masonic memorabilia; his father and many Republican leaders were Masons.

'autarchism', Spain became capitalist. The *apertura* ('opening up') which followed brought in the first tourists, but these foreigners had different ideas as well as cash: the social liberalism which had been crushed during the Civil War was in danger of clambering in through the back door. The answer was to usher in Church hardliners, with 'technocrats' trained by the Opus Dei taking on cabinet positions. '*Nos han hecho ministros,*' gloated the movement's founder, Josemaría Escrivá, on hearing the news. 'We've been made ministers.'

It was 1956 and Franco was beginning to feel his age by this time. He effectively pulled away from the business of government and spent the rest of his active years hunting, fishing and watching films: like Hitler, he considered himself something of an artist, and even wrote a film script, *La Raza*, a clunking melodrama in which two brothers – one a fine upstanding Catholic and the other a Masonic reprobate – have a huge falling-out . . . You get the picture. The Caudillo's simplistic metaphor for the causes of the Civil War got to be filmed twice, once in the '40s and again in the '50s. Both versions are as bad as each other, if interesting from a historical point of view.

It is tempting to see the Franco years as a period in which Spain was, in effect, put on ice, when the turbulence of the preceding period was suppressed with an iron fist and progress halted; while the rest of the Western world was experiencing 'the '60s', Spain was held back somewhere in the '40s or even earlier. There is some truth to this view, but underneath the rigid dictatorial regime's upper layer, the rest of the country was going through rapid and quite fundamental change, particularly from the late 1950s onwards. Tourism and the 'opening up' process saw millions of foreigners arrive,[2] but also similar numbers of Spaniards left the country in search of work, often in Germany, then booming in its post-WWII rebuilding phase. As a result, Spanish per-capita income between 1960 and 1970 rose by over 80 per cent. The austere post-war years were coming to an end, and everyone wanted to enjoy the new fruits: over a million Spaniards left the countryside during the same decade, usually ending up in shanty towns on the edges of the main cities. Although much reduced these days, they still exist in places, while a walk in remote mountain areas of the country can sometimes reveal old farmhouses abandoned during this period, with scattered scraps of the last newspapers and magazines left by their owners before they headed for the bright lights, never to return.

New levels of personal wealth and contact with liberal foreigners also brought challenges to the conservative forces trying to keep Spain at one remove from the rest of the world. While bullfighting and flamenco were requisitioned by the regime to sell Spanish 'passion' and 'difference' to bikini-clad hordes in search of holiday exoticism,[3] at the same time the Church was becoming increasingly alarmed at the side effects this was having on Spanish youth, who were discovering that there was more to life than rosary beads.

By the late 1960s, however, there were more things on the regime's mind than the sexual morals of the people. Victory in

---

2 One of them was John Lennon, for the filming of *How I Won the War* in Almería. During his stay he was visited by a local schoolteacher who used Beatles songs to teach children English. The result of this interview was that *Sgt. Pepper's* subsequently had the lyrics printed on the back sleeve, the first time this had ever happened on an LP record.

3 The phrase 'Spain is different' was coined at this time by Francoist minister Manuel Fraga to help sell the country as an exotic holiday destination to foreigners. It still rankles among many Spaniards today, who feel it demeans their country.

the Civil War might have led some to think that the ancient threat to national unity, regionalism, had been vanquished once and for all. But just as in the past it had risen from near death, so it did again now, most visibly in the shape of ETA, which aped the government it was intent on removing from the Basque Country by using violence for political ends: the group claimed its first victim in 1968 and over the next fifty years went on to claim eight hundred and sixty-four lives. Only in the spring of 2018 did it give up the ghost and disband (interestingly, at exactly the moment when Catalan separatism took centre stage on the Spanish political scene).

Things came to a head in the late '60s when the more liberal elements within Franco's government were removed, and a hard-line conservative–Catholic regime was installed which really did try to put the clock back. It was led by an ardent Franco supporter, Admiral Carrero Blanco, who became prime minister in 1973. Franco was ageing rapidly; Carrero Blanco was meant to ensure his legacy continued once the old dictator was gone. But ETA had other ideas. In December that same year they blew the prime minister's car up with so many explosives that it flew into the air, over a church and into a courtyard. Even the armoured plating of a minister's vehicle couldn't save the new head of government, and Carrero Blanco died soon afterwards of his wounds. (At the time, Moscow accused the CIA of involvement, a theory which some still defend today.)

The assassination came as a shock, but also as a relief for many. ETA, who would later leave such a bloody stain on Spanish history, had apparently done the regime's enemies a huge favour. Carrero Blanco left a large authoritarian hole which his successor as prime minister was unable to fill.

But that was of secondary importance. Franco was ever closer to death, and this 'biological imperative' – as the regime euphemistically referred to his inevitable demise – meant that all minds were focused on what would come next. What would happen to Spain without its modern-day El Cid?

TRANSITIONS

On 20 November 1975 Franco finally died. The television announcer broke down in tears, as did half the country. The other half rushed out to buy champagne and cava, emptying the nation's shelves of bubbly overnight. On the surface, everything was different, but underneath it was all the same: a country eternally divided against itself marking a key moment in its history in diametrically opposed ways. What would come next?

There were reasons to fear for the future: violent regionalism had not only made a comeback in the shape of ETA, but had done so in spectacular fashion with Carrero Blanco's assassination. Meanwhile, left-wing opposition parties had been operating in secret, waiting for the day when the dictator died and they could spring back into action. It was time to right the wrongs of the past. The Civil War had begun almost forty years before; no one could forget the wave of violence which had brought Franco to power. Or could they?

In 1969 Franco had named his successor. Despite refusing to reinstate the monarchy while alive, he would bring it back after his death. Alfonso XIII had died in Mussolini's Rome in 1941 and the natural choice would have been his heir, Juan. But Juan was unloved, having already forged and broken alliances with almost everyone – even exiled Socialists – in an attempt to get rid of Franco and claim Spain for himself. Instead of Juan, Franco decided to skip a generation and name Juan's son, Juan Carlos, as the next Spanish head of state.

Not everyone in the regime was happy with this decision. Juan still had a few supporters, while the Falangists weren't even ideological monarchists to begin with. Both mocked the future king and nicknamed him *Juan Carlos el Breve* – 'the Brief'. Few imagined that he would survive for very long.

But survive he did, and in a surprisingly short time following Franco's death, Spain moved effortlessly from being an authoritarian dictatorship to becoming a fully functioning, constitutional, democratic monarchy. Without a shot being fired . . .

Or at least that's the story that has been told, the myth, the official version of how Spain, after centuries of internal conflict and warfare and division and military coups, finally became a modern country, one in which fighting was no longer the principal means through which it addressed the great questions of state. It's a story which has worked very well, and many people still cling to it, convinced that everything is now different, that the ways of the past are gone, never to return.

But where does this assumption come from? What exactly is this belief that 'we don't do things like that any more' based upon? The habits of over a thousand years are deeply engrained and have repeated themselves time after time. Why should they be broken now?

The simple answer is that it is wishful thinking combined with a certain amount of hubris. And it is largely built on the successful storytelling around the *Transición* – the country's 'peaceful' progression from dictatorship to democracy. But that very story is now being questioned. Fewer and fewer Spaniards today accept its 'truths'. There is a growing sense that a convenient yarn has been spun, one which doesn't give the whole picture and which is starting to unravel. New versions are emerging of a far more complex process which, over forty years after Franco died, is far from complete. Did Francoism ever really go away? Is it correct, in fact, to talk of a 'transition' at all?

The man at the centre of the official version of the *Transición* is King Juan Carlos, the hero of the tale, the knight in shining armour who confounded his detractors and, in conjunction with a small group of close advisors, managed to navigate the good ship Spain through the choppy waters of end-of-dictatorship and into the calm, bright, sunlit seas of democracy and prosperity. According to this story, Juan Carlos and his friends were secretly planning from before Franco's death to turn the country into a constitutional monarchy. When the Caudillo died and Juan Carlos became the new head of state, they put their plan into action, drafting a new democratic Constitution and uniting many political factions on both left and right to bury the hatchet, put aside their differences, and help build a new country. Elections were held, and Spain marched happily into her better future. And when diehard Francoists tried to put the clock back, staging a coup attempt in 1981 by storming the parliament building, Juan Carlos was there on his steed again, a kinder incarnation of Santiago the Slayer, smiting the enemy of the new Spain down (without having to resort to violence, but the effect was the same) and assuring once and for all that democracy was here to stay, that the age of military coups was finally over. It was a success: rebellious generals were locked away, a Socialist government – unthinkable only a few years before – was voted in shortly afterwards, and Juan Carlos basked in his vindication as a force for good. Monarchy, with its long history of instability in the country, was firmly established.

And the story after that is one of continued success: Spain joined NATO and the European Economic Community, later the European Union. Earnings went up, people became wealthier and more comfortable, governments came and went, but always according to the norms of a stable democracy. Spain became a fully fledged member of the club of prosperous post-WWII Western European nations. History was buried. There were no more 'events' (or any that came would be of the slightly dull, democratic variety).

The End.

Except that it wasn't, and it isn't. Today 'history' is at the forefront of Spanish public life. Catalan regionalism has flared up again in spectacular fashion. The monarchy is back in crisis: following a long family tradition of stealing from the State it is meant to represent, the current king's brother-in-law is doing time for corruption, while there are serious questions about how Juan Carlos, who abdicated under a cloud in 2014, amassed his own fortune, allegedly squirrelled away in Swiss bank accounts. The Republican flag, which ten or fifteen years ago was a rare sight, is everywhere today – in graffiti, flying at political marches, hanging from balconies. Against this backdrop, mass graves from the Civil War are being excavated all the time, reopening wounds from a conflict which (supposedly) ended eighty years ago. And every so often some high-ranking military official is caught making interventionist-type comments that wouldn't have been out of place in the 1920s and '30s. Meanwhile, buried deep at the heart of a mountain, in a gigantic and macabre mausoleum of his own design, Franco should be turning in his grave because as I write these words the Spanish government is initiating moves to dig the *Generalísimo* up and move him somewhere less visible. Everywhere you look, the 'past' is on the move, the old patterns of behaviour rearing up once more.

And the reason is that it never went away; it was simply that, for the sake of the *Transición*, everyone pretended that it had. Spain, as she so often has, drew a veil over unwanted parts of her history in an attempt to forge a new future.

The sentiments behind the transition to democracy were largely noble: to bring about a very rare and almost impossible change of regime in the country's history without violence. To do so, all manner of compromises and deals had to be done in order to keep a people with a tendency to self-harm from turning once more to civil war. The people with the most to lose were also the most heavily armed: hard-line Francoists within the military, the *búnker* as they were called, in an echo of Hitler's last stand at Berlin. Keeping them pacified was of utmost importance. So, for example, the Francoist State was never fully dismantled: Francoist institutions were kept in place, while Francoist laws remained – and still remain – on the statute books, and were only superseded when new, democratic, laws replaced them in piecemeal fashion. The Constitution of 1978 established a democratic monarchy, but in effect this new Spain was given a blessing by the old one – without a clean break. Yet how could a state which itself had been born out of a military coup – and which was therefore illegitimate – give legitimacy to its successor?

And just how democratic is Spain? Yes, there are elections, and yes, governments come and go. But there is a congenital lack of transparency about everything. Rather than having internal elections to decide their candidates, the main traditional political parties have closed lists, unaccountable to anyone but themselves. This creates an ideal ground for corruption in which no one dares blow the whistle for fear of expulsion from the group. Not surprisingly, those cases that are investigated are often – although not always – after the person in question has left office and is in a much weaker position to cajole any potential witnesses into silence. Many millions of euros (and before them, pesetas) have been hoarded in recent decades through such schemes as re-designating stretches of countryside as 'constructible' (sometimes after an entirely accidental and fortuitous forest fire), with politicians taking large kickbacks from the speculators who then pile in and build on the site. Examples of this and many more corruption scandals (such as siphoning off funds from a charity for impoverished African children) are legion, so much so that one repentant corrupt official talks of an 'addiction', describing himself and others as 'money-junkies'. The courts go after who they can, when they can, but there is a general sense in Spain – and one that has become much worse over recent years – that anyone in a position of power has their hand in the till in some way, no matter what political persuasion they profess.

Politics, in the new Spain, is less about ideology and nation-building than a means through which to divvy up the spoils of power. You only have to watch State television for a couple of minutes to know who is in charge: any change at the top is quickly followed by a ruthless sweeping away of the old newsreaders in favour of ones more in keeping with the new ruling party's image.

The lack of accountability and sense of real democracy isn't helped by the electoral system. In a complex set-up, the parties coming first and second in the polls take the lion's share of the vote, forcing a bi-party state on a country in which – at a national level – there are now four or five principal parties which run very close to one another in the polls. Added to this is a measure intended to give greater weight to the more underpopulated areas of the country – which are generally more conservative. Which produces bizarre results in which, for example, the vote of someone from the province of Soria (total population: ninety thousand) is worth five times more than that of someone from a major city. Yet a system designed to produce political stability has more often than not caused hung parliaments, most of which have only managed to govern by doing deals with the Catalan nationalists, whose ultimate aim is to break away from the Spanish state altogether . . .

Spanish democracy is so flawed that some describe it bluntly as a 'pseudo-democracy', a sham. Even token democratic norms such as freedom of speech come regularly under threat; try criticising the king or other State institutions openly and you can quickly find yourself in jail. One Spanish rapper has sought asylum in Belgium from Spanish justice, which has given him a three-and-a-half-year sentence for, amongst other things, 'insulting the king' in one of his lyrics.

And it is precisely the figure of the king which is at the centre of this unravelling of the *Transición* fairy tale. From having been a national hero, Juan Carlos is close to becoming a pariah, while his son and successor, Felipe VI, has failed to unite the country behind him in the way that his father once managed to do.

Part of the problem is that many now question the key element in the Juan Carlos myth – his role in the coup attempt of 1981. According to the official story, it was Juan Carlos's intervention, appearing on State television in full military dress to denounce the plotters, which saved the day. Duly castigated, the rebel generals and their minions put away their guns and handed themselves in. It had been a close-run thing, but democracy had prevailed and Juan Carlos was the hero of the moment.

Today, however, many question this. According to some versions that are now told – by historians Jesús Palacios and Juan Eslava Galán amongst others – Juan Carlos was in on the plot to begin with. The government was unstable and the country, still navigating those choppy waters, appeared close to the brink once more: in stark contrast to the 'peaceful' transition story which has frequently been told, ETA was going through its bloodiest phase in its demand for Basque independence, with regionalism provoking fears at the centre of another break-up of the country.[1] Order was meant to be imposed by a 'liberal' general – Juan Carlos's close friend Alfonso Armada – who would set up a government of national unity which would include parties from both Left and Right. But the plan backfired. The man holding parliament at gunpoint, Colonel Tejero – an unwitting pawn in a bigger game – refused to cooperate when the true plan was put to him. Fifteen minutes later Juan Carlos appeared on TV, and by the morning it was all over. The coup had come to naught. But according to some, Juan Carlos wasn't the only person in the know: almost everyone, including the Socialist Party, was in on it as well. The whole thing was meant to be no more than a 'show' which would facilitate the reimposition of order.

The Spanish establishment sticks to the original version of events, with former prime minister Leopoldo Calvo-Sotelo describing Juan

---

1 In a less-than-democratic move, the State was soon to set up a terror group of its own in response, the GAL, a dirty operations unit which was meant to give ETA members a taste of their own medicine; some of the GAL's victims were indeed linked to the Basque group, but others were innocent citizens targeted by mistake. Two government ministers, including the Interior Minister, would eventually go to jail for their role in the scandal.

Carlos's role as 'brilliant'. 'That night he won his throne as his ancestors did.' But this is a view which ever fewer Spaniards appear to share.

Parallels between the Tejero coup of 1981 and Serrano's – which brought an end to the First Republic and the restoration of the monarchy in 1874 – have often been made. On both occasions the military stormed parliament, with generals sitting in the wings waiting to appear as 'saviours of the nation' at its time of need. The difference is that – ostensibly at least – the 1981 coup failed and General Armada and the others ended up behind bars. And yet the system that was installed in Spain as a result bears a close resemblance to the state created by Cánovas at the end of the nineteenth century: a constitutional monarchy with a bi-party system in which the government alternates in a generally regular fashion between Left and Right. A system which is endemically corrupt and in which large numbers of the population feel themselves to be unrepresented.

The Restoration period lasted for twenty-five years, but then came under increasing strain, first with a change of monarch (the arrival of Alfonso XIII) and then under pressure from regional groups reigniting their ancient struggles. Eventually it collapsed with Alfonso's exile, and the proclamation of a Second Republic, which in turn was immolated in the Civil War.

Does the same violent fate await today's Spain?

CONCLUSION:
THE LAST KING OF SPAIN

Felipe VI came to the throne in 2014 under a cloud; around him the reputation of the royal family was approaching meltdown. Felipe's father, Juan Carlos, abdicated two years after it was claimed that public money had been spent flying him home following an accident on an elephant-hunting trip in Botswana. A photo of the king standing triumphantly next to a dead elephant (which had been shot by someone else) was on the front page of all the newspapers. There was a collective intake of breath: Juan Carlos, who had appeared such a clever reader of public opinion, who had managed to survive so much longer than anyone had ever suspected he would, was suddenly showing himself to be totally out of step with his subjects. The combination of elephant-hunting and alleged use of public funds (calculated at 44,000 euros, roughly twice the average annual salary) for his return at a time when food banks were increasingly busy across the country was a serious blow. Not only that, the king was the honorary head of the Spanish branch of the World Wildlife Fund; killing large game didn't exactly fit, and he was subsequently stripped of his title.

All this came while Juan Carlos's own daughter and son-in-law were coming under investigation for corruption. The Infanta Cristina was later cleared, but Iñaki Urdangarín was eventually sentenced to five years and ten months in jail for tax evasion.[1] This and other rumours surrounding the Spanish royal family meant that its image was seriously damaged. Juan Carlos effectively sacrificed himself in an attempt to preserve the monarchy.

But it was too late. After his heir, Felipe, was proclaimed king in parliament, the new head of state was paraded around Madrid to his adoring subjects . . . except that there was hardly anyone present. For a split second the face of Queen Letitia (a former journalist and someone who understands the importance of these things) betrayed a sense of disappointed surprise on stepping outside to see such a small crowd waiting to greet them. State television cameras focused on the happy new monarchs, but they could not disguise the sheer absence of well-wishers lining the streets as the royal couple went on a drive through the capital. Overhead, a helicopter camera crew tracked their progress along avenues where barricades had been erected to hold back the expected crowds. But not only were these thin on the ground, there were some stretches where no one showed up at all. The vast majority of Madrileños were simply getting on with their day. For a supposedly monarchist country, the arrival of the new king was the dampest of squibs.

The fact was that the edifice of the *Transición*, with the king at its centre holding everything together, was falling apart. The complex arrangements of tacit agreements and alliances, and more

---

1 The couple lost their titles of Duke and Duchess of Palma de Mallorca before sentence was passed.

importantly a will to unite the country to facilitate the introduction of democracy, was no longer working. A new generation – people who were only children during the Transition years – was coming to power, and wasn't content with blindly carrying on in the same way.

An early sign that things were changing had come a few years before with the creation of the 'historical memory' movement, groups of people around the country who wanted to excavate the mass graves of Republicans who had been executed (or murdered) by the rebels during the Civil War. This was breaking a huge taboo and one of the building blocks of the Transition – the pact of forgetting (the most recent of several in Spanish history), under which everyone had agreed not to open old wounds. But the 'historical memory' groups disagreed. Founded in large part by the grandchildren of murdered Republicans, by the mid-2000s they felt that the moment had come to re-examine the recent past, not least because time was running out to speak to the last survivors of the Civil War before their memories were buried with them. Franco's dead had been honoured throughout the dictatorship as martyrs to his cause,[2] but the other half of Spain had never been allowed to mourn their own fallen in proper fashion, not even knowing, in many cases, where their loved ones lay.

The movement had limited success: in some parts of the country a number of mass graves were opened, while in others they remained firmly closed. Left-wing regional administrations tended to favour the projects, while right-wing ones shut them down. Debate raged about whether it was a good idea after all. Was it

---

2 Every church in the land had a plaque on the facade with the word *¡Presente!* followed by the names of parishioners who had been killed – but only those on the Francoist side. Many of these have been removed in recent years.

purely about 'history'? Or did it include an element of muck-raking for political ends, a way for the Left to garner more votes? Was it simply better to continue pretending that nothing had happened?

Around this time, a book of mine on the War and its legacy was published in Spain. The editors gave it the title *Las heridas abiertas de la Guerra Civil* – 'The Open Wounds of the Civil War'. At a presentation event in a provincial capital city, one man, a right-wing councillor, stood up sharply when he saw the front cover. Red-faced and frothing at the mouth, he made it clear to everyone that, to his mind, there were no open wounds from the Civil War, and tossed the book away. The comment that his own reaction seemed to suggest otherwise went over his head. History was very much a live topic, and having been smothered for several decades, was reawakening old emotions.

Then came the crash of 2008, and a Spanish economy which had been built on construction itself came tumbling down. 'Historical memory' was put on the back burner: people were being left destitute overnight – mostly ordinary folk who could no longer afford to pay their mortgages or bills. Some were throwing them-selves out of windows in desperation. One morning after dropping my son off at school, I saw a distraught man at the top of his block of flats about to launch himself into the void. The whole street came to a terrified standstill. Thankfully in this case the man's wife and daughter were able to talk him out of it. Others were more determined, however, and a friend in the police crime-scene investigation squad would talk in sombre tones about the human remains he was increasingly having to clear up.

The bankruptcies, food banks and a cascade of new corruption cases among the political elite made many ordinary Spaniards increasingly aware of the gap between themselves and those meant to represent them.[3] The result was the creation of what became known as *el 15-M*, the 15 May movement. On that day in 2011, thousands of anti-austerity and pro-democracy protesters staged a demonstration in Madrid's Puerta del Sol. Over several days, the rally grew, with members camping out in the square and 'occupying' it. It was a largely spontaneous outpouring of anger which quickly spread across the country. And from there to much of the Western world: within six months, 'Occupy' movements had taken over central areas of New York, London and many other important cities.

The Spanish *indignados* of the 15-M were inspired in part by the writings of the veteran French politician Stéphane Hessel, whose book *Indignez-vous* came out the previous year. But also by the Arab Spring, which began in January 2011 when the Tunisian Mohamed Bouazizi burnt himself to death in protest at government corruption. Ask many people in Western countries today, however, about the Occupy movement, and they have vague memories of the Madrid demonstrations, but have generally forgotten that the Spanish protestors were the precursors to those who sprang up in other major cities. With the 15-M, Spain's Cassandra pattern, which stretches back over many centuries, has repeated itself as recently as the last decade; and it parallels the Moorish civilisation which flourished over a thousand years ago by not only being largely ignored as a predictor of wider change, but also by having found a large part of its inspiration in the East.

With time, 15-M was transformed into a new left-wing political party, Podemos. The disaffected were given a voice and, following

---

3 At the time of writing, over fifteen hundred Spanish politicians, mostly from the ruling parties, have been implicated in corruption cases. Some four hundred have been found guilty, of whom only a fifth are currently serving prison sentences.

elections, representation in parliament. They had been corralled, brought into the system. Podemos then followed the pattern of so many left-wing parties of proceeding to chase its own tail in convoluted internal power struggles. Yet for a moment the Establishment had been worried: a brief whiff of change had been in the air. Even, dare one say it, revolution . . .

But the danger hadn't, in fact, passed: today things remain anything but settled.

Reopened wounds from the Civil War, an economy in trouble, a million Spaniards forced to seek work abroad, an endemically corrupt political class, a monarchy on the brink . . . Almost everywhere you look in Spain at the moment, history and the patterns of the past are rising to the fore. A counter-weight to Podemos has emerged on the far-right in the form of a successful and growing new party, Vox, which actually uses words like 'Reconquest' to describe its policies towards Muslim immigrants, and which calls for 'homage' to be paid to pro-Francoists.

Almost every day, news reports throw up further examples of how the wounds from the past rarely appear to heal. When Franco's only child, Carmencita, died at the age of ninety-one in December 2017, the story served to remind people of certain uncomfortable facts: Carmen had been the head of the Francisco Franco Foundation, a partially State-funded body dedicated to preserving the dictator's memory and which still refers to the 1936 military coup that kick-started the Civil War as an 'armed referendum'. Moreover, Franco's descendants are mostly very wealthy, still in possession of assets gained – or expropriated, in the eyes of some – during the dictatorship. Carmen's aristocratic title, Duchess of Franco, had been given to her by King Juan Carlos, and was inherited on her death by her daughter, the dictator's granddaughter.

Around thirty other titles, ranging from count to marquis, still belong to the descendants of Francoist generals and supporters from the Civil War, some of whom carried out multiple atrocities and massacres of civilians.

A further example comes from this morning's news as I write these words: a corporal in the armed forces is being court-martialled for signing an *anti*-Francoist manifesto with the possibility that he will spend up to a month in prison. The unfortunate corporal was reacting to a manifesto published the previous summer, and signed by one hundred and forty-four officers, which justified the coup attempt of 1936. Furthermore, in an acutely symbolic act, the current – Socialist – government in Madrid is planning to disinter Franco from his gigantic mausoleum in the Sierra de Guadarrama mountains and have him buried elsewhere. Rarely has the phrase 'digging up the past' been more apt. Yet, as in a folk tale, inside those mountains, sleeping dragons lie; they have already been roused; they may soon become fully awake.

Spain is trapped, a beautiful and dynamic country perpetually divided against itself, a nation of generous, warm-hearted people destined to be ruled by the worst elements within their own society. Moments of relative light and peace – such as the Transition – come once in a while. But they are short-lived: in the same way that Restoration Spain disintegrated, the Spanish Renaissance was crushed by the Counter-Reformation, Jewish and Islamic cultures were squeezed out by the Inquisition, or Caliphal Cordoba was destroyed by religious bigots. Spain's Transition was deeply flawed, but it worked for a while. And yet it could only ever be temporary. The country's own history makes that clear.

If the very long-standing patterns of Spanish history continue, Transition Spain will eventually fall, just as every other regime has.

But outside forces won't bring it to an end: internal tensions will cause it to self-immolate, as in the past. And the biggest threat at present to the seriously weakened state is the Catalan separatist movement.

The whole world is aware of an age-old conflict between Catalonia and the rest of Spain thanks mostly to the football rivalry between Real Madrid and FC Barcelona, a sporting clash on the turf which in Spain is known simply as *el Clásico*. All other fixtures in the calendar of *La Liga* pale in comparison, and although most Spaniards may support their own local side, the vast majority have as much emotional investment in this match as in their own.

The real tensions symbolised in this rivalry, however, were laid bare for all to see in October 2017. In that month the Catalan regional authorities organised a referendum on independence from the rest of Spain. Of those who voted, the vast majority[4] were in favour of Catalonia breaking away. The world was shocked to see the response by the Madrid government, which declared the referendum illegal and sent in riot police to try to prevent it from taking place. Santiago the perpetual 'Slayer' of Spain's Other, of those who would threaten national unity, was brought out of retirement and sent in to do battle once more. Instead of swords, this time truncheons were brought down on the enemies' heads, but the same centuries-old pattern was repeated: not Moors being crushed this time, but Catalans casting a vote on self-determination. Violent, bloody scenes flashed over the world media within moments. Internationally, there was a sense of shock: 'I thought this kind of thing didn't happen any more in Western democracies,' went the comment.

Yet anyone with a long view of Spanish history would have known that this violent reaction was inevitable. As should now be

---

4 92 per cent out of a total of almost 2,300,000 votes, with a turnout of 43 per cent.

clear, Spain is constructed through the use of violence. And violence – or the threat of violence – is the only thing which keeps it from falling apart. The Catalan referendum was the most serious threat to the unity of the country since the end of the Civil War.[5] 'Spain,' as George Borrow said, 'never changes.' And so the established patterns of behaviour reasserted themselves as they always have: violence was employed by the State to hold the nation together. Policemen in Barcelona beating voters with batons were following a long historical tradition, yet one of which they themselves were, at best, only vaguely aware.

A few weeks later Madrid withdrew Catalonia's autonomy and imposed direct rule – the first time such a move had taken place since Spain became a democracy. For a brief moment the Catalan authorities had declared a republic – just as they had done several times in the past – only to suspend it immediately. And now, regional administration and rights were being swept away by the centre, as had also happened before. Catalan politicians and independence activists were arrested on charges of 'rebellion', a crime which implies the use of violence, despite the very public violence which had been meted out by the Spanish state. History was coming alive again in multiple and disturbing ways.

The situation in Catalonia today is, frankly, a mess, a situation seeded during the Transition, when minority governments in Madrid needed Catalan votes to get bills through parliament (and frequently still do). The return favour was to grant ever more rights and freedoms to Catalonia, where a sense of 'separateness' from the

---

5 ETA's violent campaign for Basque independence, while dominating the news for so long, was ultimately doomed to failure once Spain joined the family of democratic European nations – then the EEC – in the 1980s. Thenceforth, any international support or sympathy for their cause quickly faded. In contrast, the Catalan independence movement is overwhelmingly peaceful, giving it a more morally powerful position.

rest of Spain has been fomented over decades and is now beginning to bear fruit. Many Catalans, particularly in rural areas, feel no connection with other Spaniards, thanks in part to a regionally controlled education system which has highlighted differences between them. With each generation, this is increasing, and with it the pressure for Catalonia to become a separate nation.

In Madrid, meanwhile, there has mostly been an absence of any concerted effort to 'woo back' Catalans to the national fold. In 2005, the conservative People's Party actively campaigned against a new Catalan statute of autonomy while a simultaneous, unofficial boycott of Catalan goods, such as cava, got under way across Spain. Yet this, like the use of police violence, only helps the Catalan independence cause, fuelling a centuries-old sense of victimhood. In Madrid the policy has generally been to isolate the separatists, put them in jail where possible, and wait the movement out: it worked with ETA and the Basques, so – the thinking goes – it will work again.

But ETA made the crucial mistake of using violence. So far the Catalan movement is peaceful, no matter what charges are laid by Spanish courts against its leaders. The violent ones are the 'Spanish', who, to Catalan delight, are thereby condemned by international public opinion.

Yet by now it will be clear that the Spanish state knows nothing more than to use violence in the face of a possible Catalan break-away. It is what it has always done. The gulf between separatists and centralists is now vast, each side becoming more virulent in its rhetoric. The situation has been boiled down to basic elements of 'us' and 'them', of, as ever, *blanco y negro*. These are the same warning signs which prefigure crises all over the world, but particularly so in Spain, with its long history of repression and civil conflict.

Will the Catalan crisis turn violent? The police response on the day of the referendum means it already has. The question is, how much worse will it become?

The situation might not be so gloomy were it not for seriously damaged institutions captaining the ship of State in Madrid. The key point is that Spain has always broken up when anything other than a strong, centralising and usually authoritarian force holds the country together. Yet democracies by their very nature are not like this. That the country did not split up as soon as Franco died was due in large part to the symbolic role that Juan Carlos played as the father figure of the nation, seeing it through into the new age. But Juan Carlos has gone, and the monarchy he has left behind is in serious trouble. Felipe may be admired by some, but he is loved by no one. The symbolic father figure at the centre of the nation is no more. Which means that, if Spain follows the patterns of its own history, troubled waters lie ahead.

The Catalan independence movement may wax and wane, yet its long-term trend is towards greater confidence; it has grown steadily and substantially over the past few decades, and in the form of the 2017 referendum has had the briefest of tastes of its ultimate goal. On the other side, anti-Catalan sentiment has risen sharply in the rest of Spain in consequence: giving more concessions to Barcelona is seen as a weakness and has become an electorally damaging position for any Madrid government to hold. A clash has already occurred: more are inevitably on their way.

Which means that Spain today has a stark choice: either continue as a democracy (albeit a flawed one), accept the essentially democratic idea of regional self-determination, and allow the country eventually to break apart, with Catalonia quickly followed by the Basque Country in becoming an independent nation; or turn increasingly authoritarian (in reality, if not openly) as the only means at its disposal to keep the country united. Both outcomes involve violence, for Spain has never undergone such radical change without bloodshed, and there is little sign that today's defenders of a united country would allow their opponents to succeed without a fight.

Unless the patterns of the past can be broken, these are the two paths between which Spain has to choose: democracy and existential threat; or unity and authoritarianism.

This may seem pessimistic, yet viewing Spanish history as a whole tends to lead to this conclusion: in a country perpetually divided, every century has seen at least one major civil war. Memories of previous civil conflicts weren't enough to prevent the Civil War of the twentieth century. So why should we think that memories from the 1930s today will help avoid a repeat of the bloodshed of the past? Can the twenty-first century buck the overriding trends of the country's history? I am doubtful, but certainly hope so.

And if there is a glimmer for Spain to be gleaned from her history, it is that with the darkness also comes the light. The current climate would seem to suggest that civil conflict of some description will again blight the lives of ordinary Spaniards in the not-too-distant future – either in the context of a break-up of the nation, or in a forceful holding of it together. But even in her darkest hours – during the rule of the Berber fundamentalists, or the paranoia of the Counter-Reformation – Spain frequently produces a beacon for the world. What that might be is too early to say, but just as civil violence is a part of Spain's national story, so is her ability to enlighten and surprise.

What Spain needs to do now is create a new myth, a new story around which all her peoples can unite. It has been attempted before, with the liberal Constitution of 1812, and, in part, with the Transition. In both cases common cause was found which allowed all sides to bury their differences. What might draw Spaniards together today? That is the question, and one which needs an urgent answer.

And why should this be of importance beyond Spain? Because, as this book has shown, events there have a nagging habit of presaging what will take place in other Western countries – even if those countries are unaware of this fact. The Occupy movement is just the most recent example, but this further pattern of Spanish history stretches back well over a thousand years, through the Second World War, Western colonialism, the Renaissance, the Crusades and even beyond. If Spain is set to take one of two possible paths into the future, her neighbours and partners should be watching her decisions very closely, for they will almost certainly herald in some way developments which the peoples of France, Germany, Britain, the US and many other nations will soon be facing. For at present these countries, like Spain, are facing keen problems brought about by complications with the very democratic principles upon which they are built. What those developments may be remains unclear, but Spain's role as a harbinger of things to come should not be doubted: it is a part the country has played since its beginnings.

The Trojans ignored the truth of Cassandra's predictions at their own peril. Can we afford to turn a blind eye to events in Spain?

People often boast that today we have moved on from the past, that we have learned the lessons of history, that history never repeats itself.

Perhaps it doesn't. Perhaps we really have reached a moment in human history where we can break old patterns of behaviour and forge different futures for ourselves. I certainly hope so. Current trends, however, might suggest otherwise.

Nevertheless, history need not be a straightjacket. It only binds us when we ignore it. The patterns of behaviour can be broken, even those laid down over a thousand years. But this can only happen with an increase of self-awareness and understanding of what those patterns are and how they operate.

My own fascination with Spain began with the Moorish period. From there it extended to cover all the country's history and culture. Along the way it seemed that each new facet I discovered was entirely different compared to what I already knew, and so 'Spain' itself, its essence, appeared elusive: there was always something else to learn, something which would almost certainly contradict what I thought I already understood. That journey has not ended, I'm certain, but after three and a half decades of focusing on the country in one form or another, I can see now that each facet is simply that – a different face of what is, in fact, a complete whole. Here, for me, lies the mystery and magic of Spain, a vastly complex yet somehow integrated thing of beauty that remains just beyond ordinary sight or reach. In some ways it might best be symbolised by the fruit which forms the smallest section of its coat of arms, the pomegranate; each segment, each seed may consider itself individual, yet only together do they form the complete thing itself. Spain is greater than the sum of her parts, and for her to break up into fragments would, in my own opinion, be a tragedy in so many ways. And yet the alternative is equally unappealing: dictatorship or authoritarianism of some description holding everything together by force. The problem today is intractable.

And yet if Spain's history tells a tale of perpetual conflict and bloodshed – of darkness – it also demonstrates the country's ability to illuminate. Turbulent and more violent times may lie ahead, yet her past also suggests that somewhere, somehow, new light will also eventually emerge, just as Averroes laboured away against the backdrop of Almohad fundamentalism, and *Don Quixote* was written against the leaden weight of Inquisitorial terror. The alchemical process in Spain never sleeps: it has always produced gold and will continue to do so. What Spain needs is to see this truth for herself, recognise her exceptional, crucible nature, and embrace her possibilities.

Santiago the Slayer and Santiago the Seeker are the same person; they need not be locked in perpetual conflict.

Perhaps, if they learned to accept each other, they might come to comprehend this, and in time see that, combined, they are also both a first, an original, Santiago, at the same time: James the Apostle, the Man from the East who brought to Spain a message of love.

It is in the hope that *he* may prevail that this book has been written.

Acknowledgments

Thanks to Mike Ivey for setting up the framework from which this book could emerge. Also to Matthew Hamilton and Andreas Campomar for having the *cojones* to go where others feared to tread. Mary Chamberlain remains the best copy editor one could hope for, and my thanks to her for her combined diligence and breadth of vision. Jules Stewart gave very generously of his time and experience, and helped steady things at a late stage. Claire Chesser and Clara Díaz at Little, Brown are both wonderful to work with.

This book is a condensation of many years' experience in and of Spain, and it would be impossible to thank everyone who has shaped my ideas of a country which has been my adopted home in one form or another since the early 1990s. Some, however, need mentioning, including Enrique Murillo, Alex Gómez, Vicente Tamarit, Vicente Monsonís, Marta Sol, Sandra Ferrández, and Víctor Amela. José Valdivia was the person who first opened my eyes to the richness of Spanish history and it is with great sadness that I cannot thank him today.

There is, however, one person without whom my books would never have been written, the source of my inspiration, and to her must go the greatest thanks, as always. *Gracias, mi amor.*

Index